Specters of Revolt

Specters of Revolt

On the Intellect of Insurrection
and Philosophy from Below

Richard Gilman-Opalsky

Published by Repeater Books

An imprint of Watkins Media Ltd

19–21 Cecil Court
London
WC2N 4EZ
UK

www.repeaterbooks.com
A Repeater Books paperback original 2016
1

Distributed in the United States by Random House, Inc., New York.

Cover design: Johnny Bull
Typography and typesetting: Jan Middendorp
Typefaces: Chaparral Pro, Absara Sans
Printed in Finland

ISBN: 978-1-910924-36-5
Ebook ISBN: 978-1-910924-37-2

For Robyn, for the love and companionship.

For Roscoe, for the laughter and imagination.

For Ramsey, for the sweetness and joy.

CONTENTS

It's Always *Antebellum*

The word "*antebellum*" presents an interesting idea. The word's particular historical reference is to the period in the southern US before the American Civil War, but its general etymology refers to the time before war. Technically, "*ante*" means before and "*bellum*" means war. Human history reveals every time as a time before war. It is even *antebellum during* wartime — the present war is never the last war. The war to end all wars has never happened. Whenever there has not been war, or when one is taking place, a future war remains somewhere on the horizon. Thus, times of peace cannot be called "*postbellum*," because there is no "after war," only "before war." The *postbellum* may function as a utopian touchstone, a thing that has its uses. Whereas, *antebellum* captures the sense of a present situation about to be changed by some imminent conflict. For those who dream of a peaceful world, this represents a cynical view, or perhaps, just a view held true so far.

But shifting from war to other modes of conflict and other forms of fighting, this same notion turns optimistic and hopeful. Some formulation like the following captures the point well: If we are not now rising up for something better, we will be. This book is not about war, but revolt.

Happily, there are other ways of contesting reality and relations of power than with the militaries of governments. This book explores and develops the premise that human hope, revolutionary imaginations, creativity, and critique — for however long they're in abeyance — are always eventually liberated and activated in moments of revolt. Of course, this premise will have to be borne out, and basic terms like "revolt," "revolution," and "critique" need much defining.

But entertaining the premise, for the introductory time being, we might think of every moment in between revolt as a time before revolt. Perhaps, instead of *"antebellum,"* we may speak of *"anterivolta."* Like war, revolt against the existing state of affairs also keeps on occurring, yet more than war, revolt embodies and reflects the transformative aspirations of everyday people. Whereas wars waged by states embody and reflect the interests of power and capital, which usually coincide. Inasmuch as revolt comes back, in new forms, in different places, with different stakes and demands, periods of relative passivity, times of quiet, are haunted by the specter of revolt, just as peacetime is haunted by the specter of war.

The title of this book, *Specters of Revolt*, intends an allusion to two major thinkers separated by a century: First, the title alludes to Karl Marx, who happily announced in *The Communist Manifesto*, that "A specter is haunting Europe — the specter of Communism."[1] Marx understood that the present was haunted by its future abolition. Second, this book intends to recall one of the greatest works of Jacques Derrida, *Specters of Marx*, published early into the post-Cold War period.[2] Derrida's study of the enduring relevance of Marx emerged in the wake of the ideological model of opposition between capitalism and socialism which spanned the short 20th century. The short 20th century was defined by Eric Hobsbawm as the period between 1914 and 1991.[3] In the 21st century that began in the 1990s, a new hegemony

1 Marx, Karl, *The Communist Manifesto*, trans. Samuel Moore (New York: International Publishers, 1994), p. 8.
2 Derrida, Jacques, *Specters of Marx: The State of the Debt, the Work of Mourning and the New International*, trans. Peggy Kamuf (New York and London: Routledge, 1994).
3 Hobsbawm, Eric, *Age of Extremes: A History of the World, 1914-1991* (New York: Vintage Books, 1996).

emerged around the conclusion that Marx was now irrelevant, proven wrong, and responsible (even if indirectly) for some of the worst catastrophes the world had known. Against the ascendant post-Cold War opinion, Derrida insists that Marxism

> is still necessary *but* provided it be transformed and adapted to new conditions and to a new thinking of the ideological, provided it be made to analyze the new articulation of techno-economic casualties and of religious ghosts, the dependent condition of the juridical at the service of socio-economic powers or States that are themselves never totally independent with regard to capital [but there is no longer, there never was just capital, nor capitalism in the singular, but capitalisms plural — whether state or private, real or symbolic, always linked to spectral forces — or rather capitalizations whose antagonisms are irreducible].
>
> This transformation and this opening up of Marxism are in conformity with what we were calling a moment ago the *spirit of Marxism.*[4]

Derrida is here insisting that Marxism was not killed in the Cold War, but rather, it is awaiting its next iteration, *against* previous orthodoxies and forms and *for* an analysis of the changing present. He acknowledges that the ongoing re-articulation of Marx's critical analysis of capital is a defining part of Marxism itself, which began shortly after Marx's death with all forms of rethinking the critique of capital and power in ways beyond both the imagination and the life and times of Marx himself.

Derrida observed:

> Capitalist societies can always heave a sigh of relief and say to themselves: communism is finished since the collapse of the totalitarianisms of the twentieth century and not only is it

4 Derrida, Jacques, *Specters of Marx* (New York: Routledge, 1994), p. 73.

finished, but it did not take place, it was only a ghost. They do no more than disavow the undeniable itself: a ghost never dies, it remains always to come and to come-back.[5]

Considered in terms of a communist *logos* (as opposed to a "communist government"), we might say that if there is anything sensible in the idea of communism, in its opposition to capitalist society, then the communist *logos* cannot be killed by collapsed regimes. Inasmuch as Marxism continues to express and address real disaffections about real deficits in present society and everyday life, capitalist societies will never be rid of it, no matter how much they might like to deny its existence, to proclaim its death.

Derrida's overarching argument is that, while the 20th century seemed to vindicate Marx's claim from the 19th century that the world was haunted by the ghost of communism, the 21st would yet continue to be haunted by Marx in spectral forms to be determined, to be reconsidered. Bringing the two together, I claim that both communism and Marx do haunt — and will continue to haunt — the 21st century in particular ways that this book will take up directly in its course. However, the ghosts are neither clearly communist nor Marxist all (or even most) of the time. I suggest a broader framework regarding specters of revolt, which give rise to communist and Marxist hauntings, but also, which haunt the world with other ideas about autonomy, everyday life, anxiety, experience, knowledge, and possibility, in ways that often include but are quite clearly not limited to Marxian and communist discourses, no matter how transformed.

In the fall of 1998, I was a student of Derrida's in his seminar at The New School for Social Research, "Justice, Perjury, and Forgiveness." Despite the ambitious title, Derrida's singular focus that semester was forgiveness. He was particularly interested in the notion that to be pardoned or forgiven is only actually mean-

5 Ibid., p. 123.

ingful in the face of the unpardonable, the unforgivable. To for-give someone for a minor mistake, or to say "pardon me" when accidentally bumping into a stranger on the street, is perhaps a nicety, a well-meaning mannerism or gesture, but where forgive-ness is really needed — *where it actually changes human relations* — is where (and when) it is given to the unforgivable. In this way, the power of forgiveness depends upon the unforgivable.

Since then, I have maintained a correlated interest in the acceptance of the unacceptable, in the toleration of the intolera-ble, pairings that indicate a deeper problem; deeper in the sense that humans regularly accept the unacceptable (unlike forgiving the unforgivable). People regularly accept theoretically changea-ble facts of the world that are, even by their own accounts, totally unacceptable. Adjustments and acquiescence to unhappiness and dissatisfaction are common expectations of a practical life of "doing what one has to do," and yet, it remains a basic ethi-cal instinct to say that we should not accept a life that does us and others real measurable harm — at home, at work, in school, in society. And yet we regularly do. We do, that is, until there is a revolt against the unacceptable, against the intolerable.

In this way, revolt seems to me a peculiar force *of* (or, perhaps, *toward*) justice that emerges in the crisis of the system of the repressed-irrepressible, of the accepted-unacceptable. Derrida's seminar on forgiveness, much like his famous essay on justice and the law, explored how these things (forgiveness, justice, the law) depend upon their opposites, how forgiveness requires the unfor-givable, and how what is just and legal (in French, "*droit*") requires what is unjust and illegal.[6] We may look upon revolt as a disrup-tion, often vilified as "violent," that actually comes from the vio-lence of its absence. Powerful interruptions of normal life are

6   See Derrida, Jacques, "Force of Law: The 'Mystical Foundation of Authority'" in *Deconstruction and the Possibility of Justice*, ed. Drucilla Cornell, Michel Rosenfeld, and David Gray Carlson (New York: Routledge, 1992).

typically felt to be and caricatured as "violent" when the interruptions have real and immediate effects at home, at work, in school, or in society. However, the real hope and power of revolt is that it may expose how the cooperative reproduction of the "normal" state of affairs actually conceals a range of unacceptable realities.

Whereas Derrida's *Specters of Marx* embodies and reflects a particular historicity of Marxist philosophy in the wake of the Cold War and the end of the Soviet Union, *Specters of Revolt* aims to think through how systems of oppression are always haunted by revolt, how revolt is the oppositional (and historical and liberatory) theory and practice of transformative aspirations. Thus, while it is true that the worldly impetus for the present work comes from the eventuality of recent revolt and the context of capitalist crisis, it is also true that we can theorize specters of revolt in altogether different contexts.

Consider one distant example: During the gladiatorial times of the Roman Empire, an assorted subset of "criminals" and slaves were held captive and trained as gladiators.[7] Gladiators were trained for violent confrontation with other gladiators as a form of popular entertainment tinged with the moral endorsement of public opinion — an opinion taking cover behind the concepts of "punishment" and "justice." Although some volunteered, most gladiators came from the despised regions in proximity to Rome, those deemed "barbaric" and "uncivilized" enough for the wanton killing of the "sport" — the enslaved, many of them prisoners taken by Romans during conflict with surrounding regions. Their training took place in the ludus, a gladiatorial school, often also the site of their captivity and servitude. The gladiators were

7 Gladiatorial combat may well go back to the 3rd century BCE. It thereafter became a prominent part of Roman politics and social life. Gladiator entertainment lasted for close to a thousand years, reaching its peak between the 1st century BCE and the 2nd century ACE. It was formally abolished in the 5th century.

"schooled" in severe prison conditions, regarded as subhuman, and forced to fight to the death.

One of Marx's favorite heroes, Spartacus, emerged in such a "school," in a ludus of the lanista Batiatus, in Capua in southern Italy.[8] Spartacus, the famous Thracian agent of slave revolt in 73 BCE, broke out of his confinement with less than one hundred slaves, making a revolt that led to the uprisings known as the Third Servile War (73-71 BCE). Marx, unsurprisingly, found in this an example of the oppressed "ancient proletariat" rising up against a proto-capitalist oligarchy.[9] Despite great limitations and much disagreement in our knowledge of Spartacus and the surrounding history, it is difficult to see the events otherwise. Undoubtedly, the conditions of enslavement gave incentive to the revolt of the slaves.

One could say, then, that this iconic slave revolt was the materialization of a real possibility that must have haunted every ludus. The ludus and the coliseum were equipped with cages, guards, and tunnels, as well as multiple forms of abuse, discipline, and punishment for the maintenance of order and the dissuasion of insurrectionary impulses. It is difficult to imagine the containment and cultivation of such violence, and its deployment for the pleasures of its masters, without the ongoing necessity for a repressive system to guard against the outbreak of revolt.

This suggests a certain hauntology: We do not say that the ancient and abandoned Ludus Magnus, for example, the largest arena and gladiatorial school in Rome, is haunted because of the violence that once occurred there. Rather, we understand that the whole system was haunted by the specter of its possible overthrow, *before any revolt occurred*, within the energies of the repressed and captive humanity. Such a thesis can be stated in

8   See, for one example, "Confessions of Marx" in *The Portable Karl Marx*, trans. Eugene Kamenka (New York: Viking Penguin, 1983), p. 53.

9   Marx, Karl, *On History & People*, edited and translated by Saul K. Padover (New York: McGraw-Hill, 1977), p. 304.

either humanist terms, regarding the dignity of the oppressed, or in strictly materialist terms, regarding the conditions of life. However one puts it, specters of revolt are not new. Revolt is a transformative possibility both structurally and existentially bound to all social, political, and economic systems maintained against the interests of the people they confine. This generality applies broadly throughout human history, and remains widely applicable today in schools, militaries, prisons, impoverished communities, despotic and oligarchic regimes, heavily policed neighborhoods, miserable workplaces, etc. All such locations are haunted by specters of revolt, where the "Spartacus" we wait for is less a person than an upheaval — "Spartacus" as a disruption of the system that can be identified as a feature of the system itself.[10] Simply, the basic theorization of *Specters of Revolt* may well have long predated recent uprisings and capitalist crises, though it is the latter uprisings and crises that motivate this work.

In the years since 2008, certain closures have been reopened by revolt. After the uprising of the Mexican Zapatistas in 1994 opened and set a stage for new forms of revolt against the recently liberated and expanded logic of capital, there were some large but short-lived continuations of Zapatismo in Seattle in 1999 and in Genoa in 2001, as well as in numerous other locations. But then, the closure of capital seemed to stitch things up again, resuming and restoring its hold. Yet in 2008, at the culmination of diverse global crises in economic, social, and political life, Greek revolts tore open the sutures, and since then, we have seen various real-

10 Do not read my invocation of Spartacus here, or of John Brown later, as lionizations that ignore the uglier sides of these men's histories, for example their infamous brutality and fanaticism (respectively). Although their brutality and fanaticism should be both questioned and contextualized, I never intend to stipulate with "Spartacus" (in quotes), as with Brown later, the names of personal heroes. That is, I do not mean to invoke the men themselves. Rather, I invoke figures of history associated with insurrections in thought and action.

izations of the haunting hopes of people in the so-called Arab Spring, in Turkey, Bosnia and Herzegovina, Syria, Brazil, and in Occupy Wall Street, among other places, many of which we consider in greater detail throughout this book.

How does the "Spartacus" haunt and threaten the present? An anecdote: In January 2012, I learned about the re-occupation of Zuccotti Park just as I was boarding a plane from Springfield, IL to New York City to present research at the *TELOS* conference at NYU and do a book talk at Bluestockings Bookstore. I had not been in New York since the Occupy Wall Street activities began in September 2011, and national news of activists taking over the park again in January opened up the possibility for me to participate in and observe the next iteration of occupations in Zuccotti Park. While I was able to participate in and observe some impressive Occupy activity in Springfield, I knew the first thing I'd do upon arrival in NYC was go check out the happenings at Zuccotti. It was freezing cold on the evening of my arrival, but after stowing my bags in my aunt and uncle's apartment, I made my way down to the park, only to find it empty, save for about sixty or so NYPD cops. There was a lone man with a sign standing at an outside corner of the park, but aside from him, Zuccotti was only occupied by the police.

I figured I would ask the nearest cop about what had happened, telling him that I'd heard the park had been occupied again. He said, "Yes, they were here yesterday, but it got too cold, so they left." I asked him, "Since they're all gone now, why are there so many cops in the park?" He simply replied, "Because they come back." There was a sense, in that moment, in which the absence of the occupiers and the presence of the police disclosed the hopeful expression of a ghost-like power. The park was clearly haunted by the recently departed spirit of the occupation, and its future possibility. The cops had orders to stay in an empty park, but only because the park had not been fully emptied of its contentious potentiality. After a while, of course, the cops too did leave. But the park remains a transformed and haunted site, a location that can never be stripped of its historic role as the place for a surprising expression of disaffection aimed at capital in the financial nerve center of Manhattan. The park, now even empty, suggests the other side of capital: the opposition to the values, purposes, and effects of Wall Street. Discourses of failure do not change the basic facts of this residual expectation, aspiration, and unfinished business of Occupy. On my visit, power saw fit to go on guard even in the absence of something to guard against. Capital's spaces and bases must be guarded as they are the physical locations of capitalist activity (much capitalist activity has no such physical location), representations of systems, and even demarcations of time, haunted by what they do.

Part of what enables us to speak of specters of revolt is the recognition of unfinished business from previous revolt. Thus, in Baltimore, MD in 2015 we saw a particular iteration of some of the same disaffections that were expressed in Ferguson, MO in 2014, where we found a certain rekindling of some of what was expressed in New Orleans, LA in 2005, which contained some of what was found in Los Angeles in 1992, which contained some of what was found in Watts, Los Angeles in 1965, leaving out, of course, so many critical incidents and coordinates before and in between. Inasmuch as "in between" also always designates a "time before the next one," we can speak of the *antebellum* status of revolt. Specters of revolt haunt in between, that is, both before and after, realizations of revolt. To show this well, clear and certain connections between individual coordinates of upheaval must be made more concrete and far less speculative, and that is partly what this book aims to accomplish.

But there is yet another, and perhaps more important aim of the present book, which one could say was summed up best over four decades ago in a conversation between Michel Foucault and Gilles Deleuze, published under the title, "Intellectuals and Power."[11] In the conversation, Foucault says the following in reference to the French uprisings of May 1968:

> In the most recent upheaval, the intellectual discovered that the masses no longer need him to gain knowledge: they know perfectly well, without illusion; they know far better than he and they are certainly capable of expressing themselves. But there exists a system of power which blocks, prohibits, and invalidates this discourse and this knowledge, a power not only found in the manifest authority of censorship, but one that profoundly and subtly penetrates an entire societal network... In this sense theory does not express, translate, or serve to apply practice: it is practice.[12]

Foucault's comments here mark my point of departure. The present book seeks to advance an understanding of the intellect of revolt, not to provide an analysis of revolt. While some analysis of recent global uprisings is inevitably presented in fleeting, tentative passages, I mainly pursue an understanding of what kind of analysis revolt itself offers. I consider the question, also taken up by Deleuze and Guattari, of *What is Philosophy?*[13] In so doing, I try to isolate the most basic features of what might be called "good" philosophy, and then to assess how revolt does it better than professional philosophers ever have done or could do. This thesis, captured well by Foucault, which regards uprising as thinking, upheaval as speaking, is the overarching interest and guiding concern of the present work.

11   Foucault, Michel, "Intellectuals and Power," a conversation between Foucault and Deleuze, published in *Foucault Live: Interviews, 1961–1984*, ed. Sylvère Lotringer (New York: Semiotext(e), 1996).

12   Ibid., p. 75.

13   Deleuze, Gilles and Guattari, Félix, *What is Philosophy?*, trans. Hugh Tomlinson and Graham Burchell (New York: Columbia University Press, 1994).

But because revolt is always a destabilizing activity, and because it is animated and energized also by human disaffections, there is often real fear associated with the possibility that it may lead to an even worse reality than the one it opposes. Immanuel Kant was attentive to this possibility in his famous essay on enlightenment, where he recommended public criticism (what he called "the public use of reason") within the limits of a general obedience (what he called "the private use of reason"), so as to ensure that social and political progress would not undermine the stability and functionality of the basic reality.[14] Indeed, one has to take seriously the possibility that revolt may not only fail to improve the situation, but even make the situation worse. Although, in considering that possibility, it is important to assess whether it was in fact the revolt that made things worse, or if political forces of counterinsurgency are mainly to blame. Often, when a revolt goes badly, the repressive apparatus intervenes with its defensive and normalizing violence, and that violence, allied with the ideas of punishment and "justice," makes things worse. Yet, the normalizing and punitive violence of "law and order" is typically given a peculiar kind of absolution, as if the only violence on the scene belongs to the upheaval, as if the condemnable violence is the sole property of insurrection. Nonetheless, to insist that revolt always improves the situation would be a kind of romanticization, an ideological distortion.

At the same time, nothing is simple or easy in the historical transformation of the world, nor ever has been. Every major advance, including many that we now look upon as obvious and legal, such as the abolition of the transatlantic slave trade, suffrage and women's rights, the rights of gays and lesbians, had their moments of illegal, courageous, and frightening revolt.

14 See Kant, Immanuel, "An Answer to the Question: 'What is Enlightenment?'" in *Political Writings*, trans. H.B. Nisbet (Cambridge, UK and New York: Cambridge University Press, 1991).

Whether we are talking about dangerous slave revolts against the odds of great power, the direct action of Emmeline and Christabel Pankhurst and their comrades who fought with the police, or the Stonewall uprisings against police terrorism in 1969, the risks of repression and political setbacks, and even of death, are serious concerns. Human history does not unfold in one tidy, linear direction. So, how could we know if women and gays will be rounded up and killed, how should we measure the outcomes and aspirations of the Paris Commune or Warsaw Ghetto Uprising, and how could we know if the resistance of Palestinians will result in their total extermination? Hope and fear can mingle in an eternal dance of speculation.

In any case, whether or not it could be worse is the wrong question. It could always be worse and it could always be better. I am not here suggesting we ignore real risks and the possibility of political failure in revolt. Rather, I argue that we must look centrally at the critical and philosophical content of revolt. While, on the one hand, we cannot romanticize revolt, pretending it's always a full victory, on the other hand, we cannot overlook its philosophical content out of a fear of immediate practical consequences.

For example, in the case of slave uprisings, we see clearly in hindsight that the thinking of the revolt is the better position, and we should keep in mind that present uprisings may well be looked upon with a similar clarity from future perspectives. Yet, to be governed by predictions about future perspectives and possible failure is also highly uncertain, and the politics of fear has long taken sides with the defense of the existing order. Transformative hope sides with the upheaval, however uncertain and rightfully worried that hope may be. This, it seems to me, is all the more reason to engage with the critical and philosophical content of revolt and to oppose the politics of fear that dissuades everything other than the maintenance and reproduction of what already is.

The research for this book began in 2010, when I started working on the first of what would become a series of articles on the relationships between revolt, insurrection, communism, philosophy, and capitalist crisis. These articles were not originally conceived of as a series, but ended up constituting a somewhat cohesive constellation of inquiry that spanned the time and events of the years from 2010 to 2016. What you find in this book, however, is a substantial development and synthesis of discrete researches that were previously published in various journals and magazines, some of which are difficult to find, or have miniscule readerships. The present book begins thinking in the light of uprisings from 2008 to the present, and aims to speak to and anticipate (not to predict) further iterations and occasions of revolt to come. *Specters of Revolt* is not a collection of previously published essays. I have radically reworked and expanded each piece into complete book chapters, which move them from the vague haunting of each other to a direct linking up, building upon, and theoretical synthesis. In short, this book weaves together years of research on revolt into a new cohesive whole.

The first chapter outlines a hauntology of revolt. We ask: What makes a place, a city, a building, haunted? What is the social and political history that leaves a place haunted, and what is it exactly that does the haunting? Can we speak of ghosts in a materialist language? What do such ghosts tell us, what do they do? To address these questions, we consider the kind of haunting Marx alluded to when, in the opening lines of *The Communist Manifesto*, he invoked that "specter of communism": Something that is not quite present, but looms over the existing state of affairs as a danger to it. Can we think, in a similar way, about the specter of revolt? To assist the inquiry, and to show why it matters, I draw on Félix Guattari's theory of becoming to articulate a politics of becoming-ghost. In this opening chapter, we consider how revolt, as any good ghost would do, threatens to interrupt the constituted present, bringing to light fatal injustices and indignations that have been obscured, dormant, or buried.

In the second chapter, we reconsider the old notion of the

virtue of struggle. Struggle has been valorized by radical movements for 200 years, as the name for the dialectical activity driving transformative politics. Struggle and revolution have been associated to the extent that the former is typically understood as both prerequisite to and content of the latter. No transformation without struggle. But should we valorize struggle? I argue for unpacking the other virtues of revolt. Revolt embodies and reflects other virtues of a human life that are more inviting than the hackneyed call for those who are already miserable to struggle and struggle some more. The possibility for activities others than those called "struggle" is at the same time the possibility for making a more desirable mode of action, or many more desirable modes. The old idea of class struggle runs contrary to an autonomist praxis, according to which we might develop new and joyful forms of contestation. Also in this way, specters of revolt are not always defined by catastrophe, as in the ghosts left by death, for they may also be defined by happiness, longing, and revolutionary hope. A politics that valorizes struggle is something no one wants to do; people struggle because they must. Struggle is an apt description of the default position of so much daily life. Therefore, we explore more ecstatic and less insufferable dimensions, impetuses, and purposes of revolt.

Having considered what a specter of revolt is and how revolt relates to happiness and desire, we move on in Chapter 3 to critically consider a prominent form of postmodern politics called "culture jamming." Culture jamming is clearly not any classical form of political struggle or collective action, and yet it follows a playful, fun, and autonomous revolutionary hope. It appears as a concrete example of revolt by other means, but what exactly does it do? We ask this because, in many ways, culture jamming intends to rethink revolt in light of 20th-century disaffections with conventional notions of revolution. That is, culture jamming is an attempt to rethink revolt so that it doesn't need to wait for the old class mobilizations that rarely ever come. However, I argue that culture jamming has detourned *détournement* in the wrong direction, converting a potentially radical situationist praxis into a liberal fantasy that borrows more from capitalist advertising than from Guy Debord. At the same time, we want to learn from culture jamming. What does it tell us about the position of radical critique in the existing society? What does it tell us about communication, media, visual terrains, and revolt by other means than mass action? We discuss and redefine culture jamming so that it may include seemingly spontaneous uprising and collective action, and not only depend upon a tiny cast of atomized celebrity artists engaged in the production of "subversive" marketing spectacles.

Now with a basic theoretical framework for understanding revolt — what it is and how it works — we can consider its actualization in the world.[15] In Chapter 4, we consider the promise of what appears to be the eternal recurrence of revolt in the world. The ends of revolt, its eventual ending and lasting effects, do not grasp the meaning and the power of revolt. I argue for shifted attention to the beginning and to the inevitable recurrence of revolt (instead of ending and effects), as the unit of study. This shifts our focus *from* the political accomplishments of revolt *to* its critical content. Whenever revolt is not happening, it will. This is how it haunts, this is how it happens. When revolt goes away, it does not go away for good. It goes away, but always comes back. When it ends, if the world is left much as it was before, the revolt is called a failure. But should we accept this discourse of failure? In *The Communist Hypothesis*, Alain Badiou challenges the discourse of failure that has become a convention when reflecting on the so-called communist projects of the 20th century.[16] They were not simply failures, he insists, but experiments that we learned a lot

15 However, it is not until the final chapter, Chapter 7, that a new cohesive theory of the intellect of insurrection and philosophy from below is fully articulated.

16 Badiou, Alain, *The Communist Hypothesis*, trans. David Macey and Steve Corcoran (London and New York: Verso, 2010), pp. 1-40.

from, and that also included distinct successes. While Badiou is correct to attack the ideological emphasis on communist failure, we are interested in the success/failure discourse as it pertains to recent uprisings, which have been more micropolitical and rhizomatic, and less decisively communist. In relation, specifically, to common criticisms of Occupy and the "Arab Spring," which accused them of a certain aimlessness, I argue that collective refutation of the basic principles of the existing world is always a triumph. We should consider how specific forms of revolt each and always break through the considerable ideological defenses of the existing world, and how they are realizations of very clear disaffections and aspirations.

The last three chapters of the book turn toward more positive developments of its normative arguments. In Chapter 5, for example, I argue for the necessity of 21st-century Marxism to liberate itself from 20th-century statism. Indeed, there are many Marxian trajectories, including left-communist, autonomist, and anarchist, that attempt to raise the critique of the state form to the same level of the critique of capital. In the 20th century, these theories appeared variously utopian and impractical, but now they must be recovered precisely for their necessity and practicality. How this relates to the interest in revolt is, in very basic terms, twofold: First, revolt remains the way communism works from the bottom up. We must know by now, if communist activity took the form of electoral participation, it would not be communist. Marx himself understood revolt as a historical social force from below. Indeed, his interest in revolt, in the social forces of rebellion, far outstrips his attention to the state form. There is, thus, always a certain Marxism in taking sides with the powers of revolt. Here, too, we find support for Derrida's thesis on the specters of Marx, although in other places than he looked. Second, as we are considering revolt in the context of capitalist lifeworlds, it is fundamental and necessary to consider which aspects of the capitalist present give rise to revolt.

In Chapter 5, we qualify the haunting Marxism of these arguments by calling for a non-ideological approach that is both willing and able to draw on seemingly contradictory sources from diverse milieus. What we need is not so much Marxism, but rather, a graveyard for orthodoxies. We cannot analyze and defend revolt from some decisively Marxist or anarchist position because revolt does not and will not always conform to our worldviews. If we insist on a Marxist or anarchist interpretation of revolt, then revolt will always appear to us to be for what we are for, which guarantees a misreading of events and bad analysis guided by ideology. And yet, we cannot simply avert our eyes from the abused source materials of past great thinkers, because there is a vast body of resources we can make *new* use of, if only we will allow ourselves to do so. Rather than the guidance of ideology, we should be guided by the open questioning of revolt. In fact, I argue that new global uprisings can instruct and reveal new readings of our classical and canonical sources.

In Chapter 6, "The Ferguson Revolt Did Not Take Place," I present a short consideration of the uprisings in impoverished black communities that took place in the US in 2014 and 2015. The chapter owes its brevity to the source material it detourns, Gilles Deleuze and Félix Guattari's even shorter essay, "May '68 Did Not Take Place."[17] The purpose of Chapter 6 is to confront and discuss race and class in the US, set within the context and history of black oppression and black revolt. While this book is not about the US, this chapter takes the opportunity to think through some recent and particularly intense uprisings against police brutality, racism, and classism. But Chapter 6 makes only a brief encounter with its complex and important subject matter, in order to (1) bring attention to the ongoing problem of racism

17 Deleuze, Gilles and Guattari, Félix, "May '68 Did Not Take Place" in *Hatred of Capitalism: A Semiotext(e) Reader*, ed. Chris Kraus and Sylvère Lotringer (Los Angeles: Semiotext(e), 2001).

and (2) link recent revolt in the US to past and future articulations of the struggles against racism within capitalist society. These are the particular aims of the chapter, worked out with all due modesty in relation to current and important events in the real world of revolt. However, Chapter 6 also serves the more general and overarching purpose of demonstrating the kind of analysis that my theory of revolt yields and recommends. The chapter is, in fact, an application of the general theory of the book to a reading of actual events in the world.

Finally, Chapter 7 brings a thread that runs through every chapter of this book to its full fruition. Our culminating and concluding arguments focus centrally on the intellect of revolt and philosophy from below. As a whole, *Specters of Revolt* defends revolt not so much for what it permanently changes in the world, but rather, for what it says, for how it speaks, in short, for its communicative power. In this final chapter, I argue that revolt, as philosophy from below, carries and conveys more critical content than what is conventionally called philosophy. Some days or weeks of uprising in Ferguson or Baltimore contain and communicate more critical content than a book comprised of years of research on the same subjects (including the present one). This does not demean or degrade the book, but rather, positions events as the primary sources on which good books depend.

Throughout history, we can find a defining vision of philosophy as a discursive and dialectical force against the justice and reality of the existing world. There is indeed a long list of philosophers who were openly critical of professional philosophy, dating back at least to Socrates. So, how else is philosophy done, and who else does it? I argue that revolt appears as a modality of philosophy, what we may call "philosophy from below."

To theorize revolt as "philosophy from below," it is necessary to refute its conventional vilification as irrational and violent. Rather than making an intellectual analysis of revolt, we try to comprehend revolt as intellectual analysis itself. It is an overarching contention of this book that professional thinkers have more to learn from insurrectionary movements than they have to teach them. Throughout, we aim to take seriously the communicative content of recent revolts, from Greece, to North Africa, to Wall Street, to Turkey, to Brazil, to Ferguson, to Baltimore, and elsewhere.[18]

The recurrence of revolt has been faster, with less time between global uprisings in the years from 2008 to 2016. Nonetheless, a case needs to be made for the affective *and* rational content of these movements, which are still often characterized as violent and senseless. And we must go farther. Our goal is to move from the mere appreciation of the affective and rational dimensions of upheaval, to a close reading of its philosophical content. Occupied buildings and public squares, and yes, even riots, typically do more to throw the reality and justice of the world into question than the work of professional philosophers does.

Although I define and distinguish various forms of social upheaval later on, especially (but not only) in Chapters 3, 6, and 7, a brief qualification about riots is useful here. A riot may well be part of a revolt, but it is not always a revolt in-and-of-itself. By riot, we typically mean some wave of illegal group activity that usually involves confrontations with police and property destruction. A riot can be motivated by many things, including nihilist

18 Several recently published books with some (albeit very different) overlapping interest in the theoretical work of revolt are worth mentioning here: Franco "Bifo" Berardi, *The Uprising: On Poetry and Finance* (Los Angeles: Semiotext(e), 2012); Hamid Dabashi, *The Arab Spring: The End of Postcolonialism* (London and New York: Zed Books, 2012); Marina Sitrin and Dario Azzellini, *They Can't Represent Us!: Reinventing Democracy from Greece to Occupy* (London and New York: Verso Books, 2014); Brecht De Smet, *A Dialectical Pedagogy of Revolt: Gramsci, Vygotsky, and the Egyptian Revolution* (Leiden and Boston: Brill, 2015); Brian C. Lovato, *Democracy, Dialectics, and Difference: Hegel, Marx, and 21st Century Social Movements* (New York and London: Routledge, 2016). Although these books cover very different ground, I recommend them to readers interested in some of the general and defining themes of the present work.

thrill, football hooliganism, or the visceral excitement of blackout looting, lawbreaking, etc. What makes riot an open question is that it does not always or self-consciously express a clearly legible philosophical content, at least not on its face.

But I want to resist two tendencies in thinking about riots. First, I do not regard them as "anti-social behavior." To the contrary, riots are distinctly social in that they are carried out by groups of people within society who act out together in the upheaval. They are, in fact, more "social" than reading this book. That does not mean they are good. To say something is social is not to defend it. Second, I claim that although riots do not necessarily or self-consciously express a politics of any kind, they do likely contain some political and philosophical content that can be accessed eventually. Whether or not we endorse riots in general is a bad question. I neither endorse nor condemn riots categorically, and of course, we must criticize what needs criticizing. I argue instead that basic understanding demands us to consider *why* a riot breaks out, *how* it relates to revolt against the existing state of affairs, and *what* it communicates about the social situation.

Philosophy has never produced a new world directly, but when it is good, philosophy produces epiphanies about the world, suggesting its transformation. Philosophy is the practical activity of working out the difference and distance between what is and what ought to be. Perhaps the best philosophers do not carry out their work in books and articles. Since the Greek uprisings of 2008, we have seen that the most important philosophy of our time is not written down, but acted out. What economic crises, social instability, and political impasses tell us today is that we still need epiphanies about the world and its necessary transformation. Perhaps we will always be at that historical juncture, or should be. Nonetheless, what we have to do, in so many ways, is to participate in the production of epiphanies, or in the moments of their realization. Epiphany, I argue, is a crucial part of what is called revolution.

CHAPTER 1

Becoming-Ghost

One must, magically, chase away a specter, exorcise the possible return of a power held to be baleful in itself and whose demonic threat continues to haunt the century.

— JACQUES DERRIDA, *Specters of Marx*[19]

Shit will never be the same in Baltimore.

— DEMARCUS ON TWITTER, *The 2015 Baltimore Uprising*[20]

Ghosts are real and normal. What is truly "paranormal" is their absence.

To understand the meaning of this proclamation, we start by defining, or by redefining, its key terms.[21]

I do not use the term "ghost" to specify anything supernatural or in any celestial sense. Rather, let's begin with the question of what a ghost, or a specter, does. A ghost may do many things, but

19 Derrida, Jacques, *Specters of Marx* (New York and London: Routledge, 1994), p. 120.

20 *The 2015 Baltimore Uprising: A Teen Epistolary* (New York: Research and Destroy, 2015), no page numbers.

21 I would like to thank the students in my spring 2013 class, "Postmodern Theory: Politics and Possibility," at University of Illinois, Springfield. The basic idea for this chapter first emerged in discussion with them, on a beautiful spring evening, during our final session outside by the university library. It was the students who pressed me to articulate a materialist conception of ghosts, and to realize that there was something to be done here. I hope those who were there on that night will find something useful in the directions I have taken.

its primary activity — the one which distinguishes the ghost as a ghost — is to haunt. To be haunted is to be troubled or followed by the presence of some invisible thing, some unseen entity that one nonetheless feels or knows to be present. Indeed, a ghost may haunt as an invisible presence, or as a scarcely visible phenomenon (like a faint trace), which affectively transforms the context in which one lives or acts. Ghosts are typically understood to haunt the particular locations, objects, or people with which they are associated in some intimate and historical way. All of this is quite conventional to the common definition of ghosts, and yet it is a language that can be used to describe the normal — possibly universal — experiences of being haunted by personal or political history, being haunted by the bad things we have done or that have been done to us. On the personal level, when we speak of one's "baggage," or of being troubled by a memory, by a traumatic event, people can often name the specific ghosts that haunt them. Of course, there are other ways of speaking of these things, but I argue that none of them are as useful as the language of ghosts for diagnostic and prescriptive purposes.

We do not have to go out on any shaky limbs to reclaim the language of ghosts from its supernatural and religious captors. Let us consider the meanings of the German word "*Geist*." Depending on context, "*Geist*" can be translated as the English words "mind," "spirit," or "ghost." The word *Geist* is etymologically closest to the English word ghost. The multiple meanings of the term substantiate Gilbert Ryle's famous notion of "the ghost in the machine," which he used to characterize and critique Descartes' theory of the mind in the body.[22] But for a long time, English renderings have reduced the tripartite meaning of the word to "spirit/mind" or to "spirit (mind)," and choosing which one to go with has a complex philosophical history dating back (at least) to G.W.F. Hegel's *The Phenomenology of Spirit*, or *The Phenome-*

22 Ryle, Gilbert, *The Concept of Mind* (New York: Routledge, 2009).

nology of Mind.[23] Both of these are titles for the same book that can still be found in English publication today. We cannot fully settle the choice between one and the other title, because understanding Hegel's philosophy requires both spiritual-metaphysical and rationalist connotations. Hegel's work depends upon a more robust conception of *Geist* and resists reductive translation. In cognitive science and neuropsychology, and in the philosophical work that centralizes these, for example that of Daniel Dennett, spirit has fallen off entirely, because science is more confident than ever before that everything that was mysterious enough to be called "spiritual" can now be demystified as some complexity or another of human brain function.[24] This reflects a general consensus in philosophies of the mind today.

So, we must observe the tendency in philosophy and science to strip *Geist* of all its ghostly meaning, whilst even phonetically, the word "*Geist*" is nearer to the word "ghost" than any of its more common renderings. But there is more than a phonetic force for ghosts left in the concept and meaning of *Geist*, for the ghosts that I want to speak of are those that haunt our minds, as individual persons and collectivities, in psychological, social, and psycho-social senses. The tripartite meaning of the word "*Geist*" already embodies the idea we shall be working out in the present chapter, because that meaning conceives the domain of the mind as also the domain of ghosts, and the brain (or mind) is where a haunting takes hold of us. On this point, even the most materialist cognitive science would agree, such as when the scientist debunks ghostly activity as a case of "your mind playing tricks on you." We need not refute this debunking, and can go farther to say that

23   Hegel, G.W.F., *The Phenomenology of Spirit* (New York: Oxford University Press, 1977); Hegel, G.W.F., *The Phenomenology of Mind* (New York: Dover Philosophical Classics, 2003).

24   Dennett, Daniel C., *Consciousness Explained* (Boston: Back Bay Books, 1991).

every person's mind plays tricks on them at some point. But what is meant by a "mind playing tricks" is that our brain makes certain interpretations, certain remembrances, which take us by surprise, which make us think in peculiar ways about, or rethink, something that has happened. Indeed, a mind playing tricks can lead us to see something wrongly, or just differently, through the screen of certain fears, anxieties, or other psychological preoccupations.

Recall the opening proclamation that ghosts are real and normal. What is "paranormal," I claim, is their absence. What is meant by "paranormal" here is the literal and etymological sense of the word, scrubbed of its supernatural and religious encrustations. "Paranormal" is a relatively new word, a 20th-century term that designates experiences outside of the range of normal human experience. If we consider ghosts *vis-à-vis Geist*, in the context provided above, then we can understand the assertion that ghosts are real and normal, and that their absence is paranormal. There is no semantic sorcery here, for the word-forming prefix "para" always indicates "alongside, beyond, contrary to, irregular, or abnormal," hence "paralegal" indicates action beyond, outside of, or against the law, and paranormal indicates some experience beyond, outside of, or against what is normal. As with the paralegal, what is paranormal is not always wrong, not always a deception — often normality bears those traits.

Given this, it is fair to say that some ghosts may be paranormal, but only in a differently qualified sense. For example, if you are haunted by some experience from your past that haunts scarcely anyone else, an experience that is unrelatable to others within your lifeworld, if the ghosts that haunt you are outside the common experience of your community, then your ghosts are paranormal. But they are not, for that reason, celestial apparitions. Holding off, for now, on specific considerations of some single particularly unrelatable haunting or another, we can establish the general premise that everyone is haunted by something, that every human person with a history of experiences in the world is haunted by some ghost(s). It is on this general premise that we may say ghosts are real and normal.

If we challenge the logic of fear that usually attends discussions of ghosts, we also challenge its normative underpinnings. For example, a social system full of exploitation and human suffering, we might say, *should be* haunted by the miseries it proliferates and sanctions. In this way, a ghost could indicate what we call an active moral conscience. Extreme wealth in the face of growing and widespread impoverishment should be haunted, if not on moral or ethical grounds, then on grounds of the material conditions of human suffering, or most minimally, by the threat of mutinies on the horizon. An everyday life of generalized anxiety and despair could and should be haunted by the possibility of renewed pleasure and joy. Sometimes a haunting is a good thing, as in the case of a perpetrator of an awful crime being haunted by what they've done. Sometimes the haunting is a reassuring thing, a thing that afflicts and worries the existing state of affairs.

Political systems are haunted by revolutions, whether from the past or possible ones in the future, and every hierarchical order is haunted by possibilities of insubordination. Sometimes what haunts the existing state of affairs is the possibility of a Spartacus that owes its origins to the system it threatens. I argue that ghosts can be part of what disfigures and harms us, or part of what emancipates us and transforms the world for the better. Thus, specters can be given no categorical, normative endorsement. What they are always good for, at the very least, is what they tell us about our world and ourselves.

In what follows, I argue four specific lines in relation to ghosts and what I shall call "becoming-ghost": (I) First, I argue that every human person has ghosts, and that these may be good or bad. Beyond this basic (perhaps obvious) claim, I intend to substantiate the usefulness of a language of ghosts for self-understanding. (II) Second, I argue that ghosts haunt institutions, social and political. These ghosts comprise an ethical or moral conscience,

33

and often, a revolutionary potentiality, or some structural instability; these hauntings indicate various specters of revolt. (III) Third, I argue that some ghosts need to be busted, and that ghost-busting can be a liberatory and rehabilitative praxis. (IV) Finally, I argue that every society is haunted by its ghosts, but that this haunting is too localized and anchored to particular scenes of historical crimes. The real power of a politics of haunting calls for more ghosts engaged in more deterritorialized haunting. This requires a kind of "becoming-ghost" politics, according to which existing relations of power are troubled and spooked by social forces networking beyond their geographic locations, beyond the norm, beyond the state, outside and against it, often invisible or scarcely visible, but which hope to transform the contexts in which we live.

1 Haunted persons: your/my ghosts

Each of us is haunted by something.[25] Class analysis may be of little help in determining the nature of a personal haunting. The question of what haunts a person can only be answered in highly differentiated individual contexts. Your ghosts might remain a totally enclosed private matter were it not for the fact that what haunts you colors the nature of your relationships. Either you would have to disclose what haunts you, or one might be able to guess after some sustained and intimate relationality. Your ghosts could be many things that haunt, some rather obvious. If you are betrayed by a lover you once trusted with confidence,

25   In this section, when I say "each of us," I am not mainly thinking of young children. I am thinking of the human person with an accountable history of experiences and life events that shape that person's self-understanding. In other words, I am thinking of the adult person. But there is no reliable line to be drawn here regarding the age of persons, and certainly some young children are already haunted by fears, experiences of abuse, and other nightmares.

the possibility of betrayal might haunt you. If you did wrong to another, the memory of the pain you inflicted might haunt you. You might be haunted by something that you said, something you shouldn't have said, even something you said by accident, which can nonetheless create a memory that is present and recurring throughout your life. You can be haunted in more obvious ways still, by the memory of a dead parent or friend. These ghosts have no need for supernatural explanations for they already make sense in a materialist framework. For example, Alan Turing was famously haunted by his dear friend Christopher Morcom, after the latter's sudden death at a young age. But such a haunting is understandable in materialist and even atheist terms, in the psychological contexts of regret, longing, sadness, and more happily, in the affirmation of life.

Almost any memory can haunt, because ghosts are memories, but not all memories are ghosts. Prior to consideration of the social and political dimensions of ghosts, we should establish the basic diagnostic value of the language of ghosts here.

Each of us has many memories, some of them readily available, others buried beneath the detritus of more pressing concerns at the forefront of our consciousness. Occasionally, to access a memory requires some kind of trigger or stimulus, prompting the memory to "come back to us," as we say. Within the multilayered field of memories, only some have the status of ghosts. For example, much of what we remember does *not* haunt us. The most banal memories of a person's life are not ghosts. The question of which memories haunt, and which do not, depends very much upon a person's ghosts, and is only answerable in response to highly individuated and personal questions; this is quite clearly, then, a psychological process requiring a psychoanalytic activity of question and answer, although not in any clinical sense. In the first instance, the language of ghosts can help us to distinguish the memories that haunt us and why. What haunts a person, and what does not, tells us something about that person. Is it even possible to know a person without some knowledge of their ghosts? Such knowledge of the other, as well as self-knowledge, depends upon knowing ghosts.

It is important, however, to keep in mind that a memory is not a simple fact. What one remembers has much to do with *how* one experiences a thing. In any human relationship, whether between siblings, friends, or lovers, certain facts are remembered in very different ways, and memories tend to preserve particular trans-muted realities. That is, a memory is the product of some inter-pretation of some affectation, which puts us in touch with how something seemed to us to be, or what its significance was at that particular time in our lives. Often, two siblings close in age, with the same parents and basic upbringing, remember the mother or the father in incompatibly different ways. In some cases, the memory of an apparently boring or incidental affair can haunt a person, because the subject that it haunts experienced and remembers it in a particular way, has given it a certain signifi-cation, and has thereby inadvertently converted it into an active ghost. As in: "You do not remember when our father said that because it did not affect you as it affected me."

Something must also be said about good ghosts, or "friendly ghosts." To speak in moral terms (although we could just as easily make the point in other terms), we may be reassured of a per-son's good character by the fact that they are haunted by the bad things they've done. Good ghosts can be antagonistic, too. As shall be argued below, it may be necessary to participate in a kind of "becoming-ghost," whereby our actions contribute to haunt-ing the conscience(s) of others, of institutions and their human representatives. Victims of rape, of torture, or even victims of capital, or any other of the many real victims of the world, can move beyond the law and its failings by way of haunting their perpetrators. This haunting need not take the form of vengeance, and it may well be an important part of what is called justice, or at least a perfectly sensible indignation. In another context, to be haunted by the reassuring memory of a lost loved one, by the warm memory of some experience of love or friendship, shows that certain ghosts make good company.

Each of us is haunted, and yet we cannot judge this fact as good or bad. The goodness of a haunting depends upon the nature of the ghost(s), upon how they haunt us, upon why they haunt us, and how the haunting changes things. The tricky thing about ghosts is that they can be invisible, and at the same time, can make themselves known beyond any shadow of a doubt. Each person comes with some ghosts, and usually, you cannot see them right away. If a person denies having any ghosts, they are either lying, delusional, revealing a deficit of self-understanding, or they have not yet experienced the active haunting of their ghosts. Any of these possibilities is more tenable than the assertion that absolutely none of one's memories haunts. The total absence of conscious reflection and conscientious consideration may minimize our awareness of ghosts, and might eliminate the effects of being haunted, but thoughtful people, and I would say most people, aren't spared so easily. Ghosts are a feature of the apparatus of thinking, and thinking people have them. If such assertions seem overly categorical, they should not. It is worth recalling that these assertions merely affirm the etymological and conceptual imbrications of *Geist* with both mind (the mind thinks) and ghost (ghosts haunt).

Some of a person's ghosts are not a problem and never will be. Some ghosts are welcome to stay. Other ghosts should be confronted and laid to rest for they stand in the way of our desires and obstruct our being-in-the-world until they are "exorcized," until they are busted. But the fact is that a great many of the ghosts we'd like to bust will haunt us forever.

ii Haunted commons: our ghosts

Everywhere in the world, people are haunted. Ghosts are not the private property of the cultural imaginary of just some people

37

somewhere. There are, to be sure, many differences across cultures in discourses on ghosts, but it is more to our present purposes to consider commonalities. Ghosts are typically "found" in places where horrible things have happened to people, things not easily reconciled with the various consciences and common understandings of people. We can highlight at least three tendencies:[26] (a) the ghosts of the despised, locked-up, and vilified, (b) the ghosts of exploitation, and (c) the ghosts of power and war. These tendencies often overlap. For example, despised and vilified people are often the most exploited, and war typically requires vilification of an "enemy." In what follows, I shall touch upon some of the ghosts that haunt in common ways around the world.

The overarching aim of the present discussion is to articulate an understanding of *our* ghosts, that is, haunting on the level of the social body. Quite obviously, I make no mention of most of the hauntings of the world. There are uncountable purportedly haunted sites related to freak accidents, suicides, rapes, hangings, drownings, fires, murdered and dead celebrities, and tragic lost lovers. I gloss over such locations to draw special attention to some of the more institutional and social ghosts that haunt.

(a) Throughout history, institutions have been built to incarcerate the manifold despised and misunderstood peoples, including prisoners, slaves, witches, and all those deemed "mad" or "dangerous." Throughout history, and still to this day, massive subsets of the human population are removed from the public and locked up in various spaces of privation from the world. There is a common tendency to later find ghosts wherever the despised, criminals, and misfits have been institutionalized and mistreated. Alas, one of the many problems of morality is that it often arrives on the

26 The three tendencies discussed here are not the only possible tendencies we could discuss that would reveal cross-cultural commonalities in discourses on ghosts.

scene too late. This is one of the many problems of ghosts as well, that they are an indication of a justice or right that arrived too late.

In Australia, the Ararat Lunatic Asylum was opened in 1867, where an estimated 13,000 people died. Also in Australia is the site of the purportedly haunted Beechworth Lunatic Asylum. The so-called lunatic was often the victim of the normative "reason" of the day.[27] It is not so much that we are haunted by the "lunatics" themselves, but rather, by what happened in the places where we kept them, by what happened *to them*. In Indonesia, ghost sightings have been reported in the basement of a building called Lawang Sewu, formerly a prison. In Ireland, ghost tourists can visit Leap Castle, where so many were imprisoned and executed. In the US, the list of sites haunted by the ghosts of the despised is too numerous to account for here, since every state is full of such locations, including many prisons and slave haunts. In Louisiana, for example, the former Magnolia Plantation is reportedly haunted by slaves. The Myrtles Plantation in St. Francisville is reportedly haunted by the ghost of a slave known as Chloe.

Angela Davis' concept of "abolition democracy" is useful here. Following W.E.B. DuBois, who used the term "abolition democracy" in his *Black Reconstruction*, Davis applies the idea to "three forms of abolitionism: the abolition of slavery, the abolition of the death penalty, and the abolition of the prison."[28] She argues that abolitionist politics cannot be understood as beginning and ending with the transatlantic slave system, for such a theorization would neglect the fact that institutional racism continues to function in other forms that also need to be abolished. Davis argues that full abolition must start with an understanding that

27 See Foucault, Michel, *Madness and Civilization: A History of Insanity in the Age of Reason*, trans. Richard Howard (New York: Vintage Books/Random House, 1988).

28 Davis, Angela Y., *Abolition Democracy: Beyond Empire, Prisons, and Torture* (New York: Seven Stories Press, 2005), p. 91.

when slavery was abolished, black people were set free, but they lacked access to the material resources that would enable them to fashion new, free lives. Prisons have thrived over the last century precisely because of the absence of those resources and the persistence of some of the deep structures of slavery.[29]

Indeed, the mass incarceration of African Americans today reliably reveals that black people are disproportionately profiled as criminals, policed, and arrested. And the privatization of prisons that profit from such racialized incarceration incentivize such institutional racist practices.[30] Inasmuch as the very racism of slavery remains functional, organizational, and structural in the present society, so long after the formal abolition of slavery itself, the present society cannot rid itself of the ghosts of the despised, locked-up, and vilified.

Even where the ghosts of the despised, enslaved, and abused do the haunting directly, these are typically the ghosts of those who have died from maltreatment, abandonment, or egregious disregard. In this way, the ghosts of the despised are part of a reckoning with a history of institutional — and institutionalized — violence. The ghost tours in the slave haunts of the French Quarter in New Orleans, as in many other locations, convey this sense of historical reckoning. When I visited New Orleans (several years before Hurricane Katrina), every night downtown was a booming ghost-tour business, drawing in people for stories about the ghosts of all of the abused house servants and slaves. It would be reasonable to expect that other despised and mistreated people, such as gays and lesbians who have been "bashed," detained, killed, "suicided," and sent to "heterosexualizing" programs will produce a new wave of ghosts. Indeed, inasmuch as societies have

29 Ibid., p. 92.
30 Davis, Angela Y., *Are Prisons Obsolete?* (New York: Seven Stories Press/ Open Media Series, 2003).

already become consciously haunted by their historical treatment of gays and lesbians, the becoming-ghost of despised sexualities is well underway. Would any reader be surprised to learn that, in the future, a shuttered Guantanamo Bay "Detention Camp" may be reportedly haunted too? Haunting such as this even begins as something rather tepid, like the good conscience of a liberal. The good conscience of the liberal is mainly untroubled by what the liberal order presently allows for and endorses (i.e. profit prisons, racism, sexism, capitalism, free trade, drone warfare, etc.), in defense of the existing situation; liberal good conscience prefers to show itself by condemning the positions of more conservative foes and past generations only.

Liberalism is not always a disingenuous position. Sometimes it is. During major election cycles in dominant European countries and in the US, liberals often proclaim their full faith in some single human person or political organization, which outside of the election cycle would be the target of reasonable criticism. Common sense about the failures and limitations of the established conduits for politics lapses to make way for a temporary ideological warfare initiated by the procedural apparatus. But the other side should not be ignored. Many liberals and progressives are well aware of the awful menu offered by conventional politics, but they also understand that some important things are at stake, for example, in domestic or foreign policy. And many of these policy positions matter for real people. So when labor unions and left-wing activists endorse presidential candidates, it is a smug elitism to proclaim that they are duped and deluded. Such a purist disdain ignores the fact that, despite the real limitations and inevitable disappointment, there are real stakes in the so-called politics of lesser-evilism. Lesser-evilism recognizes the awful menu, but considers that not all of the options are equally awful. Of the various positions of liberalism, this one is clearly preferable to any full ideological faith in the spectacle politics of "capitalist democracy."

Nonetheless, such a sensible and preferable liberalism is often hard to find. In the US, for example, many feminists, communists, socialists and various other radicals and leftists point out that Hillary Clinton is a militaristic, conservative, neoliberal who maintains no meaningful connection to any of their causes.[31] Indeed, Clinton liberalism represents the triumph of right-wing politics, whereby liberals come to claim Henry Kissinger's foreign policy, the dismantling of welfare, ruthlessly pro-business policy agendas, and the total freedom of capital as their own accomplishments. But it is worth considering that Hillary Clinton still represented a hopeful horizon for many millions of US liberals in the 2016 election cycle. This reveals the truly dilapidated state of liberalism today, and confirms what radical critics have long said about the Democratic Party and capitalist elections. It also helps to substantiate the case for a politics by other means than parties and elections.

Revolt, at its best, is a rejection of lesser-evil politics and a challenge to move beyond the menu. To risk an overly general formulation, we might say that whereas the vote considers the lesser evil, the revolt rejects the given choices. And of course, one may vote today and participate in an uprising tomorrow, as has been seen in many cases, such as in the wake of the 2009 Iranian presidential election. Yet, in the historical juxtaposition, liberalism appears as the beneficiary of earlier revolt. Liberals approve of the changes most emphatically after the changes are settled and done, whereas they call for order and restraint at the time of the original rupture. This is what, for example, enables liberals in the US to criticize civil-rights protestors engaged in civil disobedience as "extreme" while watching them on TV in the 1950s, but to lionize and embrace them many decades later. The radical

---

31 See, for example, Henwood, Doug, *My Turn: Hillary Clinton Targets the Presidency* (New York and London: OR Books, 2016); *False Choices: The Faux Feminism of Hillary Rodham Clinton*, ed. Liza Featherstone (London and New York: Verso Books, 2016).

critical and political content of John Brown's revolt, of the Stone-wall uprising, and in many other examples, upsets the present liberalism and shapes the future one. Thus, the liberal position is thoroughly haunted by specters of revolt.[32]

(b) A second tendency is to find ghosts wherever workers have been fatally exploited, expropriated, or abused, in the process of constructing some grand fortress or bourgeois monument, some site to be haunted later on by the very ones who built it. This tendency, as one might expect, often overlaps with the first one, for it specifies haunting by the abused. But in this category, we don't have a refrain of lunacy to confuse us about whether the haunting comes from people who we feared. In other words, the ghosts of exploitation come from the maltreatment of everyday people, "regular people" who we could relate to without much difficulty of imagination. The difference here is that the ghosts come from abuses of the unexceptional or banal lives of "regular" unnamed people.

Back again to Australia, there is Brisbane City Hall. There, stories of deaths spanning the time period of the construction of the building feed into stories about the ghosts that haunt it. During construction, many workers are said to have died while placing the foundations. Beyond this, there is haunting associated with the fact that Brisbane City Hall is purportedly built on top of a sacred aboriginal site, either a meeting place or a camp ground. In China, there are stories of the ghosts of the exploited workers who died constructing the Great Wall. Throughout the world, similar stories accompany massive undertakings, such as railroads that depend on the total exhaustion and expiration

32 Of course, we could also say that political conservatism is similarly haunted by revolt. The focus here on liberalism is due to the fact that the liberal position presents itself as the slower but more reasonable and practical alternative to revolt. This goes back at least to Kantian liberalism, and runs on up to the present form.

of human bodies. In the Brisbane example, with the aboriginal dimension of the story, we can pull out another common thread: Indigenous peoples around the world are often said to haunt their former places of being-in-the-world, places from which they were almost always forcibly expropriated by the interests of capital and foreign powers.

Within this tendency of haunting, we find a certain resistance to erasure. The ghosts of exploitation remind us that there were bodies and brains there before, and that people suffered and died to leave us some monument of human undertaking. The building or construction site (or its human representatives) might wish to erase the memory of those who died to build it, of those who were expropriated from the geographic space it rests on, yet the ghosts stand in the way of such erasure.[33] The ghosts remind us of what would be erased, or of what was "erased" in some fatal episode of violence, but the persistence of active haunting prevents the total erasure of that history. The tendency of such haunting, observable in purported haunts around the world, further explains why ghosts are often thought to be anchored to specific architectural structures. Whereas the first tendency largely regards the unconscionable things that have happened *within* physical spaces and buildings, this second tendency regards the unconscionable

33   Here, I cannot help but think of Donald Trump's campaign of 2015-2016 for the US presidency. Trump's career is fundamentally about building and buildings, about real estate, lavish and extravagant casinos, resorts, playgrounds for the rich. Throughout his campaign, he invoked all of his building and buildings. But what of their actual construction, and what of the massive service workforce that cleans and maintains them, and those thousands who wait on Trump's guests? All of that essential work that makes Trump's building and buildings into a functional reality is carried out by nameless others than Trump. Of course, they remain unnamed and even unmentioned in a campaign in which all the building and buildings are presented as Trump's sole doing, as a credit to his brains for business alone, etc. There is a whole strata of humanity that Trump's fortunes depend upon, which is invisible in his presentation. But one day they may speak just like the factory workers in China who came out to haunt the iPhone.

things that have happened *before* buildings or constructs — the exploitation and expropriation that made them possible, or more simply, their foundational violence.

(c) The third tendency, like the first two, often overlaps with them. Throughout the world, it is quite common to find ghosts wherever official political power has been deployed to torture and kill by way of militarism, imperialism, or war in general. These are things (i.e. militarism, imperialism, war) that nation-states do with great efficiency. Even if we recognize that states are instruments in the service of capital, capital needs the state and its arms for war. Historically, certain forms of violence (the most devastating forms) have been monopolized by official institutions of governance. Those who worry about the violence of revolt should remember that the most systematic and catastrophic instruments of violence are not available to everyday people. The "violence" of a riot is always and invariably dwarfed by the violence of aerial bombardment, for example. Indeed, if one were a pacifist (and I am not), it would seem necessary to take an anarchist position in light of the terrible global history of state violence. To be a statist, on the other hand, is always to reconcile oneself with various forms of violence, past and present.

In China, one could visit the so-called "Forbidden City," located in Beijing and home to the Palace Museum. For six hundred years, from the Ming Dynasty to the end of the Qing Dynasty, the Forbidden City was the Chinese imperial palace. The Forbidden City was the home of the imperial family, complete with a massive store of "concubines" and "servants." Thousands lived and died there as human fodder for the pleasures of dynastic regimes. It is no wonder that visitors and workers have long claimed to see ghosts there. In France, at Château de Versailles, home to the royal family from 1682 and 1789, there have been reports of sightings of the ghost of a beheaded Marie Antoinette. In Germany, it is hardly surprising that the Reichstag building in Berlin has been reported haunted and, in Heidelberg, the Hexenturm Witches Tower and the Nazi Amphitheatre are said to be so, too. In Malaysia, the Victoria Institution is said to be haunted, a school in Kuala Lumpur that was turned into a torture chamber for prisoners of war and civilians by the Japanese during World War II. In England, airfields around the country are claimed to be haunted by the ghosts of airmen who died fighting in World War II. In Russia, the Kremlin is said to be haunted by Lenin and Stalin, although it is possible to say that all of us (including communists) are haunted by them.

The main thing to distinguish in this category of haunting is that political power, militarism, and imperialism have been the causes of so much carnage throughout human history that they cannot but leave a legacy of ghost activity along with the corpses. Of the three tendencies discussed above, the ghosts of power and war are the most deterritorialized. That is, these ghosts are attached to human eventuality more than to architecture, physical structures, or national boundaries. In a certain sense, the ghosts of power and war have long forecasted the definition of empire made famous by Michael Hardt and Antonio Negri: "In contrast to imperialism, Empire establishes no territorial center of power and does not rely on fixed boundaries or barriers. It is a *decentered* and *deterritorializing* apparatus..."[34] Indeed, the ghosts of war, as accessories of empire, cannot but travel the world beyond fixed boundaries or barriers, following the trauma of military invasion.

To highlight the literal and materialist discourse on ghosts in the context of the ghosts of war, we may consider the recent crisis in the US of soldiers returning from Iraq and Afghanistan with dangerous and widespread outbreaks of Post-Traumatic

34 Hardt, Michael and Negri, Antonio, *Empire* (Cambridge, MA and London: Harvard University Press, 2000), p. xii.

Stress Disorder (PTSD). Of course, long before this crisis of PTSD, it was on the level of common sense that war is traumatic. But now, the epidemic crisis of PTSD haunts the wars in Iraq and Afghanistan in concrete and impactful ways.

The ghosts alluded to above may be considered real and unreal, depending on what exactly one means by ghost. Using the definition provided in the present chapter, all of these ghosts are real. Simply put, that generations of people have been and continue to be haunted by the awful things that people do cannot be gainsaid. Such ghosts are a part of historical understanding, of moral reckoning, or of what is called justice. The abovementioned ghosts can only be condemned as unreal in the sense that would specify them as celestial apparitions, although just as it is with God, we can never really prove the non-existence of such ghosts to everyone's satisfaction. But with ghosts, unlike with God, why should we need to insist on their metaphysical or celestial presence? The materialist discourse on ghosts I have been using would deprive many of their otherworldly claims, some of which are integral to religious identities and spiritual worldviews. Nonetheless, the materialist discourse on ghosts can be engaged in any milieu, on both theological and non-theological terrains, and can contribute concretely to the analysis of personal, social, and political histories.

In this book, though, my opposition to the celestial form of ghosts as metaphysical apparitions is more political than phenomenological. We mustn't only confront the metaphysical ghosts that are attached to something outside of ourselves. Such ghosts are too easily seen as external and independent, and even the assertion of their existence relieves us of the burden of having to confront collective memory and historical self-understanding. We must go farther. Indeed, my sense of the ghost is more persuasive (in psychological, historical, political, and moral terms) than the widespread sense that identifies every haunting with an otherworldly phenomenon. Every day, people deny celestial apparitions, and can always find an easy way to do so. But the PTSD that accompanies war is a reality that cannot be denied. Post-war PTSD can be established as certain a fact as any, and it is one of the many ghosts that haunt war.

It is no coincidence or surprise that the ghosts of the despised, the ghosts of the exploited, and the ghosts of war haunt the world. The question is: What to do with these ghosts? Or, what can these ghosts do?

III Ghost-busting

Ghost-busting refers to any process that brings a haunting to its end, any process that lays an active ghost to rest, such that the person or place is no longer haunted by it. In many of the examples I've described, it is actually good news to be haunted by ghosts. Not all ghosts should be busted. While, on the one hand, we might wish for victims of abuse to bust the ghosts that haunt them, on the other hand, we might find some small consolation in the haunting of the perpetrators. Some ghosts, and ultimately the ghosts of greatest interest to us, are the other side of something awful, of catastrophe, of death. *Their* absence is only bad news.

But some ghosts should be busted.

In political, cultural, and psychological contexts, certain ghosts keep us from participation; certain ghosts stymie feelings of solidarity, alienate and depress us, *both individually and collectively*. Although she does not rely in any way on the language of ghosts, Julia Kristeva has done much to help us understand the nature of the ghosts I want to discuss, and the ghost-busting that should and could be done here.

Kristeva has written a trilogy on revolt, which I regard as indispensable to any good theory of revolt today, and thus I return to her work throughout this book.[35] Kristeva wants to diagnose what haunts a culture of revolt, or more specifically, what keeps us from revolting.

> Stalinism no doubt marked the strangling of the culture of revolt, its deviation into terror and bureaucracy. Can one recapture the spirit itself and extricate new forms from it beyond the two impasses where we are caught today: the failure of rebellious ideologies, on the one hand, and the surge of consumer culture, on the other?[36]

While she does not write of specters of revolt, she is always concerned with the spirit of revolt. Kristeva then asserts that "[t]here is an urgent need to develop the culture of revolt starting with our aesthetic heritage and to find new variants of it."[37]

We should note that when Kristeva uses the term "revolt," she does not mean the politically specific sense of a civil society in revolt against its government (although her sense of revolt *is* inclusive of that more common, narrower meaning). Kristeva begins with the etymological and conceptual richness of the word and idea "revolt" from the Latin verbs *volvere* and *revolvere*, which indicate consultation, rereading, return, and repair, among other meanings. Revolt has both individual and collective meanings,

35 The trilogy on revolt is as follows: Kristeva, Julia, *Revolution in Poetic Language* (New York: Columbia University Press, 1984); *The Sense and Non-Sense of Revolt: The Powers and Limits of Psychoanalysis* (New York: Columbia University Press, 2000); *Intimate Revolt: The Powers and Limits of Psychoanalysis* (New York: Columbia University Press, 2002). In addition to Kristeva's trilogy, I also regard the short collection of interviews with her, *Revolt, She Said* (Los Angeles and New York: Semiotext(e), 2002), as an excellent introductory supplement to the major works listed here.
36 Kristeva, Julia, *The Sense and Non-Sense of Revolt: The Powers and Limits of Psychoanalysis*, trans. Jeanine Herman (New York: Columbia University Press, 2000), p. 7.
37 Ibid.

and as a psychoanalyst, Kristeva explores what she calls "psychic revolt" (discussed more fully below). What Kristeva calls psychic revolt requires, using my language in the present work, a confrontation with ghosts.

The relationship between the notion of a haunting ghost and the notion of analysis appears for us in Kristeva's description of Freud's problematic as "a remembrance and representation of the initial murder."[38] In Freudian psychoanalysis, the work of analysis is used to go back to scenes of the crime to which a person's ghosts can be traced. An analyst begins by trying to understand the nature of the ghosts that haunt the analysand, and the process of analysis attempts to return to, uncover, consult, reread, and ultimately repair the damage that was done some time ago. Considering the exploratory and revelatory dimensions of analysis, and the etymological and conceptual meanings of "revolt," we begin to understand how and why ghost-busting might require a form of psychic revolt. Thinking about revolt in a psychoanalytic context, Kristeva proposes three forms of analytical or psychic revolt: "revolt as the transgression of a prohibition; revolt as repetition, working-through, working-out; and revolt as displacement, combinatives, games."[39]

So, as we have been saying, every person has ghosts, some of which should be busted, and analysis provides certain ways of thinking about how to do that. Utilizing Kristeva's psychoanalytic theory, one way to ghost-bust may be to confront and transgress rules, including expectations for behavior and aspirations. If you are haunted by rules that constrain you to accept or suffer past trauma, and you do not want to be, then break those rules. Another way to ghost-bust may be to confront and think about the nature of one's own ghosts, going over again and again their origins, their *raison d'être*, and working through or working out

38 Ibid., p. 15.
39 Ibid., p. 16.

the issues that have left one so haunted. Finally, displacement, combinatives, and games brings us to Kristeva's interest in aesthetics and new variants of creative artistic praxis.[40] This last form involves experimentation in modes of play and expression. Revolt always involves acts of questioning, and Kristeva says that such a questioning "is also present in artistic experience, in the rejection and renewal of old codes of representation staged in painting, music, or poetry."[41] None of these figures of revolt precludes the other and, most likely, a healthy revolt employs some combination of two or three of the above.

We cannot simply rename Kristeva's "psychic revolt" as our "ghost-busting." We wouldn't want to, for the limits of psychoanalysis (readily confessed by Kristeva herself) leave out too much, and also, I am not specifically interested in our defining questions from a psychoanalytic point of view. There are other ways to bust ghosts than through the various pathways of analysis that Kristeva outlines. Some ghosts can be outgrown, forgotten, busted by love, or replaced by new ones without any warning. No practice or discipline has it all figured out. It's not easy to bust the ghosts that haunt in ways that paralyze us with fear and anxiety, and that cut us off from others and from the possibility for a culture of revolt. But inasmuch as we are talking about busting the ghosts of *Geist*, the ghosts of the human mind, Kristeva's analytical revolt is well calibrated to the task. For psychoanalysis in general, and for Kristeva in particular, *Geist* is a central unit of study.

Especially useful in the resources of Kristeva is her rejection of the dichotomy between the individual and collective crisis. The crisis of the individual is directly and causally related to the crisis of the collectivity, and vice versa, so working through problems by

40 Here, Kristeva's interest is no doubt informed by her work with the radical (at the time, largely communist) experimental artist/activist journal, *Tel Quel*, which she joined in the 1960s.

41 Kristeva, Julia, *Revolt, She Said*, trans. Brian O'Keeffe (Los Angeles and New York: Semiotext(e), 2002), p. 121.

way of revolt is a necessarily multilayered and multifarious process of individual and collective action, and never one without the other.

All of this is clear in Kristeva's numerous volumes on revolt.[42] The central point is sharply and summarily articulated in *Revolt, She Said*:

> First of all, this incapacity to rebel is the sign of national depression. Faltering images of identity (when they're not lacking altogether) and lost confidence in common cause, give rise at the national level to just what the depressed individual feels in his isolation: namely, feeling cut off from the other person (your nearest and dearest, neighbors, politics) and from communication, inertia, your desire switched off. On the other hand, people who rebel are malcontents with frustrated, but vigorous desires.[43]

But how can we make the more concretely social and political side of ghost-busting appear? What we can say, with the help of Kristeva's psycho-social theory, is that individual people and collectivities are often haunted into isolated and depoliticized states of acquiescence and hopelessness by personal and political ghosts. And, increasing precariousness and privatization around the world have only consolidated the problem. Kristeva points to the political state's (especially the European Union's) effort to rethink "the citizen" as a "patrimonial person," that is, mainly in terms of ownership, "owners of our organs" if of nothing else.[44] People are not only haunted by their pasts, but increasingly also by their uncertain futures. The widespread sense of a fragile security in

---

42 Of the trilogy, the major study that is especially relevant to this subject is *Intimate Revolt: The Powers and Limits of Psychoanalysis*, trans. Jeanine Herman (New York: Columbia University Press, 2002).

43 Kristeva, *Revolt, She Said*, pp. 83-84.

44 Ibid., p. 84.

the present, and no certain future, is largely what explains the widespread resonance of the term "precariat" throughout Europe in the early part of the millennium. Following Kristeva, we could say that a person who wants to bust her ghosts can engage in some form of psychic or analytical revolt, whereas society needs a culture of revolt in order to remain in a state of healthy questioning, renewal, and renovation. It is within this context that I claim revolt as a form of ghost-busting. By way of revolt, the ghosts that haunt can be confronted and busted. Sometimes, ghost-busting is the way to stare down what haunts us, to consider its original sources, and to make amends with some preceding trauma, some other form of violence, or even a bad conscience.

But that is only sometimes. For there is another side to the ghost story: Sometimes, what is needed is to become the ghosts ourselves, to become the ones who haunt.

IV Becoming-ghost, specters of revolt

Communism is one of the most notorious ghosts of the past two hundred years. Communism has haunted the world since the 19th century. Communists and anti-communists alike have been happy to accept that claim, albeit from opposing points of view. Marx, the great materialist, makes numerous mentions and uses of the language of ghosts, as well as of sorcery. In that most well-known line recalled already above, *The Communist Manifesto* begins: "A specter is haunting Europe — the specter of Communism. All the powers of old Europe have entered into a holy alliance to exorcise this specter: Pope and Czar, Metternich and Guizot, French Radicals and German police-spies." [45] In this

45 Marx, *The Communist Manifesto* (New York: International Publishers, 1994), p. 8.

53

context, Marx roots for the specter of communism against its determined exorcists.

Yet Marx's normative regard for this communist haunting was complicated. On the one hand, much of the fear of communism was (and still is) the result of slander and ideological misrepresentation, which Marx and Engels sought to refute in *The Communist Manifesto* and elsewhere. But, on the other hand, the specter of communism is admittedly something that *should* haunt and frighten the existing capitalist world, or what Marx and Engels called "bourgeois society."[46] If it does not frighten, then it is banal. The complexity of these two sides can only be grasped when we understand that the ideal starting position for communism would be to actively haunt the existing state of affairs. That is to say, communism aspires to threaten the constituted present in an existential way, and inasmuch as communism threatens to abolish or transform the existing world, the world is haunted by it.

The specter of communism continues to haunt, but in other locations and stranger ways than those Marx imagined in 1848. The specter of communism is today largely comprised of the incapacities of capital — capital is haunted by what it cannot do to address its own crises, to address us when we become its crisis. Also recently, the specter of communism actively haunts in the Middle Eastern and North African (MENA) states, and in Turkey, in India, in China, in Spain, and throughout Latin America. "Communism" also haunts, in especially ideological forms, in the US and the UK. (I use "communism" in quotes to specify an idea of communism that is not recognizably communist from a philosophical perspective, but that is commonly deployed as a vilification that derives its force from Cold War discourses and other propaganda. I discuss the distinctions between communism and

46 Ibid., p. 9.

"communism" at greater length elsewhere.[47] For now, suffice it to say that both communism and "communism," that is, both what it means and its spectacle form (i.e. its vilified form), retain some of their old power to haunt the world. If that were not the case, the word communism would be invoked for nothing and to no political effect.[48])

Inasmuch as the human world is governed by the logic of capital — that is, inasmuch as everyday life conforms to the logic of capitalist exchange relations and the valuations of money — the world should be haunted by its past, present, and future. Communism aside, every human person can understand that other logics than capital should govern a human life. There is so much that cannot be bought, like dignity and love, and so much that should not be bought, like the fundamental means of subsistence and basic human health. When we subordinate too much of human life to the logic of capital, something better haunts us, impressing upon us the possibility and desirability of other ways of life that threaten the existing way of life. Let's consider one particular instance, from which readers can imagine other historical and possible examples.

The uprisings that erupted in Turkey in May and June 2013 constitute a certain modality of haunting. Also, since late 2010, regimes across numerous MENA countries south of the Mediterranean Sea have been haunted by the so-called Arab Spring.

47 See Gilman-Opalsky, Richard, *Spectacular Capitalism: Guy Debord and the Practice of Radical Philosophy* (New York and London: Autonomedia/Minor Compositions, 2011) and *Precarious Communism: Manifest Mutations, Manifesto Detourned* (Wivenhoe, New York, and Port Watson: Autonomedia/Minor Compositions, 2014).

48 In contrast to the enduring power of the specter of communism, it is worth considering how much anarchy and anarchism really worry or threaten (i.e. haunt) the political constitution of the present. Inasmuch as anarchism does not haunt (and does not even function as an effective insult in politics), it can only dream of becoming-ghost.

Even where civil societies were not in revolt, the spirit of uprising that appeared to come from Tunisia was understood as a shape-shifting phenomenon that could travel across boundaries, with different nodal points in different locations. We could perhaps speak of the ghost of Mohamed Bouazizi, or at least, a mobile *Gemeingeist* that could grow and animate subsets of populations in revolt.[49]

From outside in the West, and for many on the inside, Turkey has come to be seen as a positive example of the power of capital and neoliberalism to "develop" a region close to Iraq and the MENA states in "good" directions following Western/European models. The uprising was triggered in part by contestation over the future of green public space in Istanbul, beginning with a sit-in in Gezi Park on Taksim Square, where fewer than one hundred protesters gathered on May 27, 2013. The gatherings quickly grew into fierce nationwide opposition to Prime Minister Recep Tayyip Erdogan's ten-year rule and provided an open space for the expression of society's disaffection about the country's political, economic, and social crises. Erdogan immediately forgot his publicly stated position during the earlier uprisings in Egypt and Syria, when he demanded that Mubarak and Assad yield to their people and step down. When Erdogan finally became the target of his own people, that old advice became inapplicable, as he denounced his opponents as "vandals" and "terrorists."

Given the differences between Syria and Egypt, on the one hand, and Turkey, on the other, Erdogan mistakenly took for granted the "fixity" of the spirit of revolt in neighboring and nearby countries.

49 The German word "*Gemeingeist*" is typically left in the original German because its meaning is difficult to capture in a succinct English term. *Geist*, as we have discussed, indicates mind, spirit, and ghost, whereas *Gemein* means common, commonly, and shared. *Gemeingeist* thus indicates a common or shared spirit/sensibility, a common thinking or feeling. In socialist philosophy, the terms *Gemeingeist* and *Gemeinwesen* are typically used to indicate something like a communist spirit, or a shared sense of life and its problems.

But ghosts can travel. They do not stay put as obediently as power-holders might wish. The uprisings in Turkey — like those before in the "Arab Spring" — have to do with problems that also occur elsewhere, so the tendency to describe them as "Egyptian," "Turkish," or even as "Arab," reduces and misunderstands the phenomena in dangerous ways. We are in fact looking at confrontations with rather general (or generalizable) problems of the existing world, a world increasingly governed by the global logic of capital, but also, a world in crisis (i.e. economic, democratic, ecological, political), a world that people everywhere want to throw into question for many different reasons.

In Turkey, the revolt articulates a number of widely applicable grievances clearly and directly. Consider one of them: The opposition in Istanbul, in Gezi Park and Taksim Square, to building a shopping mall was an opposition in defense of the open green space that the mall would be built upon. The uprising sprang from the peoples' defense of the common space against capital's seizure and repurposing of that space for private interests. Erdogan understood this objection well, which is why he insisted that the shopping mall would not be "a traditional mall," for it would include cultural centers, an opera house, and a mosque.[50] In the original plans, an Ottoman-era military barracks would be rebuilt near the site and the historic Ataturk Cultural Center would be demolished. Kalyon Group, a company with ties to the Erdogan government, was contracted to carry out the project. The whole idea embodies and reflects with perfect accuracy one of the most malignant lies of neoliberalism: Namely, that privatization and the logic of capital do no harm to culture, to the natural world, or to public space. Any shopping mall built on that site will be

---

50 BBC News, June 7, 2013, "Turkey clashes: Why are Gezi Park and Taksim Square so important?," accessed December 28, 2015, http://www.bbc.co.uk/news/world-europe-22753752.

haunted by the uprising of the summer of 2013, and will continue to be a site, indeed a target, for future haunting.

But do not think these ghosts immaterial! Ghosts are not only a shadowy lurking that follows the failure or death of some person or collectivity. Ghosts can be active, they can intervene in the world and change things, and often, the problem with the world is not that it is too haunted, but that it is not haunted enough. There is, after all, something rather absurd (and suspiciously convenient) about the "ghost-tour notion" of haunted sites, according to which ghosts are anchored to fixed locations where we can leave them locked in buildings we might pay to visit for an hour's entertainment. Moreover, there is something regrettable about the reduction of the ghost to a dastardly villain, instead of understanding it as a figment or interruption of the human conscience, as a possible and hopeful threat. If the global affairs of political-economy increasingly reorganize human relations according to exchange relations, and that system is not haunted, it *should be*. If space, time, and culture are increasingly subordinated to the logic of capital, then those disaffected by such subordination — the casualties — must and inevitably will actively haunt the system. It is in this broad context, although not in this context alone, that I recommend "becoming-ghost."

To develop this recommendation, I shall draw upon Félix Guattari's conception of "becoming-woman."[51] Guattari writes:

> On the level of the social body, libido is caught in two systems of opposition: class and sex. It is expected to be male, phallocratic, it is expected to dichotomize all values – the oppositions strong/weak, rich/poor, useful/useless, clean/dirty, etc.
>
> Conversely, on the level of the sexed body, libido is engaged in

51 The use of Guattari here should extinguish any false impression, possibly given by Part III of this chapter, that we are making a Freudian analysis of ghosts. We are not. We are simply allowing ourselves to make use of diverse and contradictory resources, inasmuch as they are useful.

becoming-woman. More precisely, the becoming-woman serves as a point of reference, and eventually as a screen for other types of becoming...[52]

What does this mean? In a social context, which includes behavioral expectations and human aspirations, as well as interpersonal relations, we can make class- and sex-based analyses, for example, in the classical Marxian mode of "class analysis" or in the orientations of those feminisms that look primarily at the social positions of women. Within the context of class- and sex-based analyses, critical theory (including many Marxisms and feminisms) works with certain dichotomies, i.e. you belong to one class or another, one gender or another. But the concept of "becoming" undermines the fixity of class- and gender-based analyses, and specifically, becoming-woman means that we can become more or less "feminine" or "woman-like" as an act of subversion against the sexed dichotomy. Notice in particular the designation of becoming-woman as a reference "for other types of becoming." Becoming is, for Guattari, about constructing new forms of life, new forms of being, which are not "supposed to be" according to certain rules, social, political, or cultural. Guattari was always fascinated with the politics of subversion.

Guattari's concept of becoming-woman clearly foregrounds some of the radical directions of queer theory and transgender politics today, and becoming-woman is a term that can have multiple literal and figurative meanings. Perhaps the most obvious literal meaning of becoming-woman can be seen in transgender transitions, instances of anatomically "male" persons becoming "female." But to be clear, such a becoming as this, as much as it troubles conventional tendencies within second-wave feminism, *is not at all the form of becoming Guattari intends*. Notice that

52 Guattari, Félix, "Becoming-Woman" in *Hatred of Capitalism: A Semiotext(e) Reader* (Los Angeles: Semiotext(e), 2001), p. 356.

becoming-woman in the physical and literal sense above operates *within* rather than *against* the very dichotomy that Guattari wants to throw into question by way of becoming. The man who becomes a woman is breaking one gender rule in accordance with another that reasserts and affirms dichotomous gender. Such a physical and literal becoming-woman remains trapped by one or another form of sexed becoming. Becoming, in Guattari's sense, can move between and beyond the conventional dichotomies of social analysis, which means that there are many ways to subvert the phallocratic order of the world. Becoming is about subversive forms of life — ways of being-in-the-world, and becoming-woman is only one particular subversive modality. This is why Guattari speaks also of "becoming-child in Schumann, becoming-animal in Kafka, becoming-vegetable in Novalis, becoming-mineral in Beckett."[53] He utilizes the concept of becoming-woman for the purposes of criticizing reactions to what is both seen to be and actually subversive in homosexuality.

Guattari insists on this overarching point:

> In a more general way, every "dissident" organization of libido
> must therefore be linked to a becoming-feminine body, as an
> escape route from the repressive socius, as a possible access to a
> "minimum" of sexed becoming, and as the last buoy vis-à-vis the
> established order.[54]

A politics of subversive becoming makes us slippery, makes it difficult to establish people with fixed identities, and thus makes it difficult to hold people down or to lock them out on the grounds of who they are. A politics of subversive becoming is not easy, it is fraught with difficulties and material limitations. And what about the reality of the many people who don't desire a subversive

53 Ibid.
54 Ibid., pp. 356-357.

becoming? Perhaps if everyone had that desire it would not be subversive. At the very least, subversion begins at the margins, even if it does not stay there. Some one subversion today may be commonplace tomorrow. In any case, for Guattari, becoming is an emancipatory project, and emancipation is never easy.

Also, Guattari does not want us to faithfully preserve and defend his conception of becoming-woman, for it is only one possible nodal point of becoming, of being-in-the-world. He says that "it's important to destroy 'big' notions like woman, homosexual... Things are never that simple. When they're reduced to black-white, male-female categories, there's an ulterior motive, a binary-reductionist operation meant to subjugate them."[55] Hence, even if we would become-woman in any certain way, we would need another becoming still, possible and desirable, in order to keep future emancipatory horizons open.

Following this, to speak of becoming-ghost is a perfectly fitting turn. We know the usual story that death makes ghosts, but we also know, in the case of authors and actors and artists with posthumous influence, that there is a very real sense of life after death there. We can speak of the life of ideas and arguments, we can even write the histories of their fortunes and failures. In this way, so many things live on after death, in the memories and activities of the living, as enduring impacts that have changed or rearranged environments, experiences, and understandings.

Like with Guattari's sense of becoming-woman, we too are not after a specific literal form of becoming-ghost, a becoming from which we can never return or move into any other state of being-in-the-world. Becoming-ghost means that, yes, we are haunted by some ghosts, but we can haunt too, and in subversive ways, just as Guattari spoke of becoming-woman. Guattari's basic idea was to frustrate binaries, dichotomies, and categorizations that are necessary for the organization and control of social life. What

55 Ibid., p. 357.

are the binaries, dichotomies, and categorizations transgressed in the concept of becoming-ghost? They are good conscience/bad conscience, life/death, acceptance/refusal, peace/upheaval, visible/invisible, internal/external, calm/agitate, and absence/presence, among other possibilities. In short, I regard becoming-ghost in the context of possible subversions and emancipations, just as Guattari intended with becoming-woman.

What, then, are the subversive and emancipatory forms of becoming-ghost?

In the first place, we must recognize something subversive about the discourse on ghosts presented here. On the discursive level, what is being undermined is the metaphysical, celestial, and religious ownership of ghosts, by way of a reclamation and restoration of the fuller meaning of *Geist*. We reclaim the language from a proprietary regime, and in our hands, it helps us to speak of human experience in new ways. Franco "Bifo" Berardi has done something similarly subversive with the language of the soul.[56] In this sense, we subvert the hegemonic regard for ghosts.

But, a more hopeful subversive aspiration is that, by way of becoming-ghost, more of what should be haunted will be haunted. Erdogan was haunted by his advice to Mubarak and Assad, and uprisings in other countries — such as the revolt in Brazil that took the world by surprise on June 17, 2013 — will go on to haunt regimes elsewhere. If Erdogan could be taken by surprise in a neoliberal beacon like Turkey, if the most massive uprisings in two decades in Brazil can erupt overnight, then it is not out of the question that regimes in countries like the US and UK might be similarly surprised, as indeed has happened in the US cities of Ferguson and Baltimore. Uprisings do not come from nowhere; they are manifestations of haunted regimes and, like

56 Berardi, Franco "Bifo," *The Soul at Work: From Alienation to Autonomy*, trans. Francesca Cadel and Giuseppina Mecchia (Los Angeles: Semiotext(e), 2009).

people, all regimes have ghosts. Becoming-ghost is a movement toward active haunting, a movement of ghosts making themselves known.

The ghosts in Turkey and Brazil were there before the latest active haunting of their social systems, just like the disaffected indigenous populations in the mountains of Chiapas, Mexico were living in oblivion long before the Zapatista rebellion of 1994. The Zapatistas needed to make the people of Mexico see what was previously invisible. And Mubarak's regime was haunted by Egyptian civil society for nearly thirty years before the regime was frightened into retreat. Morsi too, as we now know, was doomed by early usurpations that haunted his short reign to its swift conclusion. There are many examples of haunted systems with ghosts that need to haunt more actively. The global effect of this activity depends upon the proliferation of deterritorialized haunting, that is, of a becoming-ghost that travels across borders and takes hold of people in unexpected ways, places, and times.

There may be a temptation to say that, in the cases I've mentioned, ghosts become flesh, to say that in instances of presence and visibility the disaffected cease to be ghosts. But that would miss the point of this rather peculiar power. We must always remember what ghosts do. They are defined by their activity, and what they do is haunt. Haunting is an upheaval in an immediately understandable way: To haunt is to unsettle what was settled, to disrupt the semblance that there is nothing here to see. An active haunting shakes us and wakes us, making us see something that we didn't (or couldn't) see before. Often, an active haunting scares us, but if it is convincing, it also makes us explore, look for what is really happening, look for explanations that make sense, and reject the world as it appears on the face of it. That is what a haunting does. There is nothing new in this definition. Haunted people and places are, even on the conventional metaphysical view, unsettled people and places. Too much is too settled too often. Becoming-ghost is a way to unsettle things.

Emancipation is the more difficult issue; less can be said about it at this juncture, in this opening chapter. The question of emancipation will be considered more fully in Chapters 2, 6, and 7. The question of emancipation must always be qualified with "from what" and/or "to what," and the nature of any real emancipation is that we tend only to understand it when we see it. Nonetheless, some very general things can be said here about the emancipatory dimension of becoming-ghost.

A basic premise: Emancipation requires some kind of transformation in forms of life, in being-in-the-world. Therefore, emancipation implies becoming. There can be no emancipation without some process of becoming, without something becoming something else.

But why becoming-ghost and not becoming-woman or becoming-animal? The answer to this question, in the context of this book, is already indicated in the common logic of haunting. Ghost hunters typically engage in one form or another of ghost-busting, and to deal with the ghosts, they say that the ghosts will continue to haunt until X, Y, or Z is done. Typically, ghosts will haunt until there is some kind of reconciliation with the past, some kind of reckoning, some kind of justice, as it were. In the supernatural world of ghosts, it is often said that the spirit of some being must be set free to put an end to the haunting. Another way to put it is to say that the haunting ends only in the liberation of the captive spirit, which is to say *Geist*, the mind, ghosts. A good ghost, like revolt, always unsettles the situation and raises questions about what is going on. That is a fundamental and defining feature of a ghost (and a revolt).

Can the existing world rid itself of its ghosts without becoming something else? That is the question. Is ghost-busting a matter for public policy? Will the ghosts of the economic crisis stop haunting with the implementation of austerity measures, or with their defeat? Even without austerity, even before the latest crisis, things have been getting worse for most people everywhere:

64

there is more inequality, less opportunity, more disaffection, less security, no certain futures, not even in the stock market. Some systems are haunted without even knowing it. We should haunt them more actively, making them afraid, sharing our insecurity with them to make their own futures uncertain. This very sentiment was clearly expressed by a young insurrectionist in the Baltimore uprising: "Bet a cop be scared to kill a motherfucker in Baltimore now – instill the same fear in them as they instill in us."[57]

There is a necessarily transformative imperative at work here, which can be expressed as both an early conclusion and an overarching thesis: *The existing world cannot rid itself of its ghosts without becoming something else.*

---

57   *The 2015 Baltimore Uprising: A Teen Epistolary* (New York: Research and Destroy, 2015), no page numbers.

CHAPTER 2

Beyond Struggle

In the Marxist legacy, there has always been a relationship, even
if sometimes difficult and controversial, between dialectical
philosophy — coming from Hegel and Marx — and political
determination. And I think that this point is especially important
today, because in the present moment there is a general weakness
of revolutionary ideas. And so, when men and women today
engage in political action they are in search of an orientation…
It is not so much the question of immediate struggles which is
obscure. In many cases it is not. For instance, that you should
struggle against racist police violence is clear. But of course in the
long-term it is not enough to defend a purely negative indignation. You must have some principles, some positive will, an
affirmative determination.

— ALAIN BADIOU, "A Philosophy for Militants"[58]

The concept of "struggle" has occupied a central place in the radical
imagination. Social and political transformation have long been
understood as the products of social and political struggle. For
Frederick Douglass, all progress requires struggle, and for Karl
Marx, human history is comprised of conflict and class struggle.
Struggle has become an integral substance, and is often the crux,
of revolutionary projects and politics. Even today, influential
thinkers like the autonomist Marxist John Holloway understand

---

58   Badiou, Alain, "A Philosophy for Militants: Alain Badiou interviewed
by Aaron Hess," *International Socialist Review*, Issue # 95 (Winter, 2014-2015),
accessed January 11, 2016, http://isreview.org/issue/95/philosophy-militants.

that, fundamentally, revolution begins with a scream of sadness. From an affective point of view, however, people do not *want* to struggle or to scream with sadness. In this chapter, I explore the contradiction of desire embodied in wanting a different world without wanting to struggle. For example, is revolt not often the joyful interruption of struggle, a reaction against (and not an expression of) struggle? However we answer that question, I shall argue that there is an intractable absurdity at the heart of any politics that valorizes struggle: *If the narrative on virtuous struggle is not deconstructed, it shall always be ultimately undesirable to make the world that we desire.*

ı Struggle & pleasure: preliminary gestures

In 1979, Raoul Vaneigem — who in many ways wrote the philosophy of autonomy that helped to articulate Italian and French movements in the late 1960s and 1970s — sharply observed the general problematic as follows: "When the struggle against misery becomes the struggle for passionate abundance, you get the reversal of perspective. Doesn't each of us dream of making what gives him intense pleasure the ordinary stuff of everyday life?"[59] Vaneigem is right to call for a reversal of perspective, but the old focus on struggle has not simply been the intellectual and existential error that his polemics make it out to be. That everyday life is full of multifarious forms of struggle is not a fact of the world that can be "reversed" by taking on a different perspective. And, while Vaneigem is also right that most (and sensibly all) individual persons would prefer an everyday life of pleasure to an everyday life of pain, no single individual can make it so within his or her everyday living.

---

59 Vaneigem, Raoul, *The Book of Pleasures*, trans. John Fullerton (London: Pending Press, 1983), p. 22.

The problem, I shall argue, is better understood through a consideration of the *conditions* of everyday life, the field on which everyday life takes place. That field is colonized (though not absolutely) by capital, which means that a critique of capitalism and its culture remains indispensable.

I draw on key concepts from Félix Guattari and Franco "Bifo" Berardi — and on the joyful and even ecstatic disposition of the Egyptian uprising of 2011 and other recent revolts. I pool these resources to make the case for an autonomous conception of collective action that decenters struggle as a virtue. Struggle happens. But theory must speak instead to the cultivation of human talent in micropolitical projects, and must aim to uncover the real desires obscured by a life governed by money.

Very generally, this chapter advances three distinct yet linked reversals of perspective relating to the questions of autonomy, struggle, and pleasure. (1) First, autonomy as a form of freedom (or as freedom itself) is not reducible to the freedom of capital, to the unbounded flow of capital and its arbitration. To the contrary, the logic of capital seeks to organize everyday life such that human autonomy is severely limited and even extinguished, as our creative energies are increasingly relegated to an almost-disappeared "leisure" time. In the actually existing context of everyday life, then, autonomous action antagonizes the expectations of capital. (2) Second, autonomous action is *not* incompatible with collective action, but its relationship to the individual person must be made clearer than it currently is in the major works of autonomist Marxism. (3) Third, while capitalism does make autonomous action expendable in the harshest realizations of human precarity, autonomous action remains the possible and optimal mode for the displacement of struggle. All of the technical terms of these preliminary gestures will be clearly defined below.

In short, I aim to work out the parameters for an autonomous theory of revolution that can help revolution overcome its historic fixation on struggle. Despite the *reality* of struggle, the *virtue* of struggle must be refuted and overcome, and pleasure must play a part in displacing the worn out logic of paying for everything with pain.

II Diagnostics and praxis

The mainly diagnostic approach of the critical theorists of the 1940s did not complete — and could not have been expected to complete — the task of analyzing the problems of capitalism and its culture. Just as one hundred years earlier, Karl Marx's work did not and could not complete that very same task. This is not because of faults in *The Economic and Philosophic Manuscripts of 1844* or the *Dialectic of Enlightenment* of 1944, to mention two examples.[60] These works, and all of the theories of capitalism that surround them, can certainly be criticized, but capital's formal developments are frequent and radical enough to outflank any analysis of a period, no matter how precise the analysis in its place and time. Good diagnostic works, like those just mentioned, retain much of their explanatory value, but capitalism always out-grows them in important ways. Note that I mention the "formal developments" of capital. This is because capital's internal logic remains unchanged (to accumulate capital), while its organiza-tional modes are always changing in order to evolve the capacities of capital to organize culture, communication, production, style, work, and consumption. Very simply, capital's *operational logic* is the same, but its *organizational mode* is changing. The *operational logic* of capital refers to its invariable functioning for capital and its accumulation. The *organizational mode* of capital refers to the evolving ways life and society are organized for capital and its accumulation. Thus, when we speak of Fordist and post-Fordist

60 Marx, Karl, *The Economic and Philosophic Manuscripts of 1844*, trans. Martin Milligan (New York: International Publishers, 1997). And, Adorno, Theodor, and Horkheimer, Max, *Dialectic of Enlightenment*, trans. John Cumming (New York: Continuum, 1997).

society, we are speaking about a life and society with the same logic, in different organizational modes. This is what enables us to differentiate the modalities of 19th-century industrial capitalism and 21st-century financial capitalism without obscuring the functionality of their common operational logic.

This distinction is critical to an understanding of capital in each of its eras, and yet, many thinkers have mistaken major changes in *organizational mode* for changes in *operational logic*. For example, McKenzie Wark argues:

> The kind of mode of production we appear to be entering is one that I don't think is quite capitalism as classically described. This is not capitalism, this is something worse. I see the vectoral class as the emerging ruling class of our time, whose power rests on attempting to command the whole production process by owning and controlling information. In the over-developed world, an information infrastructure, a kind of third nature, now commands the old manufacturing and distribution infrastructure, or second nature, which in turn commands the resources of this planet, which is how nature now appears to us.[61]

But, what motivates the so-called "vectoral class," this new ruling class that still seeks, much like the previous ruling class, to command production, the old manufacturing and distribution infrastructure, and the resources of planet Earth? Perhaps Wark's description is correct, that the control of production, manufacture, and resources is now done by way of controlling information rather than by way of controlling money and the means of production. But two points are sufficient to flagging a confusion

61 Wark, McKenzie, "Digital Labor and the Anthropocene," accessed December 30, 2015, http://dismagazine.com/disillusioned/discussion-disillusioned/70983/mckenzie-wark-digital-labor-and-the-anthropocene/. Wark has further developed this argument in *Molecular Red: Theory for the Anthropocene* (New York and London: Verso, 2015).

between organizational mode and operational logic in Wark's analysis. First, those who command the most capital are those who own and control the greatest quantity of the most significant information, that is, who wield the dominant influence on the information infrastructure. The power of the vectoral class remains, fundamentally and overwhelmingly, a capitalist power. Therefore, the logic of capital remains decisive of the whole new informationalist organization. Second, it is still the logic of capital that mobilizes the interests of the vectoral class to command production, manufacturing, and distribution, and to seize the natural resources of the planet. The *mode* changes, not the basic motivation. The ruthless pursuit of such interests is made sensible only by capital within a capitalist lifeworld.

What has to be remembered is that the "mode of production" is, as the term suggests, a particular modality. There are many actual, and many more possible, capitalist modes of production. We know that the industrial modality from the late 18th century through the whole of the 19th century is not the only organizational mode that capital may take. When Wark says that we are entering a mode of production that is not capitalism "as classically described," this simply means that the now-classical descriptions Marx was capable of providing in the 19th century do not sufficiently describe the new organizational modalities of capital. Marxists, however, have studied changes in organizational mode since Marx himself, so it is hardly a revelation. It is in Wark's conclusion that the present era is not capitalism where his conflation of the operational logic with the organizational mode is made clear. The logic of capital has governed many modes of production, and continues to govern new ones. Understanding the mode of production is critical to understanding how capitalism works, but we must also understand that the history of capitalism is largely a history of the different modalities of capital.

I claim that the decisive question in understanding any period of capitalist society is to consider how much of human relationality is governed by the logic of capital. How much of human relations is/has been/is now being converted into exchange relations? How much of everyday life, that is, how much of what we do day-in-and-day-out, is decided by a real or perceived need for money and/or commodities? How much does the profit logic function as a "justification" for the decisions of national and state governments, groups, corporations, and individual persons? How much of space and time is carved up and paid for by capital? And, how much does capital assign space and time their respective values? How much is human security (personal, local, national, global) secured by money? And, for each of these questions, in what ways? Looking at how the operational logic of capital survives in new organizational modalities helps to reveal the enduring and, I think, growing relevance of capital in the governance of the world today. Inasmuch as capital still governs and organizes life and space and time, we cannot be done with capitalism.

It is a clear folly to discuss antidotes to a problem without an understanding of the problem. Still, one can only go so far in diagnostic work before bumping into the question of "What is to be done?" And often the question of "What is to be done?" is posed disingenuously. The question is not always posed in pursuit of a good answer. Many times, the question of "What is to be done?" is asked in order to invalidate critique, to point out that critique has no practical recommendations, to reveal it as being "merely" negative. Many times when my conservative and liberal students demand to know what is to be done, it is not because they want a solution to the problems revealed by critical theory, Marxism, etc., but rather, because they want a concrete reason to abandon lines of inquiry they perceive as, and hope will prove to be, dead ends. More simply, their means of refutation is to show that the theory cannot solve the very problems it diagnoses, i.e. if the critique outlines no expedient solutions, then it is useless. But that view rests on a fundamental misunderstanding of theory and its uses.

Theoretical critique, if it is any good, is never "merely" negative, even if it proposes no confident solutions to the problems it studies. In purely logical terms, a good diagnosis is not falsified by the absence of a certain cure, nor is it ever useless. No doubt, the absence of a certain cure is frustrating, as anyone who has been to many doctors knows well. But as frustrating as this can be, the diagnosis may still be right. What is the use of a diagnosis without a cure? The "use-value" of diagnosis, if you will, is as a necessary preliminary, or as a prerequisite to the best courses of action. No confident course of action is possible without a good diagnosis. Sticking with the medical example, I do not think I'm alone in *not* wanting a surgeon who is ready to do a heart transplant who cannot say for certain that the heart is the problem. The common sense one brings to the surgeon is no less useful in political theory. Good diagnostics are also necessary in cases of social and political problems, despite common obfuscations about practical politics having little to no need for theory.[62]

Let us consider capitalism as a problem. In the midst of extant and emergent global crises, capitalism aims to reconcile a 3% compound growth rate with instabilities in the growth model on every level.[63] The imperative of growth refers only to capital accumulation and therefore not to humans directly. Human societies generally are only ever the inadvertent beneficiaries of private accumulation. I have argued elsewhere that capitalism's internal logic is fundamentally problematic and immoral.[64] For now, it shall have to suffice to say that more than 80% of the

62 I would add that, even when separated from action, the negative content of critique is often a major analytical advance. We should not take for granted, for example, how hard it can be to break apart dangerous and common ideologies and correct other problematic understandings.

63 See Harvey, David, *The Enigma of Capital and the Crises of Capitalism* (New York: Oxford University Press, 2010).

64 Gilman-Opalsky, Richard, *Spectacular Capitalism: Guy Debord and the Practice of Radical Philosophy* (New York and London: Autonomedia/Minor Compositions, 2011).

world's population lives in countries where income differentials are widening. The poorest 40% of the world's population accounts for 5% of global income. The richest 20% of people account for three-quarters of world income.[65] The number of children in the world is 2.2 billion, and the number in poverty is 1 billion (every second child).[66] More recently, in his best-selling book *Capital in the Twenty-First Century*, Thomas Piketty and an international team of researchers organized out of the Paris School of Economics confirmed that the history of capital reveals structural tendencies in capitalist societies that have guaranteed the growth of global inequality.[67] According to an Oxfam International Report from 2014, the 85 richest individual persons on Earth have more wealth than the poorest half of the global population (the 3.5 billion poorest).[68] These are some of the basic features of a world organized by the logic of capital. If we are honest about macrosocial and macroeconomic realities, it is not possible to avoid certain basic conclusions; for example, that the exchange relations of the world are governed by capital, and that most people on Earth are poor. The ideological practice of thanking capitalism for all our favorite things in a technological life is killed by any consideration of the worst things that people suffer on a global scale.

This book both substantiates and accepts the premise that capitalism, which has dominated global social relations and international political economy for over two hundred years, has not managed to remedy or reverse the worst trends of impoverish-

65 2007/2008 Human Development Report (HDR), United Nations Development Program, accessed February 22, 2016, http://hdr.undp.org/sites/default/files/reports/268/hdr_20072008_en_complete.pdf, p. 25.
66 The State of the World's Children, 2005, UNICEF, accessed February 1, 2016, http://www.unicef.org/publications/files/SOWC_2005_%28English%29.pdf.
67 Piketty, Thomas, *Capital in the Twenty-First Century*, trans. Arthur Goldhammer (Cambridge, MA and London: Harvard University Press, 2014).
68 OXFAM International Report, "The 85 Richest People in the World Have as Much Wealth as the 3.5 Billion Poorest," *Working for the Few*, January 2014.

ment, maldistribution, and basic want. Further, I claim that the so-called communist projects of the 20th century were always already capitalist in varying ways, and that communism is not achieved in and by bureaucratic capitalist states that implemented state capitalism instead of the free market form that developed in the US, the UK, and elsewhere.[69] Whichever way one looks at it, one cannot simply select the most remarkable instances of abundance and personal well-being as the benchmarks of capitalism to the exclusion or neglect of the far more widespread and much bleaker global picture without doing some violence to the truth. As one such narrative may go: The financial crisis that opened up in 2008 and the BP oil spill had *nothing* to do with capitalism's deficits, but new communications technologies and new medical breakthroughs have *everything* to do with capital's empowering tendencies. Defenders of capitalism commonly credit everything that they like to capital, while disassociating capital from every catastrophe. This is the worst form of apologetics. The present work identifies capital as a root problem, even if not the only problem. If we are to address the problems of a capitalist lifeworld, we must diagnose them well.

Nonetheless, we can justify diagnostics in perpetuity. Shall we never allow ourselves to consider the question of "What is to be done?" If we wait until after we have gotten the diagnostics right on a unit of analysis that is ever-changing, until after we are in possession of total knowledge, we will never have done with the preliminaries. We must therefore break with the logic of diagnostics from time to time, for the sake of human action, even if we intend to pick up and continue our diagnostics later. In fact,

69 I elaborate this argument in my book, *Spectacular Capitalism*. Also, Cornelius Castoriadis had already poignantly skewered the idea that the Soviet Union was a communist state in the 1940s and 50s. See *Political & Social Writings, Volume 1, 1946-1955: From the Critique of Bureaucracy to the Positive Content of Socialism*, trans. David Ames Curtis (Minneapolis: University of Minnesota Press, 1988).

sometimes an active break with diagnostics is part of the diagnostic work itself.

This is what happens in revolt. A revolt is not separate from the diagnostic work, but part of it. And yet, every revolt also wants to change the problems that it diagnoses. In this way, revolt both advances the diagnosis of its participants while openly and actively confronting certain impasses, searching for a resolution. We can see this well in the Egyptian Revolution from January and February 2011. The uprising in Egypt simultaneously comes from an understanding, and works to test and to deepen that understanding. The uprising says something like, "we diagnose our problems right up to Mubarak's front door, but let's also see what we can do." It is both critical and exploratory, both reactive and creative. The same lesson is also contained within the surgeon analogy. At certain points, the surgeon will say that even though she does not have a perfect diagnosis, she must consider acting anyway, for to perpetually wait for certainty is to possibly act too late.

III Autonomy, talent, revolution

In the spirit of the above considerations, I shall now address the question of "What is to be done?" However, I want to rephrase the question as "Who should do what?" This version implicates the old question, but adds the dimensions of personality and multiplicity, and removes the passive voice. This line of questioning is not always a disingenuous quip against theory. Most critics of capital want a theory of praxis of some kind, even if their idea of revolution is more Foucauldian than Marxist. Let us try to think in a preliminary way about what we can and should do in the context of an opposition to the constituted present.

Looking out at the diverse field of humanity, we encounter a multifarious state of *potentia*, as Enrique Dussel calls it.[70] On the political field, we find many different actors, including *potestas, potentia*, and *hyperpotentia*.

Potestas refers to the organized institutional political organs of a society, such as governments and all of their parts — executive, judicial, legislative, electoral, military, etc.

Potentia refers to the capacity for political power that lies within and throughout the community.

Hyperpotentia refers to the realization of the power of the community of people, which exists, for example, when the community enters into a state of revolt.

In Egypt and Turkey and Greece, we recently saw *potentia* become *hyperpotentia*, and clearly why that matters.

Now, within the field of *potentia* (which is where I shall focus my attention), we immediately hit upon a certain fact. People have different talents, capabilities, proclivities, or, as we might call them, "gifts." I shall use the terms "talent" and "gift" synonymously and alternatively. But what do I mean by these terms? Not everyone has, or can be made to have, the same talents. At a rather young age I came to the realization that I could never be trained to draw very well, nor could I be made to desire learning high-order mathematics. With drawing, I did not have any natural talent. I could see the world, the human figure, the objects of nature, but I could not draw their lines to reproduce their shapes. I tried. I took classes as a child. Sometimes I came a bit closer, but I had little control over the outcome. Often, the very first line that I drew would determine the fate of the whole, and I knew it. Classes had no significant impact on me, and very different impacts on the differential raw talents of the students beside me. Perhaps other classes would have helped me more. However, as cognitive

---

70 Dussel, Enrique, *Twenty Theses on Politics*, trans. George Ciccariello-Maher (Durham and London: Duke University Press, 2008).

science now knows well, there is indeed a certain *gift* that some people have for drawing, a gift I do not have.[71]

With mathematics, I could do it. I could struggle to learn the rules of various forms of calculation, and I could memorize and apply certain complex formulae. But I didn't want to. I had no *desire* for the work, no innate *feeling* for it, if you will, beyond the ulterior motivations pertaining to my grade in a class or degree requirements. There are so many ways mathematics relates to human life, but none of them interested me enough for committed and sustained study. And desire is not all. I also noticed that it took me a great deal more effort to understand basic concepts and equations than it did many of my classmates, who seemed to "get it" quite naturally. I am not suggesting that I couldn't get it with hard work, only that the level of work required to do well far exceeded my desire to do it, and the distance between the two made it even harder work indeed. With philosophy I also worked through certain difficulties, but at least there I had the passion to support my efforts. Does not everyone find abundant evidence in their own lives for the existence of multifarious gifts?

It is possible to object to this particular indulgence of common sense, for example, if one sees in it a vulgar version of the Aristotelian view on natural talent, as Aristotle discussed in his *Politics* and *Metaphysics*. But, if we distinguish Aristotle's discussion from the offending context of slavery in Book I of *Politics* and a subsequent long history (still ongoing) of eugenics and racism, his basic observation about the existence of diverse abilities remains convincing and compatible with the view I am outlining. Simply put, not everyone is an athlete, nor would everyone make an equally good carpenter, artist, or mathematician, and these "differences"

71 A substantial amount of the neuropsychological research on this subject follows and develops the work of Roger W. Sperry. See, for example, *Brain Circuits and Functions of the Mind: Essays in Honor of Roger W. Sperry*, ed. Colwyn B. Trevarthen (Cambridge, New York, and Melbourne: Cambridge University Press, 1990).

are not all simply and wholly a matter of training. We do not even need, as Socrates suggested in Plato's *Republic*, to tell people that they are mixed with various metals that make them more or less suited for one form of work or another. Without any such manipulations, we spend much of our lives discerning and developing our talents in rather autonomous manners.[72]

Immediately, this appears as the old nature/nurture debate, though we should be done by now with taking either of those faulty sides. Both dimensions account, in various ways, for the real differentials of talents that we see across *potentia*. The whole range of difference can neither be described as a purely materialist exposure to experience and education, nor as a matter of the human soul or human biology. Neuroscience and biology no longer stand categorically opposed to sociology, as Frans B.M. de Waal has conceded.[73] There has indeed been substantial work on "sociobiology" since the 1970s.[74] Different people use different parts of their brains, sometimes in response to the same stimuli. There are genetic and biological aspects of the issue as well

72 To be clear, I am by no means suggesting that experience and education are irrelevant. Indeed, I wholly affirm the basic arguments of John Dewey's *Experience and Education* (New York and London: Collier Books, 1963). I argue that the discernment and development of our natural gifts requires autonomy, for otherwise what we can and cannot do very well is more likely a result of inequalities in the structures and superstructures of society. For example, I would never assume a young girl with stunted growth and brain development due to malnutrition, a girl who is struggling with reading, has no natural talent for reading. Her case is the result of particular injustices associated with deficits in other resources than talent. It is difficult, and in many cases impossible, to assess one's talent without the resources necessary to cultivate it.

73 de Waal, Frans B.M., "The End of Nature versus Nurture," *Scientific American*, December 1999.

74 Wilson, Edward O, *Sociobiology: The Abridged Edition* (Cambridge, MA and London: Belknap Press/Harvard University Press, 1975). Also see Wilson, David Sloan, *Evolution for Everyone: How Darwin's Theory Can Change the Way We Think About Our Lives* (New York: Delta Trade Paperback, 2008).

as cultural and experiential ones, and one must never leave out desire, passion, and feeling, and our distinctive psychological comportments. Because of the complexity of biological *and* social diversity, the diversity of human talent is a complex field that is almost impossible to sort out. And although social and cognitive scientists will nevertheless continue to sort out the causes of this diversity, it is not *my* aim to unravel the whole mystery.

For the time being, I only ask the reader to follow me to this conclusion: Certain activities that give you great joy may be a misery to others, as philosophy or mathematics may be a joy to one and a misery to another, as sports may be a pleasure to you and a torment to me. I only ask that the reader acknowledge the existence of a multifarious manifold of human talent, regardless of its complex genealogy and origins. It is in relation to this diversity, and in relation to a transformative social and political hope, that I ask: *Who should do what?*

When theorists think about action *against* the capitalist lifeworld and *for* something else, whether that better destination is named and described or left as an unspecified liberatory future, they are sensibly led by the scale of the problem. This has been particularly true in the Marxist trajectory of thinking through the grand antagonisms capable of setting the stage for world-historical transformation. Capitalism is a big problem and thus calls for a big solution. Thinking dialectically, its antithesis, or from a historical materialist point of view, its *real antagonist*, must be of equal or greater power — power meaning not only that of a physical critical mass, but also that of an antagonist who is reasonable, convincing, and widely appealing.

Hannah Arendt and Jürgen Habermas have argued well that *real* power, as opposed to force or violence, comes from and rests on those who occupy spaces outside the formal offices of power. For example, Arendt holds that "political institutions are manifestations and materializations of power; they petrify and decay as soon as the living power of the people ceases to uphold them."[75] And Habermas argues that, in its best moments, the "public sphere as a functional element in the political realm was given the normative status of an organ for the self-articulation of civil society with a state authority corresponding to its needs."[76] Arendt thus insists that the apparatuses of political power, whether individual public officials or state institutions, require a power outside of themselves that must empower them. They require the agonistic and active affirmation of the everyday people on whose behalf they act, or else, as both Mubarak and Morsi have seen in Egypt since 2011, their only "power" is the formal apparatus of the state, and mainly the military — to which they would not need practical recourse if they possessed *real* power. Habermas gave the name "public sphere" to this agonistic space of real power. For him, the public sphere is the mechanism through which civil society articulates its collective will and interest, so that it can substantively steer or throw into question the legitimacy of institutions and powerholders. For Habermas, because the public sphere requires collective (communicative) action, it is necessarily a state of *hyperpotentia*. This is what distinguishes the public sphere from civil society, as the latter is a field of *potentia*.

It is critical to point out that however we define power — from that of the proletariat to that of the public sphere — the radical imagination has gravitated toward the organization of a critical mass of some kind. And, as Michael Hardt and Antonio Negri have imagined with the "multitude," theorization of the grand revolutionary subject continues. The revolutionary actor we always get is a united front of some kind, by way of large mechanisms like international unions, political parties, or something more spon-

75 Arendt, Hannah, "Communicative Power" in *Power*, ed. Steven Lukes (New York: New York University Press, 1986), p. 62.

76 Habermas, Jürgen, *The Structural Transformation of the Public Sphere: An Inquiry into a Category of Bourgeois Society*, trans. Thomas Burger (Cambridge: The MIT Press, 1989), p. 74.

taneous and "bottom-up" like the outbreak of mass revolt, social and cultural movements, and the organic emergence of global solidarity. To be fair to this common inventory of radical imaginaries, thinking in such grand scales reflects much of the truth of the matter. Capitalist states, capitalist culture, and capitalist political economy cannot be undone by isolated and atomized acts, no matter how contentious. Capital demands an opponent of comparable scale. Even from the perspective of capital, such smaller acts appear temporary, aberrant, and ultimately as perfectly permissible within the limits of capitalist society. In fact, capitalists look forward to allowing such temporary aberrations to occur, since they serve as opportunities to demonstrate the tolerance and "democracy" of the existing system.

For some time, revolutionary theory has required a new imbrication, one capable of moving beyond the desperate or delusional scale of isolated and atomized acts, but which does nothing to standardize political action or constrict autonomy in the process. When Félix Guattari and Antonio Negri collaborated in the 1980s, they came close to just such an imbrication:

> From a molecular point of view, each attempt at ideological unification is an absurd and indeed reactionary operation. Desire, on a social terrain, refuses to allow itself to be confined to zones of consensus, in the arenas of ideological legitimation. Why ask a feminist movement to come to a doctrinal or programmatic accord with ecological movement groups or with a communitarian experiment by people of color or with a workers' movement, etc.? Ideology shatters; it only unifies on the level of appearance.[77]

77 Guattari, Félix and Negri, Antonio, *New Lines of Alliance, New Spaces of Liberty*, trans. Michael Ryan, Jared Becker, Arianna Bove, and Noe Le Blanc (Brooklyn: Autonomedia/Minor Compositions, 2010), p. 80. This text was originally published in French in 1985.

I suggest that this conceptual and organizational perspective is far superior to anything found in the more recent works of Michael Hardt and Antonio Negri. I do not blame the presence of Hardt for this difference, nor do I claim any contradiction in Negri's thinking; rather, I would perhaps give credit to Guattari for the better idea. But, what exactly is this "molecular point of view" I want to build upon?

Guattari and Negri's molecular point of view rejects any attempt to take distinct molecular revolutions as part of some unified revolutionary program. That is, their position reflects an honest acceptance of the smallness of certain revolts and a total rejection of the effort to make every movement appear as a self-conscious part of some ideological whole. For example, it would be an ideological sleight of hand to say that the revolution in Egypt in 2011 is orchestrated by the Muslim Brotherhood, or by a Google marketing manager, or by anarchists, or by communists disaffected with capitalism. Guattari and Negri point out that desire, on a social terrain, does not express a cohesive ideological consensus. It can only be made to look "communist" on the level of appearance, and this serves as a critical reminder to Hardt and Negri, who have retrieved the Marxian revolutionary subject position and refigured it in the multitude. I am afraid that the molecular point of view — more honest, less ideological — gets lost in the aggregate points of view of the multitude.[78]

But Guattari and Negri do go on to recommend a multiplicity of "molecular revolutions" that can link in clear and concrete ways, even if only for a limited time.[79] For them, this means the fol-

78 The obvious implication here is that there is a meaningful tension between Negri's earlier work (with Guattari) and his more recent work (with Hardt). Indeed, I think that is demonstrably true, and my own preferences align with the earlier work. But as this tension is not particularly relevant to my present research, I shall leave it to others, or for another time, to properly develop.

79 Guattari and Negri, *New Lines of Alliance, New Spaces of Liberty*, op. cit.

lowing: Real revolutionary activity is autonomous, sporadic, particular, singular, unpredictable, and demanding, but the impact of such activity ultimately depends on culminating intersections that can rise to the challenge of forcing or provoking transitions and transformations of social and political structures. Thus, while we must move beyond the old virtue of class struggle, we must also get over the self-glorification embedded in heroic notions of living a revolutionary lifestyle. Guattari and Negri insist on a molecular perspective capable of recognizing the transient and autonomous smallness of fragmentary and often desperate revolts, and of appreciating those moments as real expressions of desire and disaffection. On the other hand, Guattari and Negri understand the limitations of molecular revolutions in political terms. That is, on their own, molecular revolts comprise a politics of failure.

Today, only the most delusional of so-called anarchists and the most juvenile of activists will insist on the "revolutionary" character of their individual lifestyles, which mostly amounts to nothing more than slight modulations on the exchange of capital through consumption patterns. I aim to decenter struggle without shrinking to a lifestyle politics of consumption.

Indeed, some recent theories have aimed to decenter struggle. But at the same time, many such theories make a different kind of fatal mistake — that of decentering political agency and collective action. We could of course take any number of examples from the postmodern milieu, but let us take, instead, the "radical" theory of primitivism. Primitivists often distinguish themselves as the apex of the radical milieu.

Two fundamental positions constitute primitivism: (1) Primitivists accept the premise that all civilization is unsustainable, will therefore inevitably collapse, and that highly technological contemporary civilization is bringing itself to that ultimate crisis point. (2) Primitivists look forward to collapse as a potentially emancipatory transition to a sustainable primitive future.[80] In other words, the primitivist argues and longs for the inevitable collapse of civilization, and foresees such collapse as an opening to new/old forms of life liberated from the present technological dystopia.

But consider the question of what is to be done from the primitivist perspective. John Zerzan keeps a running inventory of the social and psychological problems and illegal acts that indicate civilization's inexorable march toward its own end. In every tragedy, ecological catastrophe, school shooting, or pandemic, Zerzan finds evidence for impending collapse. There is a peculiar deception in all of this. Zerzan, for example, recommends direct action of all kinds. But it appears to be an absurd recommendation in light of his other unwavering assertion that — *action or no action* — the end of civilization is coming. We can even do nothing at all, and that potentially emancipatory collapse will come. Collapse is always already on the horizon. As Zerzan writes in his latest book: "Civilizations have come and gone over the past six thousand years or so. Now there's just one. Various cultures, but a single, global civilization. Collapse is in the air."[81] Civilization has an expiration date, always to be determined, so it is ultimately sufficient to be prepared. For this preparation, what should we do? Practice with gardening and carpentry would be good, so that

---

80 My comments in this paragraph and the following one have in mind the works of the leading primitivist author John Zerzan, whose book *Future Primitive and Other Essays* (Brooklyn: Autonomedia, 1994) I am mainly thinking of here. Generally, though, I aim this critique at all of Zerzan's published work. To be fair, I have learned a lot from reading Zerzan (and I enjoy his radio show as well). It is also worth pointing out that a lot of the recent and fashionable attention to the concept of the Anthropocene in radical circles fails to recognize Zerzan's formative work on the subject, which he has been doing for well over twenty years. Nonetheless, these paragraphs address the real problems I find in his worldview and arguments.
81 Zerzan, John, *Why Hope? The Stand Against Civilization* (Port Townsend, WA: Feral House Books, 2015), p. 93.

we might know how to survive, and some philosophical support for the journey, which one could get from reading Zerzan, among others.[82]

Therefore, the truth about Zerzan's primitivist point of view is that despite his own praise for them, the courageous acts of the Black Bloc and other "elements of refusal" have only a cheap gloss of nobility, for they are ultimately quite unnecessary.[83] Primitivists observe acts of civil disobedience and property destruction (as well as school shootings) as signifiers of a better future arriving, as signs of the times, *but even without such acts and incidents they claim that the system is doomed by design*. Although he finds the revolt of dignity in certain forms of action, especially those acts that can be interpreted as attempts to say something against civilization, Zerzan reliably reminds us that civilization will accelerate its own collapse far more than — and regardless of — any human action.

From the primitivist point of view, and also, from similarly inflected theories of the Anthropocene, capitalism is often regarded as a red herring.[84] According to primitivists like Zerzan, critics of capitalist society are always far too Marxist (even if they're not Marxist at all) and old-fashioned.

Yet, despite Zerzan's disdain for Marxism, the primitivist approach inadvertently reifies the worst elements of Marxist sci-

82   In addition to Zerzan, readers interested in this current of thinking should consult Sale, Kirkpatrick, *Rebels Against the Future* (New York: Perseus Books, 1996) and Jensen, Derrick, *Endgame: Vols. 1 and 2* (New York: Seven Stories Press, 2006). Although Zerzan criticizes all kindred spirits within his milieu, Derrick Jensen especially, these three authors do share common premises about civilizational collapse, and taken together, substantiate the basic position.

83   Zerzan, John, *Elements of Refusal* (Columbia, MO: Columbia Alternative Library Press, 1999). *Elements of Refusal* also contains Zerzan's criticisms of Marx, in numerous places.

84   See, for example, the brief discussion of McKenzie Wark above, present chapter.

entism. Like Marx's crisis theory of capitalism, civilization is also pregnant with its own end. "Domination/civilization had a historical beginning. It may have a historical end — which would be the end of history."[85] But unlike Marx, there is no revolutionary subject position — not the proletariat, not the indigenous, not even the anarchists, the students, the multitude, or anyone else you might imagine in that role. Far more than Marx himself, Zerzan finds the inevitable future always forthcoming, all fatalistically determined by the present state of affairs. Ultimately, Zerzan's determinism mirrors Marx's, and runs deeper.

But if we cannot count on the metanarratives of Marxism or primitivism, and if we are also critical of the atomistic forms of lifestyle politics, then how do we not fall into a postmodern malaise of acquiescence and failure? It is in the graveyard of these narratives of transformative hope that I want to point out a more promising pathway beyond the old virtue of struggle. The theory of revolt developed in this book is my recommended alternative to a rich history of radicalisms, which have been either too small or too big in various ways. The preliminary goal of the present chapter is to outline a direction that reflects neither the impossible "bigness" of the grand revolutionary schemes of the past, nor the primitivist delusion that mistakes school shootings as death knells of human civilization — nor do I seek a liberal path felicitous with capitalism, one which happily allows capitalism to prove its own virtues.

We do need to get away from the "size requirements" of Marxist historiography. If we always look out for a massive counter-position, the multifariousness of human talent and desire appears as a kind of impediment. Even autonomist Marxist thinkers have conceptualized a massive revolutionary counter-position, such as Hardt and Negri's concept of the "multitude," or the "working

85 Zerzan, John, "Paradigms," *Fifth Estate*, Vol. 50, No. 2, #394, Summer 2015, p. 14.

class" as an open and heterogeneous category, as the term has been deployed by Holloway.[86] These authors in particular make major contributions to a better articulation of Marxist critique, but unfortunately, they theorize the antagonist as a refurbished, but equally problematic revolutionary class.

(a) Revolutionary Class

Let's consider Guattari's conception of the "molecular" revolution or "micro-revolutions" of "micropolitics," and Berardi's conception of the "precarious class," or "the precariat."[87] I have written elsewhere and at greater length about the precariat as both a useful and problematic concept.[88]

But consider first that "multitude" and "working class" only indicate a compositional content, by which I mean that they intend to specify a revolutionary demographic, even if that demographic is not drawn cleanly or simply over class lines. Like "proletariat," these terms *do not* indicate any particular comportment or contestatory activity. "Multitude" and "working class" do not tell us about the condition or comportment of the group (or, as it were, the group of groups) in the world. Nor do these terms indicate any particular mode of action. As a result, revolutionary theories that use such placeholders as these typically move to *prescribe* or *predict* the condition, comportment, and action of the revolutionary group that they name. The failure of this method becomes clear when — if ever the group is found anywhere in the world (and I have not yet found the "multitude" in the world)

86 See Hardt, Michael and Negri, Antonio, *Empire* (Cambridge: Harvard, 2001) and Holloway, John, "In the Beginning was the Scream" (Brooklyn: Autonomedia, 2003).

87 See Guattari, Félix, "The Proliferation of Margins" (Los Angeles: Semiotext(e), 2007) and Berardi, Franco "Bifo," *The Soul at Work* (Los Angeles: Seimotext(e), 2009).

88 *Precarious Communism: Manifest Mutations, Manifesto Detourned* (Wivenhoe, New York, and Port Watson: Autonomedia/Minor Compositions, 2014).

— the group does not identify or act as prescribed or predicted, because it is not in fact the theorized group.

In 1985, Guattari and Negri theorized the revolutionary subject from its singular characteristics instead of from generalizations, arguing that "[e]ach molecular movement, each autonomy, each minoritarian movement will coalesce with an aspect of the real in order to exalt its particular liberatory dimensions." [89] Thus, rather than *prescribing* or *predicting* how a cohesive revolutionary class may act as a critical mass, various subsets of the exploited, oppressed, neglected, and despised will show us directly how they act in their actual and diverse modes of revolt. So, taking the molecular point of view as a start, we begin with concrete and particular moments and modes of revolt. This helps us to understand the conditions of each movement, and their respective proclivities for action. This perspective is critical to the theory of revolt developed in this book, because it does not seek to subordinate every uprising to an ideological format of class conflict, and rather, actively guards against such reductions.

The theory of precariousness is capable of enriching class analysis, so long as it is not introduced as a replacement for class analysis. The precarious class, or precariat, is distinguished as a social class by virtue of its actual comportment within (and as a result of) capitalist society. The precariat is not told that it is (nor does it need to be described as) precarious, for its precarity is a measurable feature of its life. Simply put, the precariat is the class of people who lead precarious lives, whose everyday life is set within an ongoing state of anxiety about an increasingly uncertain future. The precariat cannot be given any guarantees about tomorrow, for they know too much about our "flexible" and "mobile" societies to believe such promises. The system of work, wages, and security (in all countries), *from the point of view of the*

89   Guattari and Negri, *New Lines of Alliance, New Spaces of Liberty*, op. cit., p. 66.

precarious, cannot be trusted to deliver on promises for a good life. Some people's lives are more precarious than others. Conceptually, "precariat" has an advantage over "proletariat" in that it describes a real condition of life and specifies a clear point of view — which is also the content of its condition — whereas "proletariat" does not indicate a point of view, just a position in the mode of production.

But the theory of precarity still needs to be supplemented with some form of class analysis, or else we run the risk of minimizing, or worse, neglecting, real differences that make a big difference in the lives of real people. For example, inasmuch as we can say that everyone is increasingly precarious, or that the whole society is already precarious, we are susceptible to a leveling gaze that pays insufficient attention to what makes people more or less precarious in our stratified societies marked with growing inequality, consolidated power, and different opportunity structures for different demographics. But to speak of precarity does not mean we *must* make such mistakes. Like any potentially useful concept, we can use the concept of precarity well or not.

A synthesis of Guattari's conception of molecular politics with Berardi's class analysis may surpass the limitations of an overly confident class analysis that marks the boundaries of inclusion at the point of production. Looking at the molecular politics of the most precarious among us, we can identify class formations with actual points of view. We see the possibility of class positions to generate multiple modalities of action, and the outbreak of collective action that cannot be easily predicted. We cannot always or easily predict where collective action will come from, what it will look like, or what it may demand. If we are honest, we not only have to confess, but must finally confront the fact that not every revolt is a proletarian uprising. Certain sectors of precarious people may revolt from other impetuses — such as in Baltimore in April 2015 — adding, for example, race to class, and even very particular histories of abuse and police brutality. The situation of 'impoverished black communities living in a city (Baltimore) in one of the wealthiest states (Maryland), and facing daily racism, specifies a particular precarity that is not like every other. There is undoubtedly a proletarian dimension to the Baltimore revolt, but we overdetermine the significance of that dimension to the detriment of our understanding.

For Guattari, molecular politics involves interventions, subversions, and transformations on a small scale. But molecular politics within and against capitalism can have no grandiose promise on their own. They are molecular in their smallness and their hope to be part of a larger living movement, and they function as a contamination or an interruption rather than as a revolution in any classical sense. Molecular politics can include rebellions of the precarious, as in Greece, Tunisia, Egypt, Ferguson, MO, and Baltimore, MD, but may also include transformations in personal and group identity, not only with regard to race, gender, and sexuality, but also with regard to the typical fixed poles of each (i.e. male or female, black or white, homosexual or heterosexual).[90] The molecular or "micropolitical" field is certainly biopolitical, which is perhaps one of the reasons why Foucault wrote his glowing preface to *Anti-Oedipus: Capitalism and Schizophrenia*. But Guattari was no individualist, nor was he interested in the *merely* micropolitical. Rather, he was always interested in their possible culminations. As Guattari puts it:

> Will these micro-revolutions, these profound examinations of the relationships within society only remain divided into limited spheres of the social arena? Or will a new "social segmentation" manage to connect them without imposing hierarchy and segregation? In short, will all these micro-revolutions finally initiate a real revolution? Will they be able to take charge of not

90 See Guattari, Félix, "Becoming-Woman" (Los Angeles: Semiotext(e), 2001).

only local problems, but also administrative larger economic configurations?[91]

Guattari's questions in the above passage express an accurate sense of the problem of politics in our time. Revolutionary activities are neither global nor unitary, but appear instead in fragmentary and often isolated ways, like the saturnalias of upheaval in France in the 1960s, Italy in the 1960s and '70s, or in the United States from Occupy to Baltimore. Revolutionary activity is typically sporadic and affective, ebullient and unpredictable. Nevertheless, Guattari wonders if such molecular activity could link up, if it may be possible for such connections to move the micro-revolutionary toward "real revolution." In juxtaposing "micro-revolution" to "real revolution," it is clear that Guattari retains a notion of revolution that is *both* "larger" and non-local. Only Guattari does not think that the activity of "real revolution" will be coordinated and executed as such.

We end up, then, with a variously precarious, diverse field of humanity, which nonetheless remains capable of producing new antagonistic subject positions, even if none of them appears capable of any sweeping negation on its own. While this may be bad news for the old Marxian conception of global proletarian revolution, it is closer to the truth, and promising in new ways. The good news about the present state of our precarious revolutionary politics is that, whereas the old, more confident, unified, revolutionary class has always been something we had to wait for, desperately and hopefully, the new contestations actually happen from time to time. They actually happen, and they embody and express real perspectives and living efforts for new forms of life, both possible and desirable.

None of my efforts here to rethink the concept of "revolutionary class" help to restore the dead determinism of certain strains of

91 Guattari, "The Proliferation of Margins," op. cit., p. 109.

Marxism (and certain parts of Marx's own writing). Although class analysis remains necessary to our project, determinism is dead; autonomy is not. On the one hand, we might argue for an autonomist politics; on the other hand, it's the only politics we've got.

(b) Talent and Autonomy

So, within the context of the micropolitics of the precarious: what is to be done, and who should do what? In conventional revolutionary narratives, our personal gifts and passions are indefinitely subordinated to the overarching tasks at hand, to what the "Great Cause" calls for. It may be hoped, of course, that one's talents and desires could be an asset in the service of the cause, but if that is not possible, the virtuous will always do what ought to be done, no matter how painful and undesirable that may be. In contrast to this, I argue that if such narratives are not deconstructed, it shall always be undesirable to make the world that we desire. Against the old virtue of struggle, we have got to find ways to make it desirable to make the world we desire. This is the central problem.

Vaneigem was right to emphasize an approach from pleasure, to insist that autonomous action brings together the talents and passions of actors. Revolution must be desirable.

> With attractive ease as the most natural thing in the world, our common desire for autonomy will bring us together to stop paying, working, following orders, giving up what we want, growing old, feeling shame or familiarity with fear. We will act instead on the pulse of pleasure, and live in love and creativity.[92]

The difference between Vaneigem's comportment and that of the conventional revolutionary narratives is clear. Vaneigem inverts the politics of self-sacrifice and struggle, rejects the logic of an exchange of suffering for freedom, and calls for a creative

92 Vaneigem, *The Book of Pleasures*, op. cit., p. 104.

and pleasurable activity. And, he does not outline this position only because it makes revolution more desirable, or more about our desires. More importantly, Vaneigem insists that such an approach is more effective. He proclaims: "I will strike harder and more accurately if pleasure demands it. Fires of desire burn fiercer than torches of rage or despair."[93]

In Paris in May-June 1968, in Italy in the decade from roughly 1968 to 1978, and even in Egypt in 2011, it was not simply suffering, struggle, and despair that motivated the uprisings. Indeed, in these three cases and in others, there was certainly an everyday suffering, struggle, and despair that had been normalized, and it seemed to be that everyday despair, and not some surprising crisis or offence, that made revolt inevitable. Sometimes revolt is less of a reaction to a great new situation or outrage, and more of a breaking point or threshold. And beyond the suffering and despair, desire and pleasure also have something to do with it. Capital cannot keep desire in abeyance forever.

While Vaneigem and Guattari have much in common, I find Guattari's analysis particularly useful here. His consideration of the place of desire is more fully developed and more explicitly political. Micropolitics may be playful in a dangerous way, but it is not a simple expression of desire. The micro-revolution of Guattari's "becoming-woman," for example, is not teleological toward a static end of identity. "Becoming," by definition, is a process of transformation, not a settled end state. Becoming destabilizes what is, and on a macropolitical scale becoming has revolutionary connotations. Guattari's psychoanalytic understanding of human desire makes a critical intervention in earlier forms of Marxism, and particularly in autonomist Marxism: Desire can be disfigured in various ways, it can be repressed or buried in everyday life, but desire and its disfigurations can nevertheless be understood. Psychoanalysis can help with this understanding. Desire is never

93   Ibid., p. 65.

completely disintegrated, and can be crystallized and expressed in micro-revolutionary political moments. In the political context as such, desire displaces and decenters struggle.

But struggle has long been considered a virtue. Beyond Marx's centralization of class struggle, Frederick Douglass famously said, "If there is no struggle there is no progress."[94] Douglass' observation of the facts of the world, which are for Marx the fundamental facts of human history, presents struggle as a revolutionary necessity. This has contributed to the fetishization of struggle (as has much of revolutionary theory). But who *wants* to struggle? Should anyone *want* to struggle, even if at times they must? Doesn't struggle already define too much of everyday life, and isn't struggle precisely what makes it so painful? Does it make any sense, psychologically and affectively, to make struggle the centerpiece of a revolutionary project? If ever one can find some way forward without struggle, won't that path always offer a special and sensible alternative? Is it time for revolutionary theory to stop glorifying struggle? We have given too much of human life over to struggle already; should we give it our theory and praxis too?

Of course, struggle is sometimes the cry, or the scream, of the oppressed and exploited, of those who must fight for their self-determination, their autonomy. As John Holloway says, opposition to capitalism starts with "a scream of sadness, a scream of horror, above all a scream of anger, of refusal: NO."[95] Sadness and horror: How long can we sustain a scream of sadness, horror, and anger, and how long should we wish to? We seek relief from sadness, horror, and anger, and we seize upon such relief at the first opportunities. Capitalism wants to empty the most precarious of their revolutionary feelings, so capital provides us with enough oppor-

94 From Douglass' speech at the West India Emancipation Celebration in New York, cited in *Frederick Douglass: Selected Speeches and Writings* (Chicago: Lawrence Hill Books, 1999).

95 Holloway, "In the Beginning was the Scream," op. cit., p. 15.

tunities for a temporary respite from the miseries of everyday life, sufficient (most of the time) to squelch the scream before it turns revolutionary. So again the question: Can our revolutionary aspirations find some other impetus than the scream of sadness and the pain of struggle to supplement and sustain revolutionary praxis?

Autonomous action within the limits of capital—self-directed, micropolitical, and joyful — is the scream's complement. We cannot simply choose between the screams of struggle, on the one hand, and pleasure, on the other, nor should we assert a hard separation between the two. The majority of the world's people, living on the losing end of capital, are stuck with struggle as a kind of *modus operandi*. They do not need to commit to the struggle, since the struggle is inevitably always with them. However, for a sustainable and ongoing contestation of capital and its culture, we must oppose the total negation of our desires and talents in the here and now. Struggle may be necessary, but it is never enough. As long as the fight for a better future places our desires and talents in abeyance, the fight will tire too quickly, and power has the patience to wait it out. Some of the most inspiring saturnalias of social upheaval rise up and subside over the course of a long weekend. Struggle must be decentered. If struggle remains the central modality of revolution, then only the most "selfless" and/or miserable among us will participate in revolution, and one wonders about the possibility, sustainability, and psychic health of such "selfless" and miserable individuals, of such a sad and horrible politics.

In order to advance an argument for a revolutionary theory centered on talent and autonomy, we must confront the logical core of the claim that collectivism and autonomy lead down divergent paths. Though not incommensurate, there is a real tension between collectivism and autonomy. For example, in the early years of the Soviet Union, in the first decade after the 1917 revolution, the state assessed the changing needs of society and industry, and directed and redirected human labor toward the satisfaction of those needs. One could be a seamstress for a month, then an electrician, and then could be called to work on the assembly of light bulbs. In the best divisions of labor, we can find a commendable principle of common cause at work, just as in a family or any other organization where individual members contribute their fair share to the healthy functioning of the whole. But examples of collective functionality may also illustrate a tension between autonomous and collective action. If everyone is given the autonomy to let their desires alone decide what they do, what needs to get done may not get done, and the common cause of the whole may be subverted by individual desires. Collective action falls apart wherever there is too much autonomy to secure its cohesion. We cannot simultaneously sing one song together and sing whatever song we want to sing.

Reinforcing the Soviet example, the dominant idea in the US for most of the 20th century was that autonomy (loosely construed as freedom) could only flourish under a system that promoted radical individualism. This view was sharply articulated mid-century by free market fundamentalists such as Milton Friedman and Ayn Rand, who viewed Marxism, Leninism, and Stalinism (as if those three "isms" have more in common than not) as antithetical to any concept of human freedom. "Autonomy" was not exactly claimed in name by these capitalists, but inasmuch as the term embodies notions of personal freedom and decentralized voluntary action, it seemed from their point of view to map out perfectly over capitalist approaches.

However, the demand for autonomy is *not* satisfied by capital, and autonomous action is *not* incompatible with collective action. Autonomy does not lead to nor flourish under capitalism and its culture. Ever since the industrial revolution, capitalism has progressively (i) standardized working life, (ii) standardized the products of labor, and (iii) standardized human desire for commodities on the marketplace. There is, of course, enough flexibility within capitalism to allow for variations on (i), (ii), and (iii), but too much variation is tantamount to a breakdown in the functionality of the system, and has not happened yet. For example, working life can be differentiated by specializations in cognitive labor, but each specialization is itself standardized and vetted by training or some form of peer review, in the absence of which, the specialization itself cannot be claimed. Products can be new and innovative, but new products must be highly standardized in mass production for mass markets and "quality control." And advertising may indeed fail to cultivate a desire for a new commodity, but when that occurs, the commodity fails and has a stilted lifespan in the marketplace. Indeed, the standardization and standards of capital must hold together *most of the time*, for if they do not, the market system enters into a state of crisis. This is because the functional capitalist market system depends upon a high level of demand with pre-dictable and reliable consumption patterns, backed by a corollary consumption power (ability to pay).

The above paragraph restates certain contentions of Marxism, for example, Marx's discussion of the business cycle in *Theories of Surplus Value*.[96] But we more deliberately build upon Adorno and Horkheimer's thesis of "the culture industry" in *Dialectic of Enlightenment*. At the same time that the free-market funda-mentalists were infiltrating the field of economics to profound effect, critical theory was making exactly opposite claims about the loss of individuality and autonomy (as freedom) in post-War post-Fordist capitalism. While I do not share the vision of catastrophe in Adorno and Horkheimer's famous chapter, and while I reject many of their political conclusions, the diagnosis of standardization in capitalism retains its veracity.[97] And on that

96 Particularly, see the "Crisis Theory" chapter in *The Marx-Engels Reader*, ed. Robert C. Tucker (New York and London: W.W. Norton & Company, 1978).
97 The diagnosis I am referring to is in the fourth chapter of *Dialectic of Enlightenment*, op. cit., "The Culture Industry: Enlightenment as Mass Deception."

view, which has of course been updated in later critical theory (largely from France), autonomy sharply emerges as a clear problem for capitalism. Human autonomy is a problem that capitalism cannot reconcile easily with its homogenizing tendencies (tendencies that have only intensified since Adorno and Horkheimer's analysis, in the context of the latest developments and accelerations of globalization). Whatever human activity can be standardized has been standardized, and whatever human activity cannot be standardized remains a technical problem to solve. Think of everything from automatic teller machines, tollbooths, and cars and planes without drivers or pilots, to drones and robot factories. Think also of standardized expressions of individuality on social media and technological device customization and the massive market for accessories. The motto of capital has more been "automation" than "autonomy." Autonomy, as it turns out, is fundamentally antithetical to capital. This is one part of an answer to the question: Why autonomy?

According to any substantive sense of autonomy, people must have some freedom, despite limitations, to explore, identify, and cultivate their distinctive gifts. Contrary to a well-funded and entrenched mythology, this freedom to explore, identify, and cultivate one's gifts is not abundant in our capitalist societies. Indeed, many people cannot even name their distinctive talents, or worse, wrongly think that they have no talents at all. The critical cultivation of our gifts is left to the margins of chance and spare time, which are overwhelmingly colonized by the obligations of a capitalist lifeworld (i.e. vocation/training, work, attention, consumption, sleep).

Nevertheless, at a certain point even in the most spectacular capitalist societies, we *do* discover that playing the guitar, writing, organizing events, building, gardening, exercising, public speaking, either does give us joy or does not. As you read through a list like this, you may not know what your talent is, but you probably have some sense of what is more or less desirable or joyful from your own experience and perspective. Any answer to the question of who should do what must be considered with this in mind. If, for example, planning events and hosting them is a misery to you, you should probably not be an organizer, no matter how much organizing we may need. Just as, if you are a meek and anxious person, if you lose composure under pressure, then you should probably not be the public face or spokesperson of a movement or group, and you should not be expected to do too many interviews. Of course, one could always get better at organizing or public speaking, but some will never excel in those areas, and more importantly, nor may they want to. Of the many diverse things a person can do, some of them are great joys. Capacity neither indicates nor maps out over desire. Autonomy works at the intersections of capability and desire.

By "autonomous action," I mean the exploration, identification, and cultivation of our talents as a self-determined, voluntary, and desirable project. Self-determined, voluntary, and desirable action defines the core of autonomy. In fact, it is difficult, if not impossible, to think of autonomous action that is directed by others, involuntary, or dreadful.

Autonomy is not turned on and off like a light switch. There is more or less autonomy depending on the case and context. So action that is voluntary and desirable, yet directed by managers to whom you are beholden, is neither total autonomy nor total subordination. Every dimension of autonomy matters. For example, one could have a job that they have chosen, that they choose to keep, and in which they are given considerable free reign over their daily activities, and yet this very same job could be the misery of their existence. In such a case as this, their "free" choice and "free" reign are attributes of a working life that is done for pleasures completely separate from and external to it. It is not the work itself that they desire, but the ends for which the work is a means.

This example also shows that "choice" and "free reign" cannot simply stand in for "voluntary" and "self-determined." Being provided total freedom to choose a dish from a menu with nothing but terrible options is a freedom with severe limitations, and that choice is not, properly speaking, self-determined and voluntary. The evidence lies in the fact that one would choose otherwise if at all possible. In working life, it is often the case that there are no other options on the menu, and one is considered fortunate to find any work at all. Actively choosing the single option available is hardly the zenith of voluntary action. Jobs taken in the US recently by the so-called "99'ers," a term used to describe those unemployed who have used up all three phases of unemployment benefits, find themselves making choices that are quite involuntary. Indeed, it is important to consider the range and reality of involuntary choices in everyday life.

"Free reign" in a job with supervisors who trust you, who do not micromanage what you do, who give you the freedom to determine how to organize your duties, nevertheless expect you to perform certain tasks, many of which are tasks you would never dream of doing unless constrained to do so for a wage. Thus, while autonomy is not an on/off switch, it nonetheless aims at the relative heights of self-determination, voluntary action, and desire. In short, autonomy is a kind of North Star, pointing us toward an unreachable goal in the everyday life of a world governed by capital.

To conclude this preliminary theorization of autonomy, it is necessary to be very clear about a final but major misconception, mentioned above in passing. Autonomous does not mean "alone." Whole communities can strive for autonomy, and can work collectively toward it through collaborative, voluntary, and desirable projects. Indeed, this reflects the aspirations and efforts of a number of indigenous communities, and was very deliberately a part of the political discourses of the Mexican Zapatistas and the Mapuche of Chile and Argentina. Autonomous action can be collective action, like a musical ensemble that does group improvisation, like an uprising in the streets of Athens or Tunis or downtown Cairo, like a revolt in Baltimore.

IV Revolutionary autonomy

The survival of revolutionary politics, the endurance of revolutionary perspectives, depends upon their desirability. Revolution's biggest enemy has been the fact that we don't really *want* it. To be precise, I mean this in an affective sense. That is, we may want revolution's *promises*, but its *processes* are a long, indefinite nightmare. To come to desire revolution, it must have many locations, and no single transcript of its promise. If revolution always aims toward one specific end-state or another, then revolution as a field of thought and action will fail to accommodate the multifarious and differentiated transformative desires of people. This does not mean saying "yes" to every transformative desire. But we must consider starting points. Today, a worthy slogan for revolutionary praxis could be: "Processes not end-states." This does not disqualify concrete improvements in the lives of real people. Rather, "processes not end-states" means a focus on the ways we may challenge the existing state of affairs. Processes not end-states means that, when you expect us in the streets, we may occupy your buildings, until you expect us to do that. We may be making films and poetry and doing theater. Processes not end-states means that we will never romanticize any static state of affairs, existing or possible.

But how, exactly, do talent and autonomy relate to the revolutionary perspective I have been working out in the present chapter? To answer, I shall return to a minor example and work outward from there.

In rare and fortunate cases, one might be paid money for autonomous action. But no amount of money can make an action autonomous. *Capital cannot convert subordination into autonomy.* As Marx rightly said, increasing wages for estranged labor would "be nothing but *better payment for the slave*, and would not win either for the worker or for labor their human status and dignity."[98] It is precisely in this way that severe limitations on autonomy can be made bearable by the ameliorations of capital (i.e. raises, perks, bonuses, consumption capacity). But making the absence of autonomy more bearable does not create autonomy. That is, autonomy is a real antidote to subordination, not something that makes subordination sufferable.

To take a minor (anecdotal) example: I am in that mythical group of people who love their jobs. I love reading and discussing social theory and political philosophy with interested people, and my students fall well enough into that category. I have good conversations every week, sometimes every day. We talk about capitalism and its culture, about rebellion and revolution, about politics and possibility. I also love doing research. It feels good to explore and to articulate new arguments that challenge and expand my own understanding of the world, and I think I might even *desire* to do research if I was not incentivized by the university to do it. Indeed, while scholarship is one of the formal obligations of my job, its institutional rewards are shamefully scarce. Yet it gives me great pleasure as a human person, such as I am.

This account reflects my good fortune. Should I be embarrassed by the fact, ashamed that I feel so contented with the active engagements of my everyday life while most of the world works daily in relative misery? Let's not get carried away. After all, not everyone would want to do what I do. For others, my life would be a painful and stressful existence, full of anxiety and constant obligation, wrought with the tedium of committee meetings and paper-grading, and many of my own colleagues embody and express that very feeling.

Even for me, my present situation is precarious and I know it well. I am not, for example, currently required to use textbooks or

---

98   Marx, *The Economic and Philosophic Manuscripts of 1844*, op. cit., p. 118.

to teach my classes online. Some of my colleagues *must* do those things. If I had to, and one day I might, I would likely change the evaluation of my life and work. While serving a mandatory term as Chair of the Department of Political Science, most of the joy of my everyday life disappeared, and was replaced with a seemingly infinite stream of undesirable responsibilities. Less teaching and research (sources of pleasure) and a lot more paperwork, meetings, and engagement with the administrative apparatus (sources of unhappiness). As Department Chair, for the first time in my professional life, I was required to represent and develop programs that have no relation to my interests or talents.

Outside of that obligatory and temporary role, I have had the academic freedom to propose, to design, and to teach any class I desire. I can write an article or book on any subject I would like. But if any one of these facts was to change, I might come to loathe my job, and I would certainly like it much less. I am not so naïve to think that these things cannot change, and indeed, each of them is always a proposition in circulation on my campus. The privatization of education, as it turns out, is transforming public universities at an ever-quickening pace. Many of the consequences of privatization (consumer-model education with large class caps, increasing tuition in order to compensate for diminishing public subsidies, shortened class times, and a market-driven approach to course offerings and curricula) could easily obliterate my present level of relative autonomy in a matter of months. This privatization is already well underway, and its further closure of autonomous space and time within the university is on a near horizon.[99]

The above reflection points to the precariousness of even the most enviable positions in our post-Fordist semiocapitalist soci-

99 Here, I recommend two recent studies of the capitalist transformation of higher education: Raunig, Gerald, *Factories of Knowledge, Industries of Creativity* (Los Angeles: Semiotext(e), 2013) and Giroux, Henry, *Neoliberalism's War on Higher Education* (Chicago: Haymarket Books, 2014).

eties, as Berardi names the present era.[100] Even capitalists who today enjoy their place and vocations hold a precarious position in current conditions (not that we should feel badly for the wealthy elite, whose precarity tends to come equipped with golden parachutes). There is a shrinking and nameable number of people who live beyond precarity (*Forbes Magazine* literally names them every year), but among the vast mass of capitalists and everyone else, those who live precarious lives are countless, and that is the state of the world. Looking back on my father's perpetual state of anxiety as an employee of General Electric, I now understand that his nervousness was not merely an attribute of his general psychological comportment, but rather it was the reasonable disposition of a stressed-out daily life with no certain future.

The purpose of the above storytelling can be simply stated. Autonomy is severely constrained and always subject to cancellation wherever it exists within the limits of capital. Autonomy is limited by economic constraints in a purely materialistic sense, but also by the economy of time, and by the necessities of everyday life, many of which run contrary to our desires and talents. Autonomous actions such as writing or poetry or music or painting — actions which most artists and authors do beyond the incentives of capital — can be done in the service of a revolutionary perspective. But autonomous actions such as these are extracurricular leisure activities, and they are the first to go when our already tenuous leisure time (i.e. the economy of time) evaporates. Therefore, while it is not true that capitalism snuffs out all autonomy, it is true that capitalism demarcates autonomous action as extracurricular, recreational, and as immediately expendable in the realizations of capitalist demands.

Having said that, and despite the limitations of the capitalist

---

100   See Berardi, Franco "Bifo," *Precarious Rhapsody: Semiocapitalism and the pathologies of the post-alpha generation* (Brooklyn: Autonomedia/Minor Compositions, 2009).

present, total autonomy is not possible, and is even quite difficult to imagine. My point is not merely to register a complaint against the limitations of autonomy under capitalism, nor is it to make a sweeping thesis about the possibility of total autonomy, but rather it is to highlight an irreducible tension between capitalism and autonomy, which contradicts the pervasive free-market fundamentalism of existing capitalist society. Capital does not encourage or generate autonomy, but manages and restricts it.

Milton Friedman wrote a book called *Capitalism and Freedom* in which he argued that "capitalism is a necessary condition for political freedom."[101] While he admits in the same passage that capitalism is not sufficient, on its own, to guarantee freedom, he insists that it is clearly a condition for freedom, as "history suggests."[102] Friedman made many claims about choice and freedom and the state-controlled economy, arguing that capitalism is the necessary prerequisite for many forms of autonomy. While his arguments are not new, their worldly influence took time, and was accelerated in the "neoliberalism" of the past fifty years. Today, Friedman's principle of capitalist freedom continues to restructure and organize new areas of human relations in the university, in politics, in military, in technology, and even in the domain of friendship and human health — a market logic for the "liberation" of everything. But Friedman's premise could and should be turned on its head, enabling us to reclaim autonomy for a new and more communist praxis that might finally move beyond the fetishization of struggle and the depersonalized connotations of collective action.

Contrary to Friedman's contention, the history of capitalism does not trend toward increasing freedom in the sense of autonomy I have been discussing in this chapter. If one is speaking of

101   Friedman, Milton, *Capitalism and Freedom* (Chicago and London: University of Chicago Press, 2002), p. 10.
102   Ibid.

freedom purely in terms of what Guy Debord called the "autonomous economy," an economy liberated from economic necessity, then Friedman has a point indeed.[103] But we cannot agree to define freedom merely in terms of the freedom of capital and its representatives. We need a more robust concept of freedom than that of the freedom of capital. I claim that a worthy conception of freedom includes some consideration of the manifold of human talent, desire, fulfillment, and a joyful life. Employing the more robust conception of autonomy I am using here, a conception that places people — *and not capital* — at the center of its view, we see that autonomy flourishes *against* and not *because of* capital. Capitalism, by virtue of its own internal logic, must subordinate autonomy to accumulation. We call capitalism by that name because it is a system and worldview based on the logic of capital, and if it were not, we'd call it by some other name. That is the crux of this particular rivalry. We can organize human affairs by a logic of accumulation and/or by a logic of autonomy, and where the one is dominant, the other is subordinate (or altogether foreclosed).

Consider a different rivalry, that between work and home. Marx's observation that the individual worker "only feels himself outside his work, and in his work feels outside himself," continues to ring true with each new generation.[104] Capitalism has not remedied this fundamental problem, but has intensified it at all class levels, now making everyone permanently on-call through the cellular ontology of the technological integration of work and life.[105] We are ourselves when we are off work, but if we are increasingly always at work, then the self and its home are foreclosed. One way to overcome the opposition between work and home is to obliterate the home by way of its conversion into work-

103   Debord, Guy, *Society of the Spectacle*, trans. Fredy Perlman (Detroit: Black & Red Books, 1983), Thesis # 51.

104   Marx, *The Economic and Philosophic Manuscripts of 1844*, op. cit., p. 110.

105   In *Precarious Communism*, op. cit., I refer to this as "technontology," p. 29.

space. If Marx was right of the worker that "when he is working he is not at home," then homelessness has become the general condition.[106] And yet, "home" has historically indicated a space of autonomy, a location free from the obligations of work, i.e. home as liberation from work. Inasmuch as our autonomy has really been exercised at home, in the space and time outside of work, the colonization of that space and time by work is an attack on our autonomy.

Nevertheless, as I have acknowledged, total foreclosures are unlikely. There always remains the possibility for some of the self, for some of the home, and we do have some room for autonomous action in the here and now. So, for the last time, who should do what? As you may have guessed, no marching orders can be given. We have no choice but to refuse to judge the "credentials" of those who, in the manifold of human experience, do not throw themselves into the very political activities that we might prefer, or even, that we might deem the most urgent. Any program that seeks to iron out real differences of talent, or to minimize the fact that we have distinct and multifarious gifts, is a program that must be (or inevitably will be) abandoned.

Guattari makes a highly resonant proposal along these lines:

> New social practices of liberation will not establish hierarchical relations between themselves; their development will answer to a principle of *transversality* that will enable them to be established by 'traversing', as a 'rhizome', heterogeneous social groups and interests.[107]

This means that a liberatory politics must allow for the radical freedom of its participants, for autonomous action, but with-

106   Marx, op. cit., p. 110.
107   Guattari, Félix, "The New Spaces of Freedom" in *New Lines of Alliance, New Spaces of Liberty* (Brooklyn: Autonomedia/Minor Compositions, 2010), p. 123.

out devolving to atomistic individualism. Guattari's rhizomatic approach provides one of the best ways to see the compatibility of autonomous and collective action, to see collective action *as autonomous*.

The approach I have outlined, which follows Guattari's principle of transversality, is critical to the overarching goal: For revolution to be worthy of our desire, we have to want to make it. This contention reflects the heart of the general overarching theory of this book, but we must make no mistake about its relative openness. While the general theory *does not* specify and recommend any certain course or chronology of action, it *does* disqualify much of the radical milieu that has sought and continues to seek to provide concrete revolutionary answers to social and political problems.

Moreover, while the argument functions first as a general theory (as a perspective), it ultimately and ideally functions as an *organizational mode*. And this organizational mode works against the organizational modes of capital because the *logos* of autonomy is inassimilable to the *logos* of capital — the latter of which depends on predictable patterns of consumption, labor, and recreation (autonomous action can never guarantee, and tends to destabilize, such predictability).

Capital has not totally foreclosed every space of autonomy, and it is in those spaces where we begin. We can only ever work against capitalism from within it. We can only get to the outside from the inside. As McKenzie Wark has written: "Welcome to gamespace... You are a gamer whether you like it or not, now that we all live in gamespace that is everywhere and nowhere. As Microsoft says: *Where do you want to go today?* You can go anywhere you want in gamespace but you can never leave it."[108] Autonomous action in existing capitalist societies still abides by certain game rules,

108 Wark, McKenzie, *Gamer Theory* (Cambridge, MA and London: Harvard University Press, 2007), Thesis 001.

none of which are of our own making. We may play, and we do play when we can, but even when we manage to create our own rules for our own games, we still play them within the limited space and time that capital leaves for free play.

Here, Wark's observation is important because it is indeed possible that autonomous action in the here and now could become a trap. That is to say, because we have some room for autonomy within the limits of capital, some level of relative gratification is achievable in the here and now. This, it seems to me, is part of the reason why capitalism has *not* totally foreclosed our autonomy. As shared above, I am quite happy with my everyday life in the capitalist present. But doesn't that daily disposition inadvertently vindicate the capitalist present? "Look! Even Marxists can be happy in capitalist societies!" Marxists have many complaints, but enjoy so much of what they do not complain about. If our talents can be explored, identified, and cultivated in the here and now, and if our desires can be gratified, then there is little impetus to leave the present for some unknown future.

To confront — if not to avoid — this trap, I am *not* suggesting that we refuse all gratification and happiness, according to the old tune of the virtue of struggle. Instead, autonomous action *must become self-conscious*. That is, actors must eventually come to understand that autonomy occurs in spite of or against the demands of capital that always aim to seize upon its open spaces. Self-conscious autonomous action cannot function as an endorsement of the existing system. But if autonomous action is not self-conscious, we may indeed be uncritically gratified with the precarious and ever-tenuous autonomy that exists within the limits of capital. If such gratification as this occurs, autonomous action occurs without its revolutionary character and doubles as an endorsement of capitalism instead. Hence, the revolutionary character of autonomous action depends on the actor's awareness of capital's antagonistic regard for autonomy; namely, that capital always subordinates human freedom to accumulation.

When one experiences great joy in the here and now, through love, or sexual pleasure, by epiphany or thrill, these experiences point to places where capital has not totally colonized human life. Sure, you may try to buy the thrill by paying for it, but if you show up at the gates of an amusement park fully expecting to pay and are told that the fees have been waived, the thrill remains, but is enhanced by the fact that you do not have to measure its worth in dollars. Self-consciousness reveals that the best things under capitalism are the least capitalist things. I am not going to credit the capitalist system for all of the joyful play I share with my two young children, play that occurs autonomously and beyond the interests of capital. We must not lose sight of the fact that capitalism is never undermined for as long as our autonomy remains an existential footnote to surviving. Vaneigem's distinction between surviving and living is useful here: "*Survival is life reduced to economic imperatives.*"[109] Whereas living is defined by spontaneity, desire, loving, and pleasure, all of which are the first casualties of survival. Capital is on the side of survival, but autonomy sides with living.

v Toward the hereafters

In 1968, Fredy Perlman summarized the pacifying mythology of capitalism. We are made to believe, he wrote, that "people do not have such power in *this society*, and this society is the *only* form of society; therefore it's impossible for people to have such power." Yet, Perlman rejects this, insisting: "The question of *what is possible* cannot be answered in terms of *what is.*"[110] Autonomous action in the here and now reveals the power of everyday people that is often buried and hidden in everyday life. A fine

109 Vaneigem, Raoul, *The Revolution of Everyday Life*, trans. Donald Nicholson-Smith (London: Rebel Press, 2006), p. 157.
110 Perlman, Fredy, *Anything Can Happen* (London: Phoenix Press, 1992), pp. 11 and 13.

example could be found in the uprising in Egypt in January and February 2011. It took the world's most powerful military several years to implement the very beginnings of "regime change" in Iraq, whereas the unarmed and precarious people of Egypt only needed eighteen days. While the Egyptian uprising was too heterogeneous to articulate any one ideal end-state, the resounding content of the message coming from the streets of Cairo was that the existing state of affairs must end, igniting the world's sense of the possible versus the actual. And it must be stressed that the overwhelming tone of the eighteen days of protest precipitating Hosni Mubarak's ouster was ebullient and joyful, full of desire and feeling, and was itself quite a departure from the "struggle" of everyday life.

It is also critical to emphasize that the "results" of the popular insurrection in Egypt have been overemphasized by too many observers around the world. Critics of the uprising continually ask what's next, worrying about the Muslim Brotherhood and Sharia law, the failure of Morsi, the resumption of military rule, and no real political transformation. Supporters, on the other hand, point to Mubarak and Morsi's ousters as evidence of the powers of revolt, or, in an effort to qualify their own optimism, remind us that the military's management of the government must prove temporary and transitional, and must give way to something better before any final verdict can be given. In this latter account, we still wait for a final verdict to decide the case.

In contrast to all of these discourses, I propose that there are some things we know with certainty from processes, and not from end-states: We know that the revolt was a rejection of the old lie that the existing society was the *only* form the Egyptians could possibly know, that it was a realization of the power of everyday people. Indeed, for all of its internal heterogeneity, the uprising declared unequivocally that the question of *what is possible* cannot be answered in terms of *what is* — and it did so in the form of a joyful collective action traversing diverse groups and interests.

In this way, we may have a verdict before any end: We should not look forward to the ends of insurrection, but rather, to its multiplication and continuation, to insurrection everywhere. Insurrection is good news for possibility, imagination, and autonomy, as it expresses a freedom to challenge and reject the existing situation in the hope for a new situation made by the real desires of the social body.

What are the unknown hereafters we should hope to get to from the here and now? I will not guess or predict, but I suspect that the kingdom of heaven will be no kingdom at all. I am reassured by the fact that Hobbes' Sovereign, much like Mubarak and Morsi, was never enthusiastic about the autonomy of his subjects, although all sovereigns know that the autonomous action of everyday people remains a possibility to be guarded against.[111] Realizations of that possibility — *autonomous action in the here and now* — exacerbate the living contradictions between capital and freedom. And the pleasure of autonomous acts of revolt invites us to think of revolution beyond its historic fixation on struggle. If revolution becomes desirable by way of its processes, and not by way of distant promises, then the rewards of revolution are available in the making.

111 See Chapter 21, "Of the Liberty of Subjects" in Hobbes, Thomas, *Leviathan* (Cambridge, UK: Cambridge University Press, 1996).

CHAPTER 3

Unjamming the
Insurrectionary Imagination

Or better: one is always located at a post through which various kinds of messages pass. No one, not even the least privileged among us, is ever entirely powerless over the messages that traverse and position him at the post of sender, addressee, or referent.

— JEAN-FRANÇOIS LYOTARD, *The Postmodern Condition*[112]

It is a great victory by the repressive forces when they make us doubt our creative powers to the point that it makes us denigrate them.

— RAOUL VANEIGEM, *Self-Portraits and Caricatures*[113]

Revolt does not always look like the "Arab Spring," 1968, or the Baltimore uprising, and if it had to take some common form, then its predictable limitations could be effectively anticipated and policed. To borrow a phrase from Nancy Fraser, can our "unruly practices" take on new and surprising forms?[114] Indeed, they can and must, but only without giving up the disruptive power of more common forms of revolt. That revolt can and must create

---

112 Lyotard, Jean-François, *The Postmodern Condition: A Report on Knowledge*, trans. Geoff Bennington and Brian Massumi (Minneapolis: University of Minnesota Press, 1983), p. 15.
113 Vaneigem, Raoul, *Self-Portraits and Caricatures of the Situationist International*, trans. Bill Brown (New York: Colossal Books, 2015), p. 237.
114 Fraser, Nancy, *Unruly Practices* (Minneapolis: University of Minnesota Press, 1989).

new forms of itself — that it must be experimental and creative (if not outright artistic) — is the basic claim the present chapter explores.

I begin this chapter with three premises: First, the cultural and political impasses that make culture jamming make sense as a form of action were first diagnosed by French and German philosophers in the decades after World War II. The cultural and political analyses of critical and postmodern theory explain well the stage for culture jamming. Second, the *necessity* of a politics of culture jamming was already indicated by postmodern theorists as the practicable modality of intervention given the impasses of the era. Thus, culture jamming may be defined as a postmodern politics. Third, the articulation of the logic of culture jamming, theorized by Guy Debord in the 1950s, is the version we most urgently need to recover. This last premise contains a normative claim that requires some clarification from the start. I am not interested in correcting the historical account of culture jamming by way of telling an origins story about where it really comes from. Rather, I set out to rescue the insurrectionary logic of culture jamming from the liberal complacencies that obscure it today. This requires bearing out the premises above.

I Formative impasses and impulses: postmodern theory

Marxist and post-Marxist philosophers came to some dreadful epiphanies in the decades after World War II. The 20th century almost totally convinced generations of revolutionaries of the historical impoverishment and failure of their own grand narratives about the radical transformation of the world. The anti-Stalinist and anti-statist Left could not find any good reason to continue to place their faith in political parties and classical conceptions of revolution, nor could they find any guarantee on the horizon of an emergent revolutionary movement to resuscitate their dilapidated optimism. The negativity of Theodor Adorno and Max Horkheimer's landmark study, *Dialectic of Enlightenment* (1944), would be recast in so many ways, but not easily overcome. The Nazis and Nuremberg revealed the dangers of manipulable masses, bolstering the political significance of the insights of Sigmund Freud and Wilhelm Reich.[115] Diminishing numbers of radicals kept faith that a real challenge to capitalism was emerging anywhere in the atmosphere of the Cold War. A pervasive sense of the unlikelihood of revolution characterized a new impasse facing disaffected radicals everywhere.

It is within this context of defeatism and disillusionment that the formative logic of culture jamming was best articulated. The grand idea of world-historical revolution appeared now as a corpse. But wasn't there still space and time for meaningful revolt, and could such space and time ever be totally obliterated? It is within this context that the possibility for negating the negativity of the revolutionary Left resided. Kindling these embers for a new radical optimism was necessary to the task of rehabilitating the disillusioned revolutionary milieu. In this chapter, we critically consider culture jamming as one means for such a task.

Clearly then, I shall challenge popular genealogies that trace culture jamming to its coinage in the 1980s and 1990s. I argue for expanding beyond its narrow conceptualization as a tactic of media-savvy activists. As media activism or pranking, culture jamming risks becoming a liberal fantasy that gives good news to capitalism: "This is all the Left has left." More hopeful than a desperate and defeated Left, is the insurrectionary logic of culture jamming articulated in 1956 in Guy Debord's theory of *détournement*. *Détournement* means a kind of political plagiarism, a subversive repurposing of sources, a hijacking, or otherwise rerouting of some material against itself, and for other reasons. For Debord,

115 See, for example, Freud, Sigmund, *Civilization and Its Discontents*, trans. James Strachey (New York: W.W. Norton & Company, 1989) and Reich, Wilhelm, *The Mass Psychology of Fascism*, trans. Mary Boyd Higgins (New York: Farrar, Straus and Giroux, 1980).

détournement was part of a revolutionary project "undertaken within the present conditions of oppression, in order to destroy those conditions," and he insisted that

> [a]n avant-garde cultural movement, even one with revolutionary sympathies, cannot accomplish this. Neither can a revolutionary party on the traditional model, even if it accords a large place to criticism of culture (understanding by that term the entirety of artistic and conceptual means through which a society explains itself to itself and shows itself goals of life).[116]

Debord was well aware, in the 1950s and '60s, that something like sporadic "subvertising" could never jam a culture of constant accumulation. In this context, to "jam" means to meaningfully interrupt and redirect cultural flows, i.e. the interference of an objectionable message, and communicating against it. But subvertising is too often like a skip on a record that the needle passes over with a minor interruption.

Against subvertising, I argue for culture jamming through collective action, and consider the "culture jams" of the Zapatistas, the "Arab Spring", occupation movements, and other recent revolts. This chapter explores sustained modes of culture jamming as the radical counterpart to a highly individualized constellation of subvertising.

But, before we arrive at questions of goals and efficacy, we shall explore culture jamming as the sensible response to postmodern epiphanies about the depressed state of revolutionary politics after World War II and during the decades of Cold War. Postmodern theory grew out of the disaffection of frustrated radicals whose utopian aspirations were squelched in the 20th century,

116 Debord, Guy, "Perspectives for Conscious Changes in Everyday Life" in *Situationist International Anthology*, trans. Ken Knabb (Berkeley: Bureau of Public Secrets, 2006), pp. 98-99.

giving us Jean-François Lyotard's "war on totality," Jean Baudrillard's apocalyptic crisis theories, and the micropolitics of Gilles Deleuze and Félix Guattari. These theorists and others within the postmodern milieu reflect profound estrangement from the grand narratives of old revolutionary promises.

In Chapter 2, we explored the exhaustion of classical revolutionary praxis, and attempted to shift our focus from end-states to desirable revolutionary processes instead. At its best, culture jamming proposes just such a specific process for autonomous revolutionary action today, as it invites disillusioned radicals to imagine joyful new opportunities for creative contestation, new modes of involvement and intervention. I especially ask: What is the relationship between culture jamming and revolt? I therefore explore culture jamming as one particular process in a postmodern politics of autonomous action.

To make the case for a consideration of postmodern politics, and more importantly, to grasp why this assessment is critical to questions of social transformation, it is necessary to review and explicate some of the signpost theory in the postmodern trajectory of thought and action. In what follows, I provide brief portraits of some of the key thinkers within that milieu to substantiate the claim that culture jamming is a postmodern politics. This portraiture shows how and why culture jamming responds to a tortured philosophy of praxis, and that its emergence is consistent with an extensive theoretical grounding. But, keep in mind that portraiture is portraiture, and what follows is by no means intended to be a deep treatment of each thinker's work. Instead, I intend to provide a map of impressions and indications of what we may take to be, collectively, the so-called postmodern context.

(a) Foucault Rethinks Power

Politics, which has centrally to do with relations of power, takes on new meaning if we change our understanding of what power is and how it functions in the world. Michel Foucault analyzed what he called a biopolitical form of power (i.e. biopower), which led to imagining unconventional forms of revolt.[117] Much of the basic theorization was accomplished in his 1975 book *Discipline and Punish: The Birth of the Prison*, which explores the structures of biopower that have developed in Western societies mainly since the 18th century, with a special focus on prisons, schools, and disciplinary technologies.[118] Foucault's elaboration of Jeremy Bentham's panopticon illustrated the phenomena of bodies controlled by brains, a technology of social control that functioned without armed guards, guns, dungeons, or public forms of violent punishment:

> There is no need for arms, physical violence, material constraints. Just a gaze. An inspecting gaze, a gaze which each individual under its weight will end by interiorising to the point that he is his own overseer, each individual thus exercising this surveillance over, and against, himself. A superb formula: power exercised continuously and for what turns out to be a minimal cost.[119]

It is critical to observe that Foucault understood a transition in the technology of discipline from the physical (i.e. physical violence) to the visual and psychological (i.e. surveillance and the gaze), claiming that the visual was a more direct and cost-effective (both politically and economically) means to control the physical. It is not that Foucault shifts attention from the body, for his work remains steadfastly committed to questions of the body and its

117 Foucault, Michel, *The Birth of Biopolitics: Lectures at the Collège de France 1978 - 1979*, trans. Graham Burchell (London and New York: Palgrave Macmillan, 2008).

118 Foucault, Michel, *Discipline and Punish: The Birth of the Prison*, trans. Alan Sheridan (New York: Vintage Books, 1995).

119 Foucault, Michel, *Power/Knowledge: Selected Interviews and Other Writings 1972-1977*, trans. Colin Gordon, Leo Marshall, John Mepham, and Kate Sopor (New York: Pantheon Books, 1980), p. 155.

intersubjective apparatus in social and political relations. Rather, he is interested in how certain lines of thought (and thinking more generally) can subordinate bodies within various systems of control, on the basis of sexuality, "abnormal" desire, criminality, and other transgressive practices. The visual apparatus of surveillance and the gaze carries the threat of exposure and judgment, causes an anxiety about being seen, and thus accesses our brains, which regulate our bodies. Foucault understood that the visual terrain would necessarily and increasingly become a site for politics and, therefore, contestation.

A culture jam accepts this premise about the importance of the visual terrain, and acts on it. There is, in other words, nothing neutral in a structure that organizes social life and normalizes our desires. Culture jamming attempts to intervene in the visual landscape that shapes how we think because jammers understand that everything we see sends us messages, that the visual landscape is a central feature of the psychic control mechanism of bodies in the world.

Further, Foucault discusses how the dominant concept of "power" has been disempowering. Power, in political philosophy, is typically associated with a negative, or a prohibitive idea, instead of understanding power in the positive terms of what it enables or produces. For Foucault, this confusion is tied to the fact that power is historically understood as the domain of the state, or as the domain of the "Sovereign" in the history of political philosophy. But Foucault argues that there are other locations of power, other "power relations" than those associated with the political state or the sovereign authority. These other power relations are important, Foucault insists. If we decouple our understanding of power from the state, we come up with a different understanding of politics and revolution. For example, if revolution means a transformation of power relations, Foucault's theory suggests that there can be revolutions that do not involve the state. He says of his view:

> This implies that there are many different kinds of revolution, roughly speaking as many kinds as there are possible subversive recodifications of power relations, and further that one can perfectly well conceive of revolutions which leave essentially untouched the power relations which form the basis for the functioning of the State.[120]

The good news, then, is that revolution remains possible, although it must take on a different meaning. We must think of revolution in new ways.

Foucault argues that power exercises a politics of truth in order to establish a self-supporting knowledge: "Each society has its regime of truth, its 'general politics' of truth: that is, the types of discourse which it accepts and makes function as true" and only some among us have "the status of those who are charged with saying what counts as true."[121] But those of us who are not charged with saying what counts as true, nonetheless want to speak. Culture jammers want to speak without having the status of those authorized to state the truth, and so culture jamming tries to send counter messages into the public to intervene in the existing regime of truth, to challenge the general politics of truth, to challenge what counts as true with *other* truths or *actual* truths that are otherwise obscured by dominant discourses of power.

Indeed, Foucault did retain optimism about the possibilities for everyday people to renegotiate power relations throughout society in order to transform understandings and usher in new regimes of truth. In this way in particular, Foucault's theory contributes to an understanding of the social and political context of the culture jammer.

120   Ibid., pp. 122-123.
121   Ibid., p. 131.

(b) Derrida's Playful Subversions

Jacques Derrida developed his influential philosophy of "deconstruction" in the 1960s. For Derrida, deconstruction was a method used to perform a kind of culture jam on the Western philosophical tradition. The interpretative and subversive effect of Derrida's jams on philosophy were not always welcome by philosophers. Derrida's work involved deconstructionist readings of philosophical texts. He read both classical and lesser known texts in such a way as to show that they could have meanings completely other than the meanings they are typically taken to have.

Derrida wanted to confront and challenge established authorities of knowledge. Consider what is counted as knowledge in philosophy – for example, to have knowledge of Plato or Aristotle or Foucault or anyone else. Knowledge means that you are able to read those authors correctly and to demonstrate an accurate understanding of them. Derrida's deconstructions revealed, however, that no text of any complexity has a single meaning that stands apart from the reader. The reader of a text always and invariably does something to the text and to its meaning. The same texts are read in different ways, so in the act of reading them, their meaning is produced one way or another. Derrida has said "reading is transformational." [122] The US Constitution has been and can be read for or against conservative or liberal positions, as can be seen in debates about the single-sentence Second Amendment, in Justice White's opinion on sodomy, in the Citizens United case, or in the decision on the constitutionality of Barack Obama's healthcare reform act. We could also find clear and present political significance in various interpretations of the Bible or Quran. Deconstruction seizes upon this interpretive openness to expose the instability of, and ultimately to subvert, dominant ways of thinking about certain texts, including texts

122 Derrida, Jacques, *Positions*, trans. Alan Bass (University of Chicago Press, 1982), p. 63.

in philosophy, law, and the sacred texts of religious traditions.

Derrida insists: "Why engage in a work of deconstruction, rather than leave things the way they are, etc.? Nothing here, without a 'show of force' somewhere. Deconstruction... is not *neutral*. It *intervenes*."[123] Changing the codified meanings of things is an intervention; it is a form of praxis. And to do nothing is to allow a previous force to have decided things, whether epistemological, economic, political, historical, or otherwise. Although they borrow more from *détournement* than from deconstruction, culture jammers' primary mode of intervention is to use their hijacked source material to say something else.

For all the criticisms that have accused Derrida's work of some kind of unserious charlatanism, his project has always been self-consciously subversive and anti-authoritarian. Derrida is subversive in the sense that his work attacks and destabilizes what is easily, or too easily, accepted as the settled facts of knowledge, of texts and their meanings, and of those who claim to have expertise over them. His work is anti-authoritarian because it aims to show, precisely through its exegetical subversion, that inasmuch as everyone reads or interprets the texts and symbols and images around them, everyone has a certain kind of power, and authoritative meanings are always subject to deconstruction. He has himself said that "from the first texts I published, I have attempted to systematize a deconstructive critique precisely against the authority of meaning."[124]

Derrida's work was never merely intended to be destructive (destruction is not deconstruction), but rather, to change things in an active way. Derrida sees deconstruction as a political act. He even understood his own project as a particular continuation of Marx's project. In *Specters of Marx*, Derrida wrote:

123 Ibid., p. 93.
124 Ibid., p. 49.

Deconstruction has never had any sense or interest, in my view at least, except as a radicalization, which is to say also in the *tradition* of a certain Marxism, in a certain *spirit of Marxism*... But a radicalization is always indebted to the very thing it radicalizes... It is not the only one and it is not just any one of the Marxist spirits, of course.[125]

Derrida understood well that both the theory and practice(s) of the Marxist tradition would have to be radically rethought in new historical contexts (in his case, after the Cold War), a basic position shared by so many Marxists going back at least to Antonio Gramsci. And I think Derrida was right to insist upon a radical rethinking of radical traditions, which would of course also include new forms of action, new concepts of revolution.

Despite this, Derrida's subversive reading of the subversive tradition of Marxism managed to provoke significant debate among Marxists, which one could read in *Ghostly Demarcations: A Symposium on Jacques Derrida's Specters of Marx*.[126] At the end of the symposium, which includes serious criticism from major Marxists such as Antonio Negri, Fredric Jameson, Aijaz Ahmad, and Terry Eagleton, Derrida expresses surprise at the proprietary guardianship of Marx by prominent Marxists.

What will never cease to amaze me about the jealous possessiveness of so many Marxists... is not only what is *always* a bit comic about a property claim, and comic in a way that is even more theatrical when what is involved is an inheritance, and, still more pathetic, the appropriation of an inheritance named "Marx"! No,

125 Derrida, Jacques, *Specters of Marx* (New York and London: Routledge, 1994), pp. 115-116.
126 Derrida, Jacques, et al., *Ghostly Demarcations: A Symposium on Jacques Derrida's Specters of Marx*, ed. Michael Sprinkler (London and New York: Verso, 1999).

> what I always wonder... is where the author thinks the presump-
> tive property deeds are.[127]

While I do not think Derrida's Marxism is above criticism, he is fundamentally correct to reveal the established traditionalism and authoritarianism both embedded within and around (like museum guards) anti-establishment and subversive theoretical and political currents. We face the same proprietary possessive-ness when we suggest in the present work that we should not simply inherit and preserve revolutionary traditions in the field of action. While this chapter ultimately develops a deep criticism of culture jamming, it does not do so on defensive grounds in order to protect old concepts of revolutionary organization and action. Deconstruction may well destroy a particular functional understanding, but it does this only by way of a creative produc-tion of new understanding.

(c) Lyotard's Fragmentary Rule-Breaking

Jean-François Lyotard's philosophy works out many of the major themes common to postmodern thought. As well, Lyotard was one of the most iconic figures of the disaffected ultra-Left. His hopes were invested in the resolution of the Algerian political situation, which he believed was ripe for revolution. In 1954 Lyo-tard joined the revolutionary organization *Socialisme ou Barbarie*. The project of *Socialisme ou Barbarie* was to provide theoretical resources for a new socialist revolution, and to critique other existing socialist aberrations (particularly Stalinism and the French communist party). In the mid-to-late 1960s, however, he grew disenchanted with Marxism, although he remained a radi-cal thinker and participated in the May 1968 uprisings in France (discussed more fully in this chapter).

---

127 Ibid., p. 222.

He famously defined the postmodern as the end of the age of metanarratives. Metanarratives are totalizing stories about history and the goals of the human race that ground and legitimize knowledge and cultural practices. The two metanarratives that Lyotard saw as most important in defining modernity were: (1) history as progressing toward social enlightenment and emancipation (for example, that Kantian idea and its many permutations), and (2) knowledge as progressing toward some kind of unity (for example, that Hegelian idea and its permutations). For Lyotard, modernity is defined as the age of metanarratives, and postmodernity as the age in which metanarratives are bankrupt. Lyotard developed a theory of postmodernity that clarified its meaning as an era of fragmentation and pluralism.

In the appendix to his *The Postmodern Condition: A Report on Knowledge*, Lyotard offers an essay that could serve as a manifesto for the basic politics of culture jamming.

> A postmodern artist or writer is in the position of a philosopher: the text he writes, the work he produces are not in principle governed by preestablished rules, and they cannot be judged according to a determining judgment, by applying familiar categories to the text or to the work.[128]

Lyotard offered this characterization of postmodern works in order to defend books like Deleuze and Guattari's *A Thousand Plateaus*, which was met with some hostility because it broke too many rules of philosophy and defied categorization.[129] It cannot be the case, according to Lyotard, that those who have something to say will continue to speak in old manners of speaking. Just as philosophers and artists must find new ways of speaking, so too must activists. Lyotard understood this well, and we should recall

128 Lyotard, *The Postmodern Condition*, op. cit., p. 81.
129 Ibid., p. 71.

his contention cited in the epigraph to this chapter, "that not even the least privileged among us, is ever entirely powerless over the messages that traverse and position him at the post of sender, addressee, or referent."[130]

When Lyotard writes that no one is powerless, and that we can all be senders, addressees, or referents of messages, one might think first and foremost about the blogosphere and cyberspace as realizations of his insights. However, it is worth noting that Lyotard was not terribly optimistic about the computerized society, which he links in *The Postmodern Condition* to the privatization of knowledge and the commodification of information. He understood well that the computerized storage of data, or information, would not necessarily lead to the liberation of knowledge, and I suspect Lyotard would remain skeptical of the emancipatory use of computers. He had more hope in the radicalization of philosophy, in philosophy by other means than philosophy. "A postmodern artist or writer is in the position of a philosopher: the text he writes, the work he produces are not in principle governed by preestablished rules, and they cannot be judged according to a determining judgment, by applying familiar categories to the text or to the work."[131] Thus, we need new rules, new judgment, and new categories, also in political action.

(d) Baudrillard's Infectious Thinking

There is no political hope in the works of Jean Baudrillard. In *The Soul at Work*, Franco Berardi challenges this claim, arguing that there is a prescient and exceedingly applicable politics of catastrophe in Baudrillard's work, a kind of nightmare from of crisis theory.[132] Even if we agree with Berardi, it is nonetheless

130 Ibid., p. 15.
131 Ibid., p. 81.
132 Berardi, Franco "Bifo," *The Soul at Work: From Alienation to Autonomy* (Los Angeles: Semiotext(e), 2009).

true that Baudrillard's optimism is hard to find (as is Berardi's at times), only presenting itself in fleeting moments where he imagines the poisoning of dominant systems by way of viruses, contamination, and collapse. Politics, if any is possible, would have to function like an infection, a sickness that spreads throughout existing systems — economic, political, and ideological — revealing their contradictions and instabilities. If Baudrillard would have commented on culture jamming, it is predictable what he would express: He would have no optimism for it, as it would undoubtedly strike him as too resolutely political, as yet another delusional activism.

One does not try to change things any more, for activism is a field of failure, it both comes from failure and leads to it. Only catastrophes can change things, and our own highly technological capitalist societies in the West are themselves testing the limits of their own continuation:

> Other cultures, other metaphysics, are doubtless not badly undermined by this development because they did not have the ambition, expectation or phantasm of possessing the world, of analysing it in order to control it. But since we claimed to control the totality of postulates, it is clearly *our* system that is heading for catastrophe.[133]

For Baudrillard, a culture jam would be at best a symptom of a possible reversal, showing us that there are exceptions to the totality of postulates.

For all his disavowals of politics, Baudrillard keeps an interest in the prospects for some game-changing crisis, and retains much of Marx's sense that transformative possibility is linked

---

133 Baudrillard, Jean, *Passwords*, trans. Chris Turner (Verso, 2003), p. 52. This is also discussed in Baudrillard's *Paroxysm: Interviews with Philippe Petit*, trans. Chris Turner (Verso, 1998).

to systems crisis.[134] The key difference, of course, is that whereas for Marx systems crisis is related to communist-becoming, for Baudrillard, it promises nothing. Still, and also following Marxist influences, most of Baudrillard's work zeroes in on features and problems of capitalist society. The economic crisis that opened up onto the world in 2008, which revealed the inability of governments around the world to safeguard their own populations from the upheavals of capital, has given rise to revolts in Greece, Spain, Turkey, the "Arab Spring", and the Occupy Wall Street movement. Baudrillard would likely deny these "social" events their political conceits, but he would surely see the forerunning crises in politics and economics as the cause or occasion for such uprisings. Thus, while crisis disrupts systems of life, it is in no way promising for revolution, communism, or any other political development.

For Baudrillard, politics cannot be attempted outside the catastrophe that makes it possible. That is, it no longer makes sense to "be political" in a world where such being is a failure. What can one do, then? Within Baudrillard's theorization, thinking is the only action that can always be done. Our agency is therefore realized in thought, so thinking matters; it can impact, infect, and help realize its own incompatibility with the world.

As Baudrillard puts it: "Thought must play a catastrophic role, must be itself an element of catastrophe, of provocation, in a world that wants absolutely to cleanse everything, to exterminate death and negativity."[135] The world presents to us an image of its

---

134 The reader may observe here a similar expectation of catastrophe in both Zerzan and Baudrillard. Baudrillard, however, shares none of Zerzan's normative interest in the creation of some holistic, anarchist, and primitive future and is much closer to nihilism than to primitivism. As well, Baudrillard's early work comes out of a much more self-consciously Marxian trajectory. This can be seen in, among other works, his books *The Mirror of Production* (St. Louis: Telos Press, 1975) and *For a Critique of the Political Economy of the Sign* (St. Louis: Telos Press, 1981).

135 Baudrillard, *Passwords*, op. cit., p. 92.

own immortality, the immortality, or permanence, of capitalism, its cleanliness, as a pure positivity. But Baudrillard holds that thought can expose other dimensions of existing reality, poisoning the sterilized and ideologically packaged image of the present world. In this way, Baudrillard connects two pathways essential to my project. He is a cynic, even exploring his own nihilism in some works.[136] He is a man of *ressentiment*, to be sure, but at the same time he sees the importance of a provocation, which has become central to any radical project today. Radicals must become provocateurs whose thought infects and poisons the ideological landscape of capital and its culture.

(e) Camatte and Post-Class Struggle

Jacques Camatte is a French theorist who has been associated more with the Italian Left than with the intellectual or political movements from France I've been reviewing. Camatte was a Marxist and a member of the International Communist Party, a primarily Italian organization under the influence of Amadeo Bordiga. Camatte's work develops a deep critique of political organizations, party politics, and the major "communist projects" of the 20th century. After collecting and publishing a great number of historical documents from leftist/communist currents, and analyzing recently discovered writings of Marx, in the early 1970s Camatte claimed to have abandoned the Marxist perspective altogether. However, the Marxism of Camatte's work is far more pervasive and legible than in any other French and Italian theorist from within this period and milieu of disaffected radicalisms.

Camatte argues that "revolution" is impossible. Who could make the revolution? The working class has become a feature of capital, fully integrated into capitalist production and consump-

---

136   See especially the chapter "On Nihilism" in Baudrillard, *Simulacra and Simulation*, trans. Sheila Faria Glaser (Ann Arbor: University of Michigan Press, 1994).

tion, unable to supersede its own situation, and not even interested in doing so. Increasingly, Camatte's work offered nothing programmatic for politics.

In "The Wandering of Humanity," Camatte elaborates his critique of Marx and capitalism.[137] He maintains that Marx's communism was already possible in Marx's lifetime, since at least the middle of the 19th century. Nevertheless, it never happened because the desperate "wandering of humanity" developed instead of the revolutionary proletariat that Marx predicted. People can hardly identify their real interests anymore. Hence, humanity is miserable and has no apparent capacity for properly diagnosing its miserable condition. Camatte's negativity obviously resonates with the disillusionment of many communists of the 1970s, and clears a place for thinking of new approaches to old problems. In 1973 Camatte argued that there would need to be

> a simultaneous refusal of all obsolete forms of struggle. Like the May '68 movement but more so, the lycée movement emphasized very clearly that staying within the old forms of struggle inevitably leads to certain defeat. It is now becoming generally accepted that demonstrations, marches, spectacle and shows don't lead anywhere... The methods of struggle therefore must be put through analysis because they present an obstacle to the creation of new modes of action. And for this to be effective, there has to be a refusal of the old terrain of struggle – both in the workplace and in the streets.[138]

We can accept no delusion that Camatte would invest any hope in a culture jam. Working out of the Marxist trajectory, Camatte was interested in the prospects for large-scale emergences of new

---

137 Published in Camatte, Jacques, *This World We Must Leave and Other Essays* (Brooklyn: Autonomedia, 1995), pp. 39-90.
138 Camatte, *The Selected Works of Jacques Camatte* (New York: Prism Key Press, 2011), p. 159.

transformative antagonisms in an era in which nothing could be planned or controlled by a political party, and class struggle had proven obsolete. He wrote of the uselessness of all "old forms of struggle" and that demonstrations and marches no longer can accomplish anything. He called for "the creation of new modes of action" and "a refusal of the old terrain of struggle." These themes run through all of Camatte's work, and at least provide some of the rationale for a politics of culture jamming, which for all its desperation and limitations, attempts to answer the call for new forms of action. The failures of culture jamming, which I shall critique in the present chapter, are nonetheless part of the reckoning with obsolete forms of struggle.

(f) Deleuze and Guattari's Rhizomatic Model

Gilles Deleuze famously said: "Underneath all reason lies delirium, and drift." [139] What lies beneath reason is all the complicated turmoil of human psychology. Rather than seeing philosophy as the pursuit of truth or universal principles, Deleuze defines philosophy as a painful attempt to create useful concepts out of an almost incomprehensible mess. In Deleuze's view, philosophy more closely resembles creative artistic production than any scientific description of a preexisting world.

Félix Guattari developed an analysis of human subjectivity — of what makes us who we are, what changes us, and how we relate to one another — called "schizoanalysis." Schizoanalysis refers to a process that critically transforms Freud's psychoanalysis, by way of Jacques Lacan, into a more political, experimental, and collective approach. Schizoanalysis was introduced widely to readers in the 1972 book by Deleuze and Guattari, *Anti-Oedipus*. [140] But

139 Deleuze, Gilles, *Desert Islands and Other Texts: 1953-1974*, trans. Michael Taormina (Los Angeles and New York: Semiotext(e), 2004), p. 262.
140 Deleuze, Gilles and Guattari, Félix, *Anti-Oedipus: Capitalism and Schizophrenia*, trans. Robert Hurley, Mark Seem, and Helen R. Lane (New York: Penguin Books, 2009).

schizoanalysis was developed over a much longer period, dating back to Guattari's first experiments in psychotherapy. Most simply, schizoanalysis rests on three premises: (1) the psychological condition of a single person is better analyzed and understood within social contexts as a wider social condition (rather than as the condition of an isolated individual within his or her childhood and family development). (2) Schizophrenia is conventionally defined as "a disintegration of the process of thinking, of contact with reality, and of emotional responsiveness."[141] But that seemed a fitting characterization for the general condition of everyday life in contemporary capitalist societies. Thus, making a "schizoanalysis" of society should help us to better analyze society and its afflictions. (3) The generalized psychological condition of society cannot eliminate or completely bury human instincts for desire, love, and sexual gratification, but can only repress these instincts. Therefore, in some instances, these desires and instincts will break through the surface. All analysis and politics should work toward cultivating such outbursts or breakthroughs.

Deleuze and Guattari's work was always in some way about opening up new horizons for political and creative resistance to the homogenizing tendencies of capitalism.[142] When Deleuze and Guattari thought about politics, they used the concept of the rhizome. A rhizome is a subterranean plant that grows like a root or a stem, which grows horizontally, and sends up shoots through the ground at various unpredictable points. The rhizome provides a model for a non-hierarchical (or horizontal) politics that Deleuze and Guattari recommended. Autonomously organized "micropolitical" acts of revolt comprise the discrete sections of

141 See *Concise Medical Dictionary: Eighth Edition* (Oxford and New York: Oxford University Press, 2010), p. 657.
142 See Chapter 6 for a more direct application of some of these ideas from Deleuze and Guattari to recent uprisings in the US. We have already made indispensable use of Guattari's work in Chapters 1 and 2.

an underground growth that aims to break out into the above-ground world of society, culture, and politics. "Let's sum up the principal characteristics of a rhizome: unlike trees or their roots, the rhizome connects any point with any other point, and none of its features necessarily refers to features of the same kind."[143] The rhizomatic theory of politics developed by Deleuze and Guattari lends itself to autonomous forms of organization and action. Culture jamming is but one example of micropolitical action, and necessarily occurs in rhizomatic form.

•

It should need no repeating that the above portraiture of the development of some small part of the formative philosophies of postmodern theory is far from exhaustive. Again, I have offered only a series of fragments intended to provide a framework for understanding why culture jamming appears as a viable modality for subversive political action today. The idealized mass collective action of an international class toward the classically conceived revolutionary transformation of the world, spreading from one geographic location to another, is no longer a convincing pathway or sensible expectation. The old revolutionary aspiration has become an article of faith for those diminishing numbers practicing a dead religion, for those more committed to asserting their hackneyed political identity than to confronting the complexities of the capitalist present. The picture painted in many colors by the above theorists represents both a general and generational loss of faith in all conventional forms of political action.

In the last several decades of the 20th century, we were left with an understanding of the shrunken and frustrated, but still-living, hopes of radical and revolutionary politics. The political imagination has been in pursuit of new forms of action since the dis-

143 Deleuze, Gilles and Guattari, Félix, *On the Line*, trans. John Johnston (New York: Semiotext(e), 1983), p. 47.

illusionment of radicals dating to the Cold War decades, many of whom saw their last old hopes flounder and fade in Algeria, in the US, in France, and elsewhere. The postmodern turn does not extinguish that persistent hope for a different world, but rather, inscribes new words on its banners: creativity, subversion, autonomy. No more historic role for a class of proletarians. No more following the official parties of the Left. No more subordination of one's desires and talents to the collective movement that promises everything and achieves nothing. Culture jamming represents one desperate new line of creativity, subversion, and autonomy. How does revolt participate in a politics of creativity, subversion, and autonomy?

II *Détournement*: the insurrectionary logic of culture jamming

One must not introduce reformist illusions about the spectacle, as if it could be eventually improved from within, ameliorated by its own specialists under the supposed control of a better-informed public opinion. To do so would be tantamount to giving revolutionaries' approval to a tendency, or an appearance of a tendency, in a game that we absolutely must not play; a game that we must reject in its entirety in the name of the fundamental requirements of the revolutionary project, which can in no case produce an aesthetics because it is already entirely beyond the domain of aesthetics.[144]

There can be no question that, for Guy Debord, the author of the theory of *détournement*, the theory and practice of culture jamming should have been developed in the service of new revolutionary projects. Debord was a thinker within the milieu of the

144 Debord, Guy, "For a Revolutionary Judgment of Art" in *Situationist International Anthology*, trans. Ken Knabb (Berkeley: Bureau of Public Secrets, 2006), p. 394.

postmodern trajectory in France, although he too often remains relegated to the footnotes of the story. In many ways, his work stood on the precipice of the postmodern turn and informed the work of most of the thinkers reviewed in Part I of the present chapter.[145] Debord's work came early in the trajectory, expressed many of the insights that would come to define postmodern theory, and yet retained certain revolutionary commitments.

In the passage cited above, Debord issued a clear warning against reformist activity disguised by the veneer of insurgency. He understood well that revolution has its spectacle (a mythological form that functions as reality), that there will be political action that wants to look like revolution — that may actually look like revolution — but that, when explored, is seeking nothing more than liberal legislation that is ultimately permissible within the limits of capital and its culture. For example, if the San Andreas Accords on Indigenous Rights was the sole aim of the Zapatista uprising, the upheaval in Chiapas would have only been a spectacle of revolution. Likewise, if the tumult of the Civil Rights movement in the US is embodied and reflected in the capstone achievements of the Civil Rights and Voting Rights Acts of 1964 and 1965, then that tumult had no real revolutionary character, even though it was often mixed with revolutionary language and imagery. What is the character of real revolution today? The question, for Debord and many others, is an old one in revolutionary theory: that is, how to discern the difference between revolution and reform?

---

145   Of the postmodern thinkers reviewed in Part I, there is little evidence that Debord had any influence on the work of Foucault and Derrida, which puts them in the category of rare exceptions. Nonetheless, there are many theoretical resonances between Foucault's and Debord's interest in subversion, and between Derrida's deconstruction and Debord's *détournement*. These theoretical resonances may well be a product of the streams of thought of that generation's intellectual and political developments, which could be explored further in a different work.

Debord's contention that "[a]rt criticism is a second-degree spectacle" should be taken as a warning to culture jammers today.[146] Is the successfully detourned billboard a second-degree spectacle? Is it a spectacle that outsmarts the advertising savvy of the original with a wittier advertising savvy? Is the successfully detourned billboard the one that survives long enough to generate a buzz among local passersby? Or, perhaps the successfully detourned billboard is the one that very few people see because it is quickly deemed impermissible by the advertisers or their guardians and is scrubbed from the landscape at once. What are the aims of culture jamming? These questions are unavoidable when considering culture jamming through the lens of Debord.

One of the most important essays Debord wrote about the prefigurative politics of culture jamming, or *détournement*, was his 1963 "The Situationists and the New Forms of Action in Politics and Art." In that essay he wrote about linking people and experiences together "to help unify such groups and the coherent basis of their project," and so that their shared commitment would inhere in "the critique of the existing world."[147] We must keep in mind that Debord worked to build a Situationist International, which attempted, however unsuccessfully, to achieve just such a coherent linking up of avant-garde activists within the radical milieu of his era. Debord argued that although the new forms of action in politics and art would have to be autonomously organized in a fragmentary way, often sporadically, and by disparate individuals taking no orders from any central command, such new forms of action should aspire to concretely coordinate with one another to avoid marginalization, cooptation, or total irrelevance.

There are indications that culture jamming today has lost this

---

146 Debord, "For a Revolutionary Judgment of Art," op. cit., p. 395.
147 Debord, "The Situationists and the New Forms of Action in Politics and Art" in *Situationist International Anthology* (Berkeley: Bureau of Public Secrets, 2006), p. 403.

critical sensibility. Culture jamming is often accessed and associated with its breakthrough stars, a coterie of notable personalities, The Yes Men, Reverend Billy, Banksy, Andrew Boyd, the artist-activists Packard Jennings and Steve Lambert, maybe a dozen other people. I have enjoyed the creative and autonomous work of artist-jammers like Steve Lambert, whose interactive sculpture "Capitalism Works For Me! (True/False)" is a provocative installment that produces an interesting interruption of the capitalist landscape.[148] But if the "new activism" is led by a small cast of celebrity activists, including maybe one hundred to one thousand assistant-workers behind the scenes, culture jamming becomes a voyeuristic politics, where few do while most watch. This preserves too much of the current notion of "being political" in the age of 24-hour cable news, where to "be political" is essentially the same as to know what is happening in the world of politics. To be political means to know what a politician said in a speech, to be up on official scandals and controversies. Debord sent warnings into the future that the new radical movements must not be any small coterie of hip marketing geniuses, some of whom are later hired for actual marketing jobs. A politics that trades collective action for a sparse campaign of media pranks coordinated by a band of professionals is a form of art criticism, a second-degree spectacle at best.

As a point of contrast, consider Debord's favorite examples of creative, subversive, and autonomous action. He wrote about students in Caracas who made an armed attack on an exhibition of French art, stealing paintings, and offering to return them only in exchange for the release of political prisoners; he discusses pirate radio broadcasts that made "official" warnings about the real dangers of nuclear war that the real officials would never

148 Lambert, Steve, "Capitalism Works For Me! (True/False)," accessed January 4, 2016, http://visitsteve.com/made/capitalism-works-for-me-truefalse.

broadcast; he commends an English group of activists, the "Spies for Peace," who discovered and divulged the secret location of a bomb shelter exclusively built for government officials. These acts are aimed to captivate attention and to force a critique of a culture in which bourgeois paintings are considered equivalent bargaining chips for prisoners, the radio is a *de facto* authority, and real preparations are made to protect presidents from bombs while the general population is locked out. Can we call this a "critical art?" According to Debord, we must. He insists that

> a critical art can be carried out within the existing means of cultural expression, from cinema to painting—even though we ultimately wish to destroy this entire artistic framework. This critical art is what the situationists have summed up in their theory of *détournement*. Such an art must not only be critical in its content, it must also be self-critical in its form.[149]

If we follow Debord, culture jamming cannot be defined as the *détournement* of billboards, as subvertising, media pranks, or any other "type of act," although all of these things may well be *examples* of culture jamming. One is reminded of Plato's insistence that we do not mistake "the good" for any particular "good act."

In the 1956 "User's Guide to Détournement," Guy Debord and Gil J. Wolman state that there are

> two main categories of detourned elements... These are *minor détournements* and *deceptive détournements*. Minor détournement is the détournement of an element which has no importance in itself and which thus draws all its meaning from the new context in which it has been placed. For example, a press clipping, a neutral phrase, a commonplace photograph. Deceptive détourne-

149 Debord, "The Situationists and the New Forms of Action in Politics and Art," op. cit., p. 406.

ment, also termed premonitory-proposition détournement, is in contrast the détournement of an intrinsically significant element, which derives a different scope from the new context.[150]

In the first case, then, *détournement* is about utilizing other peoples' resources for one's own purposes, taking what is available, regardless of its intended context, and making it say something else as you wish. In the second case, *détournement* addresses through some kind of critical derailment the intended context, making it turn on itself, or contradict its claims. Detourned billboards fall into the latter category, as does the work of Reverend Billy, who manipulates the context of the religious sermon, exploiting the preacher's world, but using it beyond and against the scope of that world in order to comment on consumerism and capitalist culture.

The first category, minor *détournement*, is in some ways the broader of the two, for it even includes graffiti, which is a way of speaking on city walls without having to pay advertising fees. Corporations are involved in what should be considered legally contracted graffiti. Indeed, illegal graffiti shows the openness and accessibility of *détournement*, for it involves all of the meaningful vandalisms of uprisings and gives voice to words that speak to the whole city, to all who see them, often written by those who have no conventional artistic prowess, little money, no contracts, and nothing to sell, but something to say nonetheless.

To explore more concretely the purposes of *détournement* in connection with Debord and his generation, we should consult René Viénet's small treasure of a book, *Enragés and Situationists in the Occupation Movement, France, May '68*. This book was originally published in 1968 in French, long before being translated for English publication in 1992. Viénet's book includes photo-

---

150   Debord and Wolman, "A User's Guide to Détournement" in *Situationist International Anthology* (Berkeley: Bureau of Public Secrets, 2006), p. 16.

graphs of detourned walls, comics, and paintings, many of which were done by students who were reading the texts of Debord and Vaneigem, among others. These examples, beautifully arranged and explained by Viénet, show us why there can be no narrow sense of culture jamming. In May 1968, the walls detourned into *communiqués* rarely involved image-play, but were nonetheless full of creative minor *détournement*. On the side of a church: "How can one think freely in the shadow of a chapel?"[151] On many walls: "Beneath the paving stones, the beach!"[152] The comics of the period were very creative, but the makers of the detourned comics did not, and presumably could not, draw them, so they took to changing the content of the text bubbles instead. A part of the culture jamming of May 1968 could be seen in the city on the day after the fiercest street protests. In Viénet's book, photographs of street scenes show burnt cars stacked by the sidewalk, shopping streets converted to rubble, police cars and vans on fire. The participants in these uprisings did not take control of the city's institutions, but rather attacked its features, transforming its appearance. Here we find revolt as a creative activity, as *détournement*, autonomous, subversive, and artistic. Why? What reason lies beneath this revolt, or what delirium, what desires, what disaffections, what grievances?

We can be sure of one thing from the start: The messages of May 1968 were not written by those who wanted reform, but by those who wanted something more radical, some kind (or many kinds) of structural transformation. The uprising appears irrational from the point of view of power, for it is speaking a different language. Debord and Wolman insisted that "*Détournement is less effective the more it approaches a rational reply*."[153] It is worth

151 Viénet, René, *Enragés and Situationists in the Occupation Movement, France, May '68*, trans. Loren Goldner and Paul Sieveking (New York: Autonomedia, 1992), p. 60.

152 Ibid., p. 80.

153 Debord and Wolman, "A User's Guide to Détournement," op. cit., p. 17.

considering that riot and revolt are typically characterized as irrational or senseless, as in the case of the "riots" around London in the fall of 2011. The demand to "be rational" is much like the demand to "be practical," which essentially means "play by the rules of the game." But it is precisely such rational-practicality that the radical elements always reject. *Détournement* as culture jamming is carried out in search of other rationalities and practices, against what Debord referred to as the ruling order's "uninterrupted monologue of self-praise."[154] Culture jamming, at its best, wants to expose and give voice to other discourses than those proliferated by the dominant narrative. It is therefore not a coincidence that Debord had an enduring interest in Hegel and dialectics: The fact that rationality turns into its opposite and vice versa is critical to his theory of the spectacle.

Debord and Wolman insist that

> détournement not only leads to the discovery of new aspects of talent; in addition, clashing head-on with all social and legal conventions, it cannot fail to be a powerful cultural weapon in the service of a real class struggle... It is a real means of proletarian artistic education, the first step toward a *literary communism*.[155]

Therefore, *détournement* can never be the private property of graphic designers, professional artists and philosophers, expert musicians, or other specialists. If *détournement* is "a real means of proletarian artistic education" and a real step toward "literary communism," this means that its purpose is to give every member of any neglected, impoverished, repressed, and alienated community new ways of speaking, of discovering what they can do, of finding new forms of struggling against their own conditions of

154 Debord, *The Society of the Spectacle*, trans. Donald Nicholson-Smith (New York: Zone Books, 1995), p. 19.
155 Debord and Wolman, "A User's Guide to Détournement," op. cit., p. 18.

life. Yet, in the same essay, Debord and Wolman say: "It is obviously in the realm of the cinema that détournement can attain its greatest effectiveness and, for those concerned with this aspect, its greatest beauty." [156] This seemingly contradictory (i.e. does the proletariat have the cinema to make use of?) sentiment clearly reflects Debord's own biases, as he made filmic *détournements*, including a detourned adaptation of his most influential book *The Society of the Spectacle*. Viénet also made feature-film-length *détournements*, and his best movie, *Can Dialectics Break Bricks?* is an excellent example of detourned cinema. But perhaps the assertion about cinema is not as contradictory as it seems. If ever there was a proletarian filmmaking, it would be through *détournement*. Viénet's movie is a detourned martial-arts film, over-dubbed with new dialogue in French. This approach takes much work and creativity, but not necessarily much money, and even less so today when *détournement* is a common methodology on YouTube and elsewhere on the Internet, where everyday people are increasingly involved in making movies.

Perhaps the most important line in Debord and Wolman's text is the one that concludes it. "In itself, the theory of détournement scarcely interests us." [157] Indeed, Debord was *not* interested in the defense of a theory, or in some proprietary situationist method, but rather in thinking through the ways that we might destroy spectacular society. And this is where I want to anchor the overview of the present chapter. *Détournement* is a particular, possible resource, which recommends what Debord and Wolman call the tactic of "extremist innovation" that intervenes in the spheres of civil disobedience and direct action. [158] Debord understood the opportunistic nature of *détournement*. Its sole function was what Debord and Wolman saw as a transformational potentiality, a way

156 Ibid., p. 19.
157 Ibid., p. 21.
158 Ibid., p. 14.

to let revolutionary desire speak. Culture jamming, which centralizes the logic of *détournement*, must therefore (a) be broadly enough conceived to include the burnt, stacked cars and graffiti in the streets of riots and revolts and (b) must understand itself as a minor composition within the broader conduction of a revolutionary politics.

In the foundational text of the Situationist International, "Report on the Construction of Situations and on the Terms of Organization and Action of the International Situationist Tendency" (1957), Debord wrote:

> Our concern is precisely the use of certain means of action, along with the discovery of new ones that may more easily be recognized in the sphere of culture and manners but that will be implemented with a view to interaction with global revolutionary change.[159]

Thus, some things were clear from the start: *Détournement* was to be counted among the tools of a new activism, which functioned primarily in the "sphere of culture." *Détournement* could be carried out autonomously by individuals, but what matters most is that it is done "with a view to interaction" as part of a broader international politics committed to "global revolutionary change." I am not convinced that Debord's interest in revolution and international action has been carried through to the present interest in culture jamming. Possibly, culture jamming leaves revolution and international action purposely behind in its comportment as a postmodern politics. I claim that the more revolutionary and transformative aims of Debord's method have been eclipsed and supplanted by an uncritical and unconscious liberal appropria-

159 Debord, "Report on the Construction of Situations and on the Terms of Organization and Action of the International Situationist Tendency" in *Guy Debord and the Situationist International: Texts and Documents*, ed. Tom McDonough (Cambridge, MA and London: The MIT Press, 2002), p. 29.

tion of the radical intentions of *détournement*. I say "unconscious" because I do not mean that liberals had any deliberate designs to render culture jamming a curiosity for academics interested in the aesthetic appeal of media pranks. By "unconscious" I mean that culture jamming has become inadvertently more liberal as a result of the rigor mortis in the corpse of the previous generation's radicalism. But such claims call for evidence and demonstration.

Debord insisted that the Situationist International

> must support, alongside the workers' parties or extremist tendencies existing within these parties, the necessity of considering a consistent ideological action for fighting, on the level of the passions, the influence of the propaganda methods of late capitalism: to concretely contrast, at every opportunity, other desirable ways of life with the reflections of the capitalist way of life; to destroy, by all hyperpolitical means, the bourgeois idea of happiness... We must introduce everywhere a revolutionary alternative to the ruling culture; coordinate all the enquiries that are happening at this moment without a general perspective; orchestrate, through criticism and propaganda, the most progressive artists and intellectuals of all countries to make contact with us with a view to joint action.[160]

Debord was resolutely committed to a passionate praxis linked to the initiative of "fighting the propaganda of late capitalism." Capitalism was still identified as the problem. With much uncertainty about the future, a refutation of classical Marxism, and with much in common with Foucault, Derrida, Lyotard, Baudrillard, Camatte, and Deleuze and Guattari, Debord nonetheless demanded "joint action" with the most extreme elements of ultra-Left groups, internationalism, global orchestration, and collective action. The key here — as was argued more fully in Chapter 2 — is

160   Ibid., pp. 49-50.

to understand that autonomous action does not imply individualist, isolated, disconnected activity. Autonomous action could and must aspire to develop new linkages, to create not only new forms of action, but also new lines of alliance in rhizomatic ways, as proposed by Deleuze, Negri, and Guattari.

Vaneigem — once a close comrade of Debord — made some distinct contributions to thinking about what a postmodern politics could be. Like Debord, Vaneigem warned against the centralization of leadership in a cadre of leaders, while advocating a kind of insurrectionary poetry. "I have already said that in my view no insurrection is ever fragmented in its initial impulses, that it only becomes so when the poetry of agitators and ringleaders gives way to authoritarian leadership."[161] Vaneigem consistently encouraged poetic forms of expressing the insurrectionary desires of everyday people. He insisted that every person has "an irreducible core of creativity."[162] And Vaneigem helped Debord articulate the approach of *détournement*. Mainly, Vaneigem adds the importance of poetry to the discussion of creative revolutionary activism. For Vaneigem, *détournement* is all about "reversal of perspective." "The reversal of perspective entails a kind of anti-conditioning. Not a new form of conditioning, but a new game and its tactics; the game of subversion (détournement)."[163] And for Vaneigem, this subversion must be fun, daring, and should make us feel good doing it.

Poetry, for Vaneigem, is a form of expression that breaks rules. Upheaval and revolt are poetic because they speak to us in unconventional ways, using forms of communication inflected with impassioned desire, outrage, and spontaneity. Vaneigem insists that "poetry rarely involves poems these days. Most works of art are betrayals of poetry. How could it be otherwise, when poetry

161   Vaneigem, Raoul, *The Revolution of Everyday Life*, trans. Donald Nicholson-Smith (London: Rebel Press, 2006), p. 174.
162   Ibid., p. 192.
163   Ibid., p. 188.

and power are irreconcilable?"[164] Poetry is, for Vaneigem, an irrepressible force. "Everywhere repressed, this poetry springs up everywhere... It plays muse to rioters, informs revolt and animates all great revolutionary carnivals for a while, until the bureaucrats consign it to the prison of hagiography."[165]

The importance of the style of expression was of course not lost on Debord either. In *The Society of the Spectacle*, Debord writes of *détournement* as an "insurrectional style."[166] What Vaneigem called the poetic form, or Debord called the insurrectional style, was central to the situationist praxis of *détournement*. And, as the title of the present chapter reveals, it is precisely the insurrectionary content of *détournement* that I seek to recover. Therefore, I must finally say what I mean by it, and what I mean by the term "insurrectionary imagination."

When I speak of insurrection, much like Debord, I do not mean to invoke the idea of an armed revolt of some militant faction of society in a mortal stand-off with the state. Instead, I want to recover the word's 15th-century meaning, which embodies the idea of "a rising up." The rising up of insurrection starts from within a system or place, and goes against from the inside — insurrection is an internal, not an external force, even when it aims at a possible destination outside the system or place from which it starts. Philosophers like Derrida engaged in what Debord would call an "insurrectionary style," going against from within a text. Insurrection may contain elements of riot and rebellion, but it is not synonymous with either of these. Insurrection delivers a message, even if that message is disqualified as irrational by opponents. Thus, riots may be more or less insurrectionary, depending on what they have to say about the existing state of affairs. Rebellion can be an insurrectionary form too, but not if it

164 Ibid., p. 201.

165 Ibid., p. 203.

166 Debord, *The Society of the Spectacle*, op. cit., p. 144.

is only demanding (in an insurrectionary style) a new law, or some particular exercise of an old law.

Rebellion occupies a space in between reform and revolution in the following way: Rebellion is a mode of action that emerges from the frustrations and failures of conventional measures. Thus, one becomes a rebel only after meeting with the impasses of reform. In this way, rebellion may be a more contentious means of making reform. People become rebellious when conventional appeals to power go unheeded for too long. Rebellion may therefore present itself in an insurrectionary style but have no revolutionary content. Whereas insurrection is always closely related to revolution because it is a rising up of revolutionary energy. Insurrection moves in the direction of revolution, or at the very least, wants to move in that direction. Though, unlike the event of revolution, insurrection is a revolutionary flourish, a moment of revolt, an attempt, an experiment, an expression, that does not carry out a total transformation. That is, it does not *institute* a new social or political reality. One could say, then, that insurrection is the activity of revolutionary aspirations in the society, and not a revolution as such. An insurrection is a revolt, or more precisely, the adjectival (insurrectionary) and energetic (insurrectionist) dimension of the thing, revolt. Insurrection specifies certain contents of revolt, particularly the *affectively* revolutionary content that at the same time knows it is not *effectively* revolutionary. Riots and rebellions, on the other hand, may not embody and reflect any revolutionary content, for they can occur in response to contested election results, court decisions, or electrical blackouts. This does not diminish the insurrectionary potentialities of riot and rebellion, but rather, specifies and highlights the revolutionary content of insurrection.

Today, the revolution, of which insurrection is a fragment, is not focused on seizing the apparatuses of power. That classical conception of revolution does not survive the basic insights of the so-called postmodern era. Revolution mainly appears today in the fragments of insurrection. What does remain from the old idea is the grand aspiration for a structural transformation of the world from what it is into some version of what it ought to be, but with none of the faithful anticipation that once accompanied that notion. Insurrection materializes the substantive hopes of such transformation, a revolutionary substance without a revolutionary form. Yet, insurrection happens even when it fails to make revolution, and it mostly does fail to make revolution. Why should we speak of insurrection instead of revolution? First of all, we speak of insurrection in order to have something to speak of. There is much insurrection in the world, little revolution. To speak of insurrection is to speak of certain processes of revolution, and not so much the goals of an overarching project(s).

If we find a potter sitting at the wheel with her hands molding spinning wet clay, is it not reasonable to ask what she is aiming to make, and would it not confuse us if she told us that she didn't know yet what the clay would become? Yet such a potter is a good analogy here. We participate in the processes of making something without yet knowing how it will turn out. Indeed, we know we want to make something new. We use our creative energy and see how ideas may guide it. The whole project is precarious, marked by an uncertainty from the start. This is the only position revolution can take, from the perspectives of postmodern disaffection, from the experiences of the ultra-Left after WWII, to philosophers like Foucault, Lyotard, and Baudrillard.

The difficulty and even undesirability of some single unitary vision for an overarching project to remake the world does not preclude the possibility of insurrection, which always suggests new horizons for politics and culture as it happens. Postmodern theory casts a dark cloud over revolution, but says nothing against the reality of ongoing insurrection. Thus, insurrection is the more hopeful term today, and needs the help of imagination. We can see many failed revolutions, or we can see many successful insurrections; there is certainly a "glass half full" part of this theorization. At its very best, culture jamming participates in the revitalization of the insurrectionary imagination. A good culture jam tries to say: "Look, we can see things differently. The insurrectionary imagination can come to life, and we are not through with revolution."

Viénet showed how the French insurrection of May 1968 enlivened the imaginations of radical students in London, the latter of whom sent a letter to French workers and students that read: "Comrades, you have reanimated the traditions of 1871 and 1917."[167] In June of 1968, the student strikers at Columbia University in New York City wrote: "For more than two weeks twelve million French workers and students have led a mass general strike against the same conditions which confront us in America... Their fight is our fight."[168] Viénet himself pointed out that by the end of May 1968 "occupations of university buildings had taken place in Germany, Stockholm, Brussels, and at the Hornsey Art College in London. Barricades had gone up in Rome on May 31st. In June the students of Tokyo... occupied their faculties and defended them against the police."[169] Viénet goes on to highlight occupations, demonstrations, and civil disobedience, all enlivened by the French situation, in Switzerland, including riots in Zurich, Buenos Aires, Dakar, Madrid, Peru, Brazil, Uruguay, Argentina, Turkey, and the Congo.[170]

It cannot simply be said that 1968 was a different era and that none of this can happen today. Fifty years after Viénet's catalog of insurrection, students at The New School for Social Research (and elsewhere around the world) occupied university buildings in solidarity with the Greek revolt of 2008. After that, we saw the "Arab Spring" and the Occupy Wall Street movement, which

167 Viénet, *Enragés and Situationists in the Occupation Movement*, op. cit., p. 118.
168 Ibid.
169 Ibid.
170 Ibid., p. 119.

had a similarly "contagious spreading" as did the examples from 1968. There are other notable examples in between 1968 and 2008, including the 1994 Zapatista uprising (discussed in more detail below), which had very particular international resonances in the movements against capitalist globalization in Seattle in 1999, DC in 2000, and Genoa in 2001. Uprisings such as these intervene critically and publicly on the terrain of the cultural-valuational norms of society, showing to their own societies, as well as to others elsewhere, that many things that are taken for granted can be thrown into question. I want to think of such insurrections as the general intellect of culture jamming.

III A *détournement* of the Wikipedia entry on "culture jamming"

Debord wrote, "Ideas improve. The meaning of words has a part in the improvement. Plagiarism is necessary. Progress demands it. Staying close to an author's phrasing, plagiarism exploits his expressions, erases false ideas, replaces them with correct ideas."[171] Following this, I shall now synthesize a number of my foregoing arguments in a *détournement* of the Wikipedia entry on "Culture Jamming."

It doesn't matter when the term "culture jamming" was officially coined, unless the history that is written about it obscures its meaning and aspirations. We have seen that the logic of culture jamming, *détournement*, was worked out as a means of insurrection in the mid-1950s. As it turns out, tracing culture jamming to the renaming of *détournement* in 1984 *does* obscure the historical context I have unpacked, and most importantly, the revolutionary aspirations of that history. Culture jamming is said to refer to a tactic used by many anti-consumerist social movements to disrupt or subvert mainstream cultural institutions, including

171 Debord, *The Society of the Spectacle,* op. cit., p. 145.

corporate advertising. But what is almost always missing from the discourse on consumerism and corporate advertising is one key word and idea: capitalism. Any definition of culture jamming that obscures the antagonistic relationship between *détournement* and capital is a problem. It is not as guardians of a sacred origins story that we should go back well before Mark Dery's definition of culture jamming, or Negativland's "original" approach, all the way to the situationists. Such work is worth doing only to dig out lost moorings, meanings, purposes, and impetuses, which once lost and buried, can convert a radical praxis into an intellectual or artistic curiosity.

Culture jamming in the form of subvertising is a liberal fantasy. Failures notwithstanding, the first month of Occupy Wall Street had far greater "cultural impact" than any detourned billboard. (We must not accept the narrative that *AdBusters* magazine started Occupy Wall Street any more than we should accept *Time Magazine*'s assignment of the sole authorship of the slogan "We are the 99%" to anthropologist David Graeber.[172] UC students in Berkeley and Santa Cruz and students at The New School in New York City kicked off the recent wave of occupations in 2008 and 2009, and protest slogans are written by those who publish them in the streets.) One of the concerns of culture jamming as liberal fantasy has to do with its integration into the liberal trend of treating conscientious consumption as political action. How is the moral sensibility of the liberal expressed today, but to buy local and organic, from health-food stores, CSAs, and farmer's markets, to use compact fluorescent light bulbs, to recycle, to vote as progressive as allowed, and to drink "fair-trade" coffee? Where is the critique of capital? The perpetual-growth logic of capital remains the operational logic of most—if not all—societies today. Capitalist societies deal well with their own ironies, even happily

172   See "The Protester" by Kurt Andersen, *Time Magazine*, Wednesday, Dec. 14, 2011.

pointing out their tolerance for every criticism that leaves their logic alone. If culture jamming is compatible with capital, then it belongs to the system it critiques, and even becomes a feature of that system's openness. If, on the other hand, culture jamming is an insurrection, its creative interventions may help to develop a revolutionary praxis. Let us consider both sides of the question.

"Crowd sourcing" now invites people to make *détournements* of corporate logos, as GAP, for example, recently invited from its customers. GAP even encouraged people to express their disgust at the old logo, to refigure the logo in any blasphemous way they would like, so that the company could generate news stories about itself and avoid hiring designers to fashion the new branding.[173] Subvertising, defined as the activity of "re-figuring logos, fashion statements, and product images as a means to challenge the idea of what's cool," could also just be defined as "advertising!" Indeed, professional advertisers today are already expert subvertisers.

Such culture jammers do not transform the capitalist mass media, for they engage in parodist and parasitic *détournement*. In this way, culture jamming is not as independent an act as it might seem, for it depends upon the dominant form that is detourned. I refer again to Viénet's detourned movie, *Can Dialectics Break Bricks?* His *détournement* required substantial work, a good script retrofitted to the filmic sequences, and actors to perform and record the overdubbed dialogue. Yet, Viénet's film would not have existed without the 1972 martial-arts original, *The Crush*, by Tu Guangqi. Although this may not be true in the particular case of Viénet's film, detourned works are generally far less widespread than the original source material. Culture jamming offers a way to infiltrate the public sphere on a small scale. It is a joy to see a detourned billboard of the Billboard Liberation Front, and it does empower even the least privileged among us to post uninvited

---

173 See "New Gap Logo Hated by Many, Company Turns to Crowdsourcing Tactics" by Mike Isaac, *Forbes Magazine*, Oct. 7, 2010.

messages, to interject, to interfere, and to intervene. The problem is that every liberated billboard is surrounded and outnumbered by the unjammed billboards that are only slightly less noteworthy on the visual landscape. In the world of billboards, this is a mismatch of scale, to say the very least. From a political point of view, we would have to romanticize the heroism of an anarchist David vs a corporate Goliath. Such a situation is as catastrophic as it is noble. This is largely why I insist on treating culture jamming broadly enough to include a wide range of interventions on the cultural terrain, including those moments of insurrectionary activity mentioned above.

Mark Dery, often associated with the introduction of the idea of culture jamming, makes some unfortunate betrayals of the good idea he is credited for. Dery agrees with Carrie McLaren's criticism of *AdBusters* magazine, which rightly challenges the magazine's founder Kalle Lasn for "branding his magazine as the house organ of the Culture Jamming Movement®, peddling anti-consumerist swag through the magazine's website..."[174] Yet, Dery's unhappiness with *AdBusters* is unlike McLaren's inasmuch as Dery takes special offense at Lasn for not crediting him personally for introducing the idea that the magazine is founded upon. Dery complains: "I introduced editor/publisher Kalle Lasn to the term 'culture jamming'" and "Lasn took the concept and ran with it," while neglecting, "in too many interviews, the role my work played in bringing the concept to his attention."[175] Why should Dery care about anyone running with the concept of culture jamming, about being credited for the idea? Many of the situationists used pseudonyms or published their writings without attribution to their authors, and they were not, for all their faults, terribly worried about keeping *détournement* as the pri-

---

174 Dery, Mark, "Culture Jamming: Hacking, Slashing, and Sniping in the Empire of Signs," accessed January 5, 2016, http://markdery.com/?page_id=154.

175 Ibid.

vate property of their movement. Moreover, the concept of culture jamming did not come into the world in 1990 through Dery's pen and *The New York Times*. By no means am I suggesting that Kalle Lasn and *AdBusters* win the dispute; I have criticized that magazine elsewhere.[176] The point is that we must break with the proprietary interests of all these post-Cold War culture jammers, understanding that the social, political, economic, and cultural impetuses for culture jamming preceded all of the "major figures" of the current wave. Such disputes exemplify the problem: culture jamming as an individualist star system. Culture jamming is only worth defending if it flows in countless directions beyond anyone's grasp.

Any culture jammer who thinks they can effectively disrupt the unconscious thought processes of consumers who might experience an epiphany after seeing detourned advertising needs a better understanding of human psychology and ideology. Subvertising culture jammers cannot reasonably expect that the memes of their actions will evoke behavioral change and political action. Ideology is resistant to critique, resilient and malleable enough to survive strong refutations. Ideology does not shatter like a mask when confronted with logical contradictions, statistical data, and other information, because ideology is central to peoples' political self-understandings. Fox News fans will not have their worldview shattered by Rachel Maddow any more than Maddow's fans would abandon their worldview in the face of the shocking exposés of Sean Hannity. The affective appeal of speaking to people through sonic/visual media is important to seize upon, but it does not promise anything. The fact is, Viénet's movie appeals to situationists and their admirers, and probably to other assorted activists interested in radical theory. But it is not hard

176 See Gilman-Opalsky, Richard, *Spectacular Capitalism: Guy Debord and the Practice of Radical Philosophy* (New York and London: Autonomedia, 2011), pp. 81-85.

to see that it would confuse a general audience that does not get all the in-joke Trotsky and Foucault references that punctuate its dialogue. Ideology, which thinkers like Wilhelm Reich, Karl Mannheim, Erich Fromm, Herbert Marcuse, Guy Debord, and Slavoj Žižek diagnose well, is not one subvertisement (or one hundred subvertisements) away from being shattered.

Perhaps the worst of all possible fates for the good idea of *détournement* is culture jamming as a tool of "social consumer movements." What is a "social consumer movement?" This essentially refers to socially conscious shopping, a "movement" of consumers not only armed with dollars, but with a liberal conscience. This so-called movement actually generates a new specialized market based on treating righteous consumption as political action, and has proven to be a boon for capital, providing it with more than new market demand with the endorsement of former critics. The business world has become expert at creating two models of every commodity, a bad version ("classic" or "traditional") and a "green" version for socially conscious consumers. Social consumerism means you can live a totally privatized life of individuated consumption that nonetheless reassures you of your good conscience. You may even feel, after a particularly "green" shopping spree, that you have just been involved in political action.

AdBusters' own "true cost" campaign falls happily into this trap. The campaign aims to get people to see the "true cost" of the products they buy, adding to the sales costs of various commodities the human and environmental costs required to make them. The best part of this campaign is that it aspires to shake up a narrowly conceived academic economics, which leaves out human and environmental costs because it only measures cost in terms of money. The "true cost" campaign should be commended for presenting a powerful, savvy critique of the sanitized mythology of free-market capitalism. But any assumption that neoliberal and neoclassical economists will adopt and repeat a critique of their own ideological narrowness in light of the "true cost" campaign is a tall order of delusion. And the claim that *AdBusters* can be accused of such delusion is well argued in Max Haiven's superb article, "Privatized Resistance: AdBusters and the Culture of Neoliberalism."[177] Haiven criticizes *AdBusters*' "plans to create and sell the Black Spot, a Portuguese-made canvas sneaker with a two-fold agenda: to 'kick [Nike CEO] Phil Knight's ass,' and to 'do no less than reinvent capitalism.'"[178] So the iconic organ of the culture jammer press is going to compete with and beat Nike at making and selling sneakers and also reinvent capitalism? That the Black Spot could kick Nike's ass is clearly, at the very gentlest, a ludicrous feat of wishful thinking, but the fact that *AdBusters* wants to reinvent capitalism helps to substantiate the claim that the magazine and its editors are fairly well integrated into the pseudo-politics of socially conscious shopping.

Haiven also rightly questions the efficacy of the "social consumer" demands raised by "Buy Nothing Day" and "TV Turnoff Week" which he attributes to the magazine's "iconic 'brand' of cultural resistance."[179] When culture jamming becomes a tool for bringing about a more conscientious consumer culture that runs for only 364 instead of for 365 days a year, it becomes a caricatured cooptation of the situationist idea of *détournement*, and inadvertently acquiesces to the most defeatist realizations of the postmodern era.

Nonetheless, with all these criticisms piled high, I want to advocate culture jamming everywhere, but a culture jamming wrested from the hands of liberal entertainment. Culture jamming appeals to that irreducible creative core Vaneigem wrote about, and provides everyday people with a way to act without

---

177 Haiven, Max, "Privatized Resistance: AdBusters and the Culture of Neoliberalism" in *The Review of Education, Pedagogy, and Cultural Studies*, 29:85–110, 2007.

178 Ibid., p. 85.

179 Ibid.

having to wait patiently for mass movements to emerge. Culture jamming shows us what can be done in between major transformations, what can be done almost anywhere, what can be done by almost anyone. Culture jamming attracts activists who are drawn to the risks of civil disobedience, who are not necessarily transfixed on outcomes, but interested in the joyful, witty, and even funny side of political engagement. This captures something important. As asked in Chapter 2, what are the prospects for creating a world we desire if all the old ways of trying to make such a world are completely undesirable? Culture jamming utilizes an "insurrectionary style" but can escape vilification by way of wit and aesthetic appeal. We need processes that are open, autonomous, fun, funny, and that can be carried out anywhere, any time; culture jamming is one possible modality for exploring and enacting these processes, if it is redefined.

So I am also calling for a recalibration. Effective forms of jamming should not be measured by the successful transmission of their messages. The most effective forms of jamming are those that show people (the jammers as well as those who view the culture jam) that they can speak a discourse of defiance, of rejection, of radical criticism. Consumers do not need culture jammers to make them aware of the negative body image perpetuated by big-name apparel brands. Everyone in a body already knows this. Rather, culture jamming can be about the sporadic revitalization of new forms of civil disobedience, which can be woven into the fabric of other insurrectionary movements.

IV Reinventing revolution, not capitalism

Creative collective action, radical critique, ongoing performances that discover new means of communication and new ways of connecting with people through humor and wit and by means of exposé *can* effectively "jam up" (i.e. interrupt, refute, rethink) the cultural-valuational norms of capitalist society. Creative revolt inspires insurrectionary imaginations. If such is the place of culture jamming, *we must culture jam*. But the jam cannot be limited to fugitive consumption patterns or other liberal fantasies. The problem is not only that a liberated billboard, a day off from shopping, a week without television, leave the existing culture exactly as it is. The problem is that such jams affirm the normality of the culture they claim to oppose by accommodating the slogan from May 1968, *"retour à la normale,"* return to normal.[180] Such jams both accept and presuppose a return to the conditions of everyday life they oppose, and thus, they reify the permanence of the capitalist lifeworld in their opposition.

But revolt is a different kind of jam. Diverse global uprisings, all kinds of social upheaval, occupied shopping malls, and often even riots, typically do better to raise enduring questions about the dominant culture, deep questions that don't go away so easily. What we need are jams that cannot be washed away with soap and water.

The Mexican Zapatistas forced much of Mexico (and much of the world) to consider the "indigenous problem" in many countries throughout the 1990s. The Zapatista rebellion jammed the culture, and even contained many experimental and aesthetic dimensions that culture jammers revere. To conclude the present chapter, I shall briefly discuss this example, and make mention of more recent examples of revolt as culture jam. It is not my intention to provide a broad overview of the Zapatista uprising, for there are better sources for that. I have myself dedicated numerous chapters to an in-depth analysis of the Zapatistas in my book, *Unbounded Publics: Transgressive Public Spheres, Zapatismo, and Political Theory.*[181]

In the 1980s, the international media paid no attention to

180 This slogan is defined and discussed more fully in Chapter 7.
181 See Gilman-Opalsky, Richard, *Unbounded Publics: Transgressive Public Spheres, Zapatismo, and Political Theory* (Lanham: Lexington Books, 2008), especially Chapters 6, 7, and 8.

the problems of Mexico's Mayan population,[182] and the details of the struggles of indigenous Mexico were not widely known in Mexican or international public spheres. Because of the dearth of publicity, the aspirations of indigenous politics went largely unrealized for most of the 20th century, until January 1, 1994, the day of the Zapatista uprising, and the inauguration day of NAFTA (North American Free Trade Agreement), which the Zapatistas famously condemned as "the death certificate for the ethnic people of Mexico."[183] After the Zapatista uprising, all kinds of media publics were made aware of the Zapatistas, although often with the heavy bias of the Mexican government that sought to characterize them as terrorists. But one strength of an uprising such as that of the Zapatistas is that it is unignorable, just as subsequent upheaval was unignorable afterwards in the streets of Seattle in 1999, in Greece in 2008, in Tunisia and Egypt from 2010 through 2012, in the Indignados movement in Spain from 2011, and in the 2011 riots in the UK.

Effective culture jams do not ask the media for favors, but if the jams are unignorably disruptive, they will command media attention on some level. In the case of the Zapatista uprising, its meaning exceeded the media, escaped it while commanding its attention at the same time. The Zapatista uprising was not understood through the media, but rather, had to be understood more fully, more slowly, and more widely elsewhere, with the help of multifarious theoretical and practical resources. The creativity, appearance, and poetry of the uprising helped it elude the usual caricature of terrorism, a caricature with which the Zapatistas were notably misfit. The meaning of the Zapatistas is still being explored today.

182 Weinberg, Bill, *Homage to Chiapas: The New Indigenous Struggles in Mexico* (London and New York: Verso, 2002), p. 99.
183 Cited in Ross, John, *The War Against Oblivion: The Zapatista Chronicles 1994-2000* (Monroe, Maine: Common Courage Press, 2000), p. 21.

From Mexico, Subcomandante Marcos extended an invitation to the people of the United States, to those who had learned of their movement and wondered how they, living in the country whose government heralded NAFTA, could respond constructively to the uprising: "We need people in the United States to create counter-propaganda to that of the Mexican federal government, and get out the truth, against the lie of Salinas."[184] "Getting out the truth" was a major part of the Zapatista strategy. This is one of the reasons why the Mexican government could not effectively establish the Zapatistas through the media as terrorists or as a conventional revolutionary movement, because instead of behaving like terrorists or conventional revolutionaries, they spent significant time reading poetry aloud and sharing imaginative stories that delivered their arguments with humor and popular appeal. The fact is, most of what the world received from the Zapatistas, most of the movement's output, were explanations in text and images — explanations of who they are, what they want, and why they are doing what they are doing. The Zapatistas used words and images as weapons to make a guerilla seizure of the public sphere, of the common imaginary, of indigeneity and insurrection. The Zapatista revolt was theatrical, artful, poetic, and joyful — difficult to vilify.

Harry Cleaver confirmed this when he wrote of the Zapatistas, "This has been a war of words, images, imagination, and organization...Vital to this continuing struggle has been the pro-Zapatista use of computer communications."[185] Discussion in topical common spaces was rarely had with the Zapatistas directly (aside from brief and infrequent *encuentros*), but rather, with and about their texts and images:

184 Weinberg, *Homage to Chiapas*, op. cit., p. 128.
185 Cleaver, Harry, "The Zapatistas and the Electronic Fabric of Struggle" in *Zapatista! Reinventing Revolution in Mexico*, ed. John Holloway and Eloina Peláez (London: Pluto Press, 1998), p. 81.

El Sup had a rifle, yes, but he hardly used it. His bullets took the form of faxes and e-mails, cluster bombs in the shape of communiqués, and nonstop e-mail midrashim through the Internet. He wrote in a torrent, producing hundreds of texts, disproving Hannah Arendt's claim that 'under conditions of tyranny it is far easier to act than to think.' In less than twelve months, during sleepless sessions on the word processor in the midst of fighting a war, El Sup generated enough text for a 300-page volume.[186]

In August 1996, in La Realidad, Mexico, at the first *encuentro*, Subcomandante Marcos said:

Who can say in what precise locale, and at what exact hour and date this Intercontinental Encounter for Humanity and Against Neoliberalism began? We don't know. But we do know who initiated it. All the rebels around the world started it. Here, we are only a small part of those rebels, it's true. But to all the many walls that all the rebels of the world break every day, you have added one more rupture — that of the wall around the Zapatista Reality.[187]

The Zapatistas understood that their rebellion was just one form, one nodal point, in the evolution of an insurrectionary response to the development of capitalism, in this case, an opposition to the accelerated phase of neoliberalism that took off at the end of the Cold War. The Zapatistas understood well that they were just one manifestation of a radical critique that predates — and that would certainly postdate — their own uprising. Their project was about the refusal to accept a world organized by the logic of capital, a sentiment that has recently reemerged in Greece, in

186 Stavans, Ilan, "Unmasking Marcos" in *The Zapatista Reader*, ed. Tom Hayden (New York: Thunder's Mouth Press/Nation Books, 2002), pp. 388-389.
187 Weinberg, *Homage to Chiapas*, op. cit., p. 161.

the years of revolt that made Syriza a viable political party, in the "Arab Spring," in Bosnia and Herzegovina, Occupy Wall Street, and in Turkey, just to mention some other examples.

In the mid-to-late '90s, the term "Zapatismo" was used to capture the idea of a contagion of resistance acted out in solidarity with the Zapatistas in other ways and places. Zapatismo could mobilize people elsewhere and differently than took place in the mountains of Chiapas in Mexico, just like Viénet's catalog of acts that were inspired around the world by the French occupations of 1968. Today, we know that the rebellion in Tunisia could take place in other ways in Egypt and Syria, just as Occupy Wall Street could take place in countless cities without a Wall Street.

Over twenty years after the 1994 uprising, the Zapatista movement is still functional in Chiapas, and has effected some concrete achievements beyond the reading of the original revolt. Perhaps the most major accomplishment has been the decades of practical self-government in the autonomous zones. Hilary Klein, who has researched the situation of the Zapatistas in recent years reports:

> Land takeovers carried out after the 1994 uprising - where large ranches were occupied by the Zapatistas and reapportioned to landless peasants - impacted the distribution of wealth in Chiapas and continue to affect living conditions for Zapatista villages farming on reclaimed land. The Zapatista structures of indigenous autonomy have meant that rural villages in Chiapas have gained access to rudimentary health care and education... The Zapatista movement also offers a viable example of local alternatives to global capitalism.[188]

188   Klein, Hilary, "Celebrating 22 Years of Zapatismo," accessed January 5, 2016, http://www.telesurtv.net/english/opinion/Celebrating-22-Years-of-Zapatismo-20151231-0026.html.

Klein has also done substantial research into the transformative effect of the gender politics of the Zapatistas.[189]

Inasmuch as culture jamming represents a radical praxis of the present, honed for previous impasses and emergent from the revolutionary pessimism of postmodernity, perhaps it could describe whatever intervenes in, with an aim to radically transform, the pervasive cultural-valuational norms of existing society. Culture jammers could participate in what Brian Holmes has called "reverse imagineering."[190] When Holmes discusses rebellions and uprisings like those of the Zapatistas and against the WTO in 1999, he reflects: "These kinds of actions are about as far as one could imagine from a museum; yet when you approach them, you can feel something distinctly artistic. They bring together the multiplicity of individual expression and the unity of a collective will."[191]

Culture jamming aims to develop new forms of "struggle" in its turn away from conventional forms of protest and toward rhizomatic and playful subversions that are thus even difficult to regard as struggle. In line with Lyotard's thinking, we can say that culture jamming is postmodern in that it rethinks power, breaks rules, and is informed by the failures of old revolutionary narratives while insisting on revolution by other means. Insurrection is revolution by other means — it is the frustrated and fragmentary activity of revolution making its way into the world today. Like Debord in the 1950s and '60s, culture jamming must not totally give up the radical aspirations of previous generations and movements, but rather rethink and recast them. Culture jamming serves as just one example of a concrete modality for an autonomous and joyful political engagement,

189   Klein, Hilary, *Compañeras: Zapatista Women's Stories* (New York and Oakland: Seven Stories Press, 2015).
190   Holmes, Brian, *Unleashing the Collective Phantoms: Essays in Reverse Imagineering* (New York: Autonomedia, 2008).
191   Ibid., p. 56.

for it invites guerrilla creativity and artful subversion. But, none of this positivity describes the culture jamming of the present and preeminent little cast of activists, authors, and high-priced magazines sold at Whole Foods.

Following Holmes and our discussion of the Zapatistas above, it is quite clear that we can find artistic critical content in the unignorable disruptions of revolt. Those are the jams we need — jams that aspire to reinvent revolution, not capitalism.

CHAPTER 4

The Eternal Recurrence of Revolt

What, if some day or night a demon were to steal after you into your loneliest loneliness and say to you: "This life as you now live it and have lived it, you will have to live once more and innumerable times more"... Would you not throw yourself down and gnash your teeth and curse the demon who spoke thus? Or have you once experienced a tremendous moment when you would have answered him: "You are a god and never have I heard anything more divine"... The question in each and every thing, "Do you desire this once more and innumerable times more?" would lie upon your actions as the greatest weight.

— FRIEDRICH NIETZSCHE, *The Gay Science* [192]

The riots ain't over.

— #SUCKAFREE on Twitter, *The 2015 Baltimore Uprising* [193]

I A fragmentary constellation of models

Revolution can have many meanings. Despite the unbridgeable chasms between them, when John Locke, Edmund Burke, and Karl Marx wrote of revolution, they had a familiar and classical conception in mind: Revolution occurs when a critical mass of insurrectionary social forces confronts existing powerholders and

---

192   Nietzsche, Friedrich, *The Gay Science With a Prelude in Rhymes and an Appendix of Songs*, trans. Walter Kaufmann (New York: Vintage Books, 1974), pp. 273-274.
193   *The 2015 Baltimore Uprising: A Teen Epistolary* (New York: Research and Destroy, 2015), no page numbers.

takes over the apparatus of the state. In the classical conception, there was an inevitable violence to revolution, so Locke preferred reform, Burke blamed the revolutionaries for the violence, and Marx blamed the counterinsurgent capitalist state. This basic view of revolution was common from the 17th century through the 19th, although some peculiar alternatives were proposed.

The most notable of the unconventional ideas of revolution, I think, is Henry David Thoreau's concept of "peaceable revolution" as described in his essay "Civil Disobedience." [194] This concept of revolution is notable for a number of reasons, starting with the fact that it was published in 1849, one year after *The Communist Manifesto*. Thoreau defines revolution as the culminating force of a critical mass of civil disobedience, which he proposes as tax resistance. We might ask, however, if what Thoreau calls "revolution" isn't really a misnomer, since he is arguing for an end to the North American war on Mexico and the abolition of slavery. He says himself that he is not calling for "no government, but *at once* a better government. Let every man make known what kind of government would command his respect, and that will be one step toward obtaining it." [195] In this way, Thoreau's "revolution" is more about improving the existing society through changes in domestic and foreign policy, much like Burke's suggestion that "the change is to be confined to the peccant part only" so that we can avoid a revolution. [196] According to the position taken in the present book, civil disobedience can indeed participate in revolt and typically does, even though Thoreau's notion of "peaceable revolution" is problematic.

Marx understood a revolutionary confrontation with the state to be inevitable in almost any case, but that does not mean he

194 Thoreau, Henry David, *Civil Disobedience and Other Essays* (New York: Dover, 1993), pp. 9-10.

195 Ibid., p. 2.

196 Burke, Edmund, *Reflections on the Revolution in France* (Indianapolis: Hackett Publishing Company, 1987), p. 19.

was a "statist." He insisted that communism is "not a stable state which is to be established," but rather that communism is "the *real* movement which abolishes the present state of things."[197] Set within Marx's theory of historical materialism, this meant that communism consists of the antagonistic forces that transform society and politics on an ongoing basis, never leaving the present state of things as it is for too long. There are many places where Marx expresses his critical view of the state, where he calls the state "merely the organized power of one class for oppressing another."[198] Marx rejected the notion that communism could or should be wielded by states, perhaps most fundamentally, because he understood that capitalism was already global, already beyond the reach of any one nation-state, and that therefore any revolution against capitalism must also be global (in principle and in practice beyond the borders of nation-states). He dealt with the global imperative in many places too.[199] Also, Marx understood revolution as coming from *underneath* state power, from civil society, and passing through the state only at critical necessary moments.

While it is true that Marx insisted, unlike his anarchist critics, on the necessity of instrumentalizing the state for the purposes of revolution, it is also true that he simultaneously insisted that such purposes were transitory — like crutches necessary to regaining one's ability to walk — useful only until one is up on her own legs. Instead of an uncritical enthusiasm for state power, Marx remained cautious and concerned about the use of state power, understanding and warning against the dangers of abuse. After all, he saw how useful a tool the state was for capital. Despite this,

---

197 Marx, Karl, "The German Ideology" in *The Portable Karl Marx* (New York: Viking Penguin, 1983), p. 179.

198 Marx, "Manifesto of the Communist Party" in *The Portable Karl Marx* (New York: Viking Penguin, 1983), p. 228. See also the concluding paragraphs of Marx's *The Poverty of Philosophy* (New York: Prometheus Books, 1995).

199 See "Manifesto of the Communist Party," op. cit., and *Critique of the Gotha Programme* (New York: International Publishers, 2002).

many (certainly not all) anarchists have been as idiotic as Glenn Beck in confusing Marxism with statism, or the other peculiarity, in confusing Karl Marx with Joseph Stalin. As a social and political force of historical materialism, revolution comes from below, not from above, and for Marx, the insurrectionary activity of revolt is precisely where revolution begins. Marxists and anarchists today (and not only them) would do well to remember this.

But this point is necessary to properly calibrate our thinking about revolution, so that we continue to work with the idea of revolution as *a process* that is dangerous to the existing state of affairs, which also includes real danger to existing political states. Marx wrote more about the abolition and overthrow of the state than he did of its takeover.[200]

Although he was not the statist his opponents claimed him to be, we must acknowledge that Marx's theory of revolution does vigorously defend passage through the state against anarchist criticism. Indeed, Marx's contention that revolutionaries must be willing and able to recognize the necessity of seizing state power for defensive, organizational, and transitional purposes was his biggest disagreement with anarchists like Michael Bakunin (who beautifully recounts this dispute with Marx in *Statism and Anarchy*).[201] Marx felt that his position was vindicated in the experience of the 1871 Paris Commune.[202] Yet, Marx's insistence on the indefinite use of state power was not only unacceptable to the anarchists, but also proved catastrophic in some of the most infamous abuses of state power in the 20th century.

And there have been other ways of thinking about revolution. Errico Malatesta and Pierre-Joseph Proudhon focused on social

---

200 See, for example, "The German Ideology," op. cit., p. 179 and especially p. 195.
201 Bakunin, Michael, *Statism and Anarchy*, trans. Marshall S. Shatz (Cambridge, UK: Cambridge University Press, 1994), pp. 177-181.
202 Marx, Karl, *The Civil War in France* (Peking: Foreign Languages Press, 1966).

revolution instead of political revolution. Malatesta argued that revolution works "to change social conditions in such a way as to produce a change of will in the desired direction."[203] Malatesta argued that if we could radically transform society from within itself, there would be no need to wield the power of the state.

Much later, Michel Foucault answered an interviewer's question about whether or not prisoners — those who were most on the losing end of power — should make a revolution and take over the disciplinary system's apparatus. "Oh yes, provided that isn't the final purpose of the operation. Do you think it would be much better to have the prisoners operating the Panoptic apparatus and sitting in the central tower, instead of the guards?"[204] What Foucault meant by this was that we should indeed confront and even take power, but never merely to operate its formal institutions. Instead, Foucault provided what we might consider a more nuanced and philosophical version of Malatesta's position, that there is power in all social relations, in the family, in the community, there is power in between us, and that we can make revolutions without passing through the state. While Foucault never discounts the importance of the state, radical transformations within the field of human relations are ultimately more important than the reallocation of institutional powers.[205]

More recently still, Enrique Dussel has made some useful distinctions, pointing out that in the leftist tradition, "it was understood that if an activity was not 'revolutionary' then it was 'reformist.'"[206] Dussel argues that the real opposition is between "reform" and "transform." He points out that revolution is only

203 Malatesta, Errico, *At the Café: Conversations on Anarchism*, trans. Paul Nursey-Bray (London: Freedom Press, 2005), p. 83.

204 Foucault, Michel, *Power/Knowledge: Selected Interviews and Other Writings 1972-1977* (New York: Pantheon Books, 1980), pp. 164-165.

205 See Parts 6 and 8 in *Power/Knowledge*, op. cit.

206 Dussel, Enrique, *Twenty Theses on Politics* (Durham and London: Duke University Press, 2008), p. 111.

one mode of transformation, but that there are other ways as well. With this, Dussel combines (inadvertently) all of the above theories of revolution, and allows for many more as we might be able to imagine or develop them.

The above constellation of thinking about revolution is far from exhaustive. It is a miniscule smattering of some of the many different prominent conceptions.

Let us consider a general formulation: *Revolution consists of the diverse processes of the radical transformation of the existing state of affairs, working from "what is" toward "what ought to be."* The term "radical transformation" indicates the abolitionist and structuralist content of revolution. Revolution works against the existing state of affairs and toward some conception of what ought to be. Who answers the question of "what ought to be?" Who decides the better possible future that we should aim to create? Revolutionaries have different answers. Some revolutionaries have no answer to this question, for they only know that the present state of affairs is immoral and/or intolerable and must be opposed. In some cases, even in the streets of actual upheavals, the participants themselves give different answers side by side. But the question of who decides what ought to be conceals the fact that the past, present, and future are already determined and will continue to be determined by *some* peoples' conception of what ought to be. Human history and society are shaped by effective human action. So, even if the answer to the question of what ought to be is "to be determined," shouldn't everyday people with real grievances claim a role in that determination? If they don't, others will.

Instead of faulting diverse revolutionary aspirations for failing to unanimously identify a single ideal end-state, we can defend revolution as an open-ended process of transformation that can address its own failures through further transformation. Revolutionary activity does not require agreement on an ideal end-state. This contention can be juxtaposed to the short-sighted and reactionary demand in the US — widespread in October 2011 — that the Occupy Wall Street contingent and solidarity occupations across the country should say exactly what they want and should articulate a specific platform for the consideration of those in positions of power. The same demand for itemized demands has more recently been made (by media commentators and liberal/conservative critics) to the Black Lives Matter (BLM) movement in 2014 and to the protestors at the University of Missouri in 2015. The purported expectation of the very targets of the protest takes the form: "if they want something, they should tell us what they want." The anxiety surrounding this frustrated expectation can rather easily be given expression: Those watching the occupations and protests want the unruly elements to establish a dialogue with powerholders, which both reassures and reifies the relationship of the actors to powerholders in a familiar, paternalistic way, as the rebellious child in a clear standoff with a mother or father. Clearly, specific demands would reduce complexity, making the expressions of revolt both easier to discuss and easier to dismiss in a simple way. If, for example, the child demands a higher weekly allowance, the request can be rejected as inappropriate. But if the child expresses general unhappiness with the basic features and arrangements of her home life, the parents are at a loss.

Unspecified disaffection creates an impasse for the conciliatory efforts of power — it is difficult to reconcile or to placate a multifarious aversion that cannot be easily diagnosed. The occupiers knew why they should continue to respond to the invitation for a particular agenda with a joyful silence, because they could see that generalized disaffection cannot be refuted in logical or ideological terms. This is why every itemized list of demands ever put forth by Occupy X contingents has been fraught with contention and rejection.[207]

It is also clear that the recommendations to articulate a platform come originally from outside the uprisings themselves, and that the presence of an internal impetus for enumerated demands mainly reflects an interest in gratifying external criticisms, or the presence of liberal/conservative tendencies from within the movement. These were some of the biggest threats to the Occupy X movement. It would be unwise to conclude, in agreement with the general consensus, that the occupations movement is totally finished. We are talking about a generation of young people who were radicalized by the occupations, young people who felt their collective power with great intimacy and a historical urgency, people who are still everywhere around us, watching what is happening in the world today, watching new revolts in Ferguson, MO and Baltimore, MD, and participating wherever possible. Whether or not the US-based occupations movement will feed into future insurrectionary activity remains to be seen, although some of the same social energies animate Black Lives Matter, and certainly, all those unruly energies will not be fully channeled into procedural

---

207 I use the term "Occupy X" to refer to the wave of occupations following and inspired by the Occupy Wall Street activity in New York in September of 2011. The term "Occupy X" is intended to name the particular period of international occupations, general assemblies, and protest that began with the targeting of growing inequality and poverty, coupled with diminishing opportunity in the US, on Wall Street in 2011. Of course, as expressed in the many discussions throughout this book about May 1968 in France, the Mexican Zapatistas, the "Arab Spring," and other global uprisings and anti-austerity protests throughout Europe, I do *not* claim that the occupations movement is somehow cut off from earlier revolt, or even distinctly American. Indeed, in many ways Occupy Wall Street comes from outside the US. Nonetheless, by "Occupy X" what I intend to capture is the fact that the disparate wave of Occupy Wall Street protest activity was not anchored to the physical location of Wall Street in New York.

politics and election cycles. Even though the occupations have dissipated, their reemergence on the horizon is far from unthinkable. They were, after all, in many ways themselves a reemergence of scattered occupations in solidarity with the Greek uprising of 2008, and were undoubtedly inspired by insurgent elements of Middle Eastern and North African and European civil societies. What seems less like a prediction, and more like a settled fact, is that such expressions of disaffection cannot be fully gratified (and thereby pacified or extinguished) within the limits of the capitalist present.

Those who were asking with feigned concern for the purposes of the occupations would never be gratified with a clear answer. They did not really want one. Their questioning did not come from a position of solidarity or even basic agreement, for they preferred to point out the absence of a plan, or to have a plan only in order to reject its "impracticality." Critical to the caricature of the occupations were the vacillating claims that no-clear-agenda-means-incoherence and that any-radical-agenda-is-irrational. Media commentators could not understand that such clarity of purpose is not desirable from the insurrectionary perspective. The insurrectionary energies of everyday people, when they fracture the repressive conditions of everyday life, are not meant to be *clearly grasped*, but rather, to be dangerously beyond anyone's grasp. This is indeed precisely what makes a world haunted by specters of revolt so frightening to the administrations of social control (i.e. law enforcement, political power): Revolt is only revolt when it is out of their control.

Let us take this particular virtue of revolt farther: We should not conceive of, propose, and defend ideal end states. There are many reasons for this, some historical, some matters of principle. For now, let's just observe that every state of affairs can be better, and to dream of an ideal end is to dream of the end of revolution. Let us dream of the beginnings, and not the ends, of revolution.

11 Why revolution?

We established in Chapter 3 that we are thinking more about insurrection, and less about revolution, because insurrection is the actual exercise of revolutionary activity today. Revolutionary theories must therefore shift a bit from their historic and defining subject in order to make insurrection the central focus. As we have discussed, insurrections move in the direction of revolution and work through its possibilities, without themselves being effective revolutions in any conventional sense of a world-historical structural transformation. But, at the same time, this confesses an enduring interest in and commitment to revolution, despite past failures and present impasses. Why revolution?

In June 2015, the International Monetary Fund (IMF) published a report acknowledging that the fundamental premises of neoliberal capitalism are now demonstrably false.[208] The report, entitled "Causes and Consequences of Income Equality: A Global Perspective," documents not only growing inequality around the world, but also that this inequality is a basic feature of the unbounded freedom of capital. The old lie about the rising tide that lifts all boats has finally been recognized as such in IMF research. "Specifically, if the income share of the top 20 percent (the rich) increases, then GDP growth actually declines over the medium term, suggesting that the benefits do not trickle down."[209] Over 165 years ago, Marx made a similar claim in *The German Ideology*, that the impoverished proletarian, "within his own class, has no chance of arriving at the conditions which would place him in the other class."[210] Marx understood that trickle down and upward mobility were cherished and important lies of a capitalist mythol-

208 International Monetary Fund (IMF) June 2015, "Causes and Consequences of Income Equality: A Global Perspective," accessed January 6, 2016, https://www.imf.org/external/pubs/ft/sdn/2015/sdn1513.pdf.

209 Ibid., p. 4.

210 Marx, "The German Ideology," op. cit., p. 195.

ogy designed to keep the poor more hopeful and patient than disaffected and revolutionary.

And now, after decades of ideological resistance, in a slow crawl to catch up with the basic insights of the young Marx, the IMF appears to be losing faith in its own religion of upward mobility. Unfortunately, this research epiphany breaks through after more than seventy years of the IMF's imposition of neoliberal policies attached to conditional loans that have contributed to the very problems they study. But maybe it is better late than never, and perhaps we should be happy for all the radical reforms, indeed, for all the total reversals in global banking policy to come. Think again. The June 2015 research is prominently stamped with a disclaimer announcing that the IMF researchers' conclusions do "not necessarily represent IMF views or IMF policy."[211] And, although it was both researched and published by the IMF, the research "should be attributed to the authors and not to the IMF, its executive board, or its management."[212] While that may be a refreshing bit of honesty, it highlights the difficulty, if not the egregious naiveté, in placing faith in any international consortium of bankers, policy-makers, and capitalists to address growing problems of inequality and poverty, among other things. The fact is that so many critics of capital remain loyal to it nonetheless, as could also be seen in Thomas Piketty's book, *Capital in the Twenty-First Century*.[213] After over four hundred and sixty pages of documenting that capital has reliably generated (and cannot help but to generate) growing global inequality and consolidated existing inequality, Piketty concludes with a call for the same regulated capital and social democracy that has fought and lost against the logic of capital for two hundred years. The IMF is just as clear

211 IMF, op. cit., p. 2.

212 Ibid.

213 See Part Four of Piketty, Thomas, *Capital in the Twenty-First Century* (Cambridge, MA and London: The Belknap Press, Harvard University Press, 2014).

that their new research, which agrees with the research of Piketty and the Paris School of Economics, is not meant to interfere in their work, and so it functions only as a ghost that haunts (one hopes, at least) the good conscience of liberals. How does this help answer the question, why revolution?

I have mentioned some of the basic features grounding a basic premise: revolutionaries object to the existing conditions and want to see them radically transformed. We have an understanding of the macroeconomic reality, which is increasingly bleak for most of the world's people, and we understand the alienation and delirium of everyday life, among other problems (including but not limited to racist, ecological, and sexist issues). Revolution is the aspiration that follows this critical phase and rests on the frustration and failure of reform.

Nonetheless, and despite meaningful differences that I have insisted (and will continue to insist) upon, the old leftist question of reform versus revolution should be abandoned. Both sides of the question have been conceived such that neither side appears as a satisfying answer to the problems of the present. Very generally, reform appears as not enough, whereas revolution often appears as too much. Revolution, it is often worried, cannot promise not to create new problems just as big as the ones it opposed. "Reform" has meant changing laws and policies, changing certain attitudes and valuations, leaving the very structures (social, political, economic, and cultural) more or less intact. And, newer definitions notwithstanding, "revolution" has mainly been mistaken to mean overtaking the law-making powers directly, the state being the target par excellence.

Dissatisfaction with a choice between reform and revolution has led to proposals for "radical democracy." Some of the key proponents of this school have been Ernesto Laclau and Chantal

Mouffe, Jürgen Habermas, and Andrew Arato and Jean Cohen.[214] What does "radical democracy" mean? Essentially, "radical democracy" argues that elections are merely a procedural piece of democracy, and do virtually nothing to help ensure a vibrant democratic culture full of critique and contestation. The theorists mentioned above are interested in seeing a more substantive and contentious form of democracy — one that does not wait for elections and the good will of politicians. Radical democracy requires a democratic culture that is ongoing, that takes place in between elections, often in the streets, in the occupation of streets and buildings, in civil disobedience. Radical democracy includes uprisings and social upheavals, taking place somewhere in between reform and revolution, or perhaps, beyond both. The idea of a politics beyond procedures is a step in the right direction.

But there is one persistent problem with theories of radical democracy: Radical democracy is possible within, and ultimately compatible with, the capitalist organization of life. It is true that Laclau and Mouffe see radical democracy as the centerpiece of socialist strategy, and their conception of socialism does not implicate an antithetical externality to capitalism. If capital trends against democracy, and we work to deepen and expand democracy, then the socialist antithesis works from the inside. Yet, this approach recommends a democratization of capital, which capitalist societies can accommodate within certain limits. A philosopher like Habermas, as well, does find a potentially disastrous tension, but not a total contradiction, between capital and democracy. While Habermas recognizes that capital disfigures and diminishes existing democracy, he ultimately claims

214 See, for example, Laclau, Ernesto and Mouffe, Chantal, *Hegemony and Socialist Strategy: Towards a Radical Democratic Politics* (London and New York: Verso, 1985); Habermas, Jürgen, "Further Reflections on the Public Sphere" in *Habermas and the Public Sphere*, ed. Craig Calhoun (Cambridge, MA: The MIT Press, 1992); Arato, Andrew and Cohen, Jean, *Civil Society and Political Theory* (Cambridge, MA: The MIT Press, 1992).

that it is possible to satisfactorily democratize the global economy within the limits of capital. Habermas' view is much better than John Rawls' contention that it is perfectly possible to create a "fair capitalist society," which Rawls' calls "justice," and thinks is essentially achievable through reformist measures with strong liberal commitments.[215] But both Habermas and Rawls share a general disregard for a revolutionary politics, old or new.

Capitalists have been speaking of "fair capitalist society" at least since the 18th century, when industrialization was getting up on its legs and already needed active apologists for every setback of "free labor." With more than two centuries of hindsight, and growing disparities globally, it is time to acknowledge the possibility that all meaningful conceptions of fairness will either impede or directly contradict the very logic of capitalism: *to accumulate capital.*

Certainly, fairness exists in gradations, and there is more or less fairness in different capitalist societies, even in different parts of the same capitalist society. Can we not establish without controversy that we want to maximize fairness? Such a thin humanism — lost more on politicians than young children — scarcely needs argument. But if we work toward optimal fairness it is only a matter of time before we run up against the logic of capital directly. Endless accumulation follows a different logic (growth and private wealth) than the logic of fairness (equality of opportunity, a common wealth). But let us not make the same mistakes of earlier socialists who hijacked and deformed the good name of socialism to mean nothing more than capitalism regulated by some sense of fairness. Government cannot guarantee fairness, and the seizure of state power must never again be the goal of a revolutionary politics. Georg Lukács understood this well in 1920,

---

215 See Parts II, III, and IV of Rawls, John, *Justice as Fairness: A Restatement* (Cambridge, MA and London: The Belknap Press, Harvard University Press, 2001).

and warned against the fetishistic obsession with the state that was prominent among communists he called "pseudo-Marxist opportunists." Lukács argued that "by viewing the state as the object of the struggle rather than as the enemy they have mentally gone over to bourgeois territory and thereby lost half the battle even before taking up arms."[216] Of course, revolution is no guarantee of fairness either. Revolution may not succeed, but it is the necessary basic framework for contesting and transforming the existing conditions we object to. Consider Emma Goldman's observation *vis-à-vis* Oscar Wilde that "it is exactly the existing conditions that one objects to, and any scheme that could accept these conditions is wrong and foolish."[217]

A revolutionary perspective is indispensable because it does not only observe the catastrophe of existing conditions, and it does not only condemn such conditions, like the IMF and Piketty. Rather, a revolutionary perspective insists on abolishing such conditions through human action.

III The poverty of primitivism revisited

Some of the newer revolutionary perspectives pointing out new avenues, attempting to move beyond the old classical formulations of the Marxian milieu, lead to dangerous dead ends. I have already treated primitivism as just such a dead end in Chapter 2, but I revisit it here for different reasons. A lot of the insurrectionary theory of our times has a certain neo-anarchist character that trends toward atomistic individualism and holier-than-thou (or, more-radical-than-thou) moralizing. Here, I want to briefly touch upon some of the other problems with that tendency, and

216 Lukács, Georg, *History and Class Consciousness: Studies in Marxist Dialectics*, trans. Rodney Livingstone (Cambridge, MA: The MIT Press, 1988), p. 260.
217 Goldman, Emma, *Anarchism and Other Essays* (New York: Dover, 1969), p. 49.

to insist that an insurrectionist and autonomist theory of revolt need not abandon politics, class analysis, the critique of capital, and collective action.

Primitivism, as introduced and criticized above, has appeared as a kind of touchstone of contemporary radicalism, as the outermost reach of the radical milieu. After all, what could be more radical than opposing the entirety of human civilization? Mixed into this "totally revolutionary" perspective are ultimate solutions to the ecological crisis, to patriarchy, power, and capital. There is nothing reformist in this categorical position, and so from its location, everything else appears as insufficiently revolutionary, as basically reformist. From a critical consideration of primitivism, it is clear that we should beware all positions that put their comparative radicality forward as an argument in their own defense.

Primitivism has helped to impoverish anarchism and to absorb revolutionary energies more than any other influential development in recent years. While primitivists often make very important points that we should heed with serious attention, the ultimate problem is that primitivism condemns human agency and collective action while denying that it does so.

John Zerzan speaks frequently of direct action, of rebellion, providing a laudatory weekly inventory of "action news" on his radio show. He has written about the need for "a conscious turn against the symbolic and civilization," and yet, his work invalidates all forms of action.[218] Behind Zerzan's expressed interest in direct action hides a decisive position *against* human action, one which fundamentally makes primitivism a kind of "post-agency" theory.

As summarized in Chapter 2, the primitivist critique of civilization entails: (1) accepting the premise that all highly technological societies evolve toward their own collapse; and (2) looking for-

218   Zerzan, John, *Twilight of the Machines* (Port Townsend, WA: Feral House, 2008), p. 55.

ward to that collapse as an emancipatory transition to a sustainable and primitive future.[219]

The first premise is more convincing than the second contention. The first premise may well be a simple statement of fact. We cannot assume the infinite perpetuity of the Anthropocene. If a socio-geological epoch of human life is unsustainable and must come to an end, then we will know that when it's actually ending in catastrophic ways. For as long as the proverbial "end of the world" remains on the horizon, it remains merely a future possibility. And even if it is not a distant future, there are observable social and psychological reasons why humans will not act as if the end of the world is happening until it is indeed happening in immediate and existential ways. Countless disaster movies have depicted this part fairly well. What the primitivist premise means, then, in practical terms, is that while we may discuss the imminence and reality of the end of the world with great seriousness — with geological and ecological science, for example — we must mostly wait and see.

In any case, the concerted human action of a subset of the world population cannot reverse the end of our Anthropocene epoch any more successfully than the dinosaurs could have organized against the Cretaceous extinction. Even if the dinosaurs had our beloved human reason, what could that mental faculty have done against asteroids, comets, or violent volcanic explosions? Humanity has a long speciesist history of overestimating its distinguishing faculties. It is hard to make political oppositions against tornadoes, tsunamis, and earthquakes, so we are left with

219 I consider the basic theory of primitivism to have been best laid out in Zerzan, John, *Future Primitive and Other Essays* (Brooklyn: Autonomedia, 1994). The underlying theoretical groundwork is more rigorously worked out in Zerzan, John, *Elements of Refusal* (Columbia, MO: Columbia Alternative Library Press, 1999). In many ways, *Elements of Refusal* is the better of the two, but *Future Primitive* provides the clearer articulation of the primitivist position.

a politics of monitoring the disturbances. It is in exactly such a manner of monitoring disturbance that Zerzan counts up all of the illegal acts that indicate, from his point of view, civilization's inexorable march toward its end.

Zerzan observes: "To many, it seems there will be no escape from the dominant reality, no alternative to an irredeemably darkened modernity as civilization's final, lasting mode. We are indeed currently trapped, and the nature of our imprisonment is not subject to scrutiny."[220] Thus, on the one hand something is going to happen, as Zerzan reliably asserts in his claim that civilization has entered its "final mode," while on the other hand, the situation remains inescapable and "not subject to scrutiny." He claims: "The deep malaise and melancholy of modernity, its dreariness and distancing, have spread everywhere; there is less and less room for escape."[221] From a primitivist perspective, as well as from the perspective of much Anthropocene theory, it would appear that we are positioned for the end times much like the dinosaurs were, but with one unfortunate distinction: We may consciously expect the end of our human epoch, equipped with an awareness of our impending end, yet not with any political response, or sufficient collective human action. Revolt is certainly not a meaningful response to the end of the human epoch—it is too social, too small, merely a symptom of a catastrophic problem we cannot touch.

In this way, the primitivist position—a purported acme of radicalism—is an acknowledgement of a possible catastrophe accompanied by a desperate hope for a "good" outcome. Zerzan's idea of an emancipatory catastrophe contains much from the Christian faith in the lake of fire or kingdom of heaven. Indeed, Zerzan observes property destruction and miserable adolescents who

220 Zerzan, John, "Paradigms," *Fifth Estate*, Vol. 50, No. 2, #394, Summer 2015, p. 13.
221 Ibid., p. 14.

shoot up schools and movie theaters as evidence of the end times for this civilized world. There is even a peculiar pleasure taken in finding such fatal "evidence" that a possible better future is nigh.

This religious dimension of primitivism partly explains why Zerzan has been embraced by the "Jesus Radicals," a network of Christian anarchists who read both the bible and Zerzan for eschatological theses on the end times.[222] In light of this, the insurrectionary direct action of anarchists expresses a certain nobility, like that of the fighter who cannot possibly win (who will not be raptured) but who makes the stand on principle.

I revisit primitivism here because it very precisely exemplifies the central problem with the neo-anarchist insurrectionary thinking that we must both reject and distinguish our present theory from: Revolt and insurrection, for the neo-anarchist primitivist, is merely symptomatic, and is not capable of addressing, let alone of solving, any of the pressing problems of our time. Insurrection is thus merely an outburst that indicates a problem, like a telltale pain in a body at the terminal stage. Not for us. I claim that revolt and insurrection are activities of the general intellect at work, producing not only real theory and analysis, but also new forms of action, exploring new possibilities for revolution in the context of its time. As in the case of the Zapatistas, an uprising aims not only to reconfigure thinking, but living too. It is not an alternative to collective action, but an open, experimental, and creative modality of collective action. In its fragmentary ways, that is the real and necessary power of insurrection.

Meanwhile, so much of Zerzan's writing is a catalog of misery, crime, and dire psychological downturns, leading to increasing suicides and growing rates of depression. For Zerzan, this whole catalog — which includes riot, revolt, and insurrection — is the

222 See the group Jesus Radicals, accessed January 6, 2016, http://www. jesusradicals.com. See also the journal of anarcho-primitivism and Christianity, *In the Land of the Living*, accessed January 6, 2016 http://www. inthelandoftheliving.org/

writing on the wall: *the system is doomed by its own designs*. Human action is dwarfed by the long, deeply rooted history of a human civilization that will do itself in (even if we do nothing). Nonetheless, primitivism is no less self-assured of its defining prediction than Marx was of his. Indeed, in all of Zerzan's hostility toward Marx, he is the more deterministic of the two, the more susceptible to religious optimism, and the more dismissive of human agency.

It was easy to predict the primitivist trope on the spree of North African uprisings that has been referred to as the "Arab Spring," and one can easily guess the primitivist take on the occupation movement in the US. Like all social upheavals and acts of rebellion, these uprisings are reliably interpreted to indicate impending final problems of civilization. In this way, the primitivist trope preserves too much of the ideological strategy employed by the socialists of the *International Socialist Review*, who always interpret every uprising as evidence of disaffection with capitalism, even when there are young businessmen in the streets.

In pursuit of revolutionary alternatives to revolution, and in light of a history of revolutionary aspiration and failure, we seek new forms of creative activity, human agency, and sustained, collective engagement. A theory that views revolt as a superfluous symptom of an already-doomed system has no need for revolt. We must not follow the preachers of catastrophism who espouse the radicalness of waiting around for the plate tectonics of civilization to rearrange our world and to address our problems at their roots. To the contrary, I argue that revolt is a critical activity necessary to transforming relations and understandings in the world; indeed, necessary to remaking the world. Revolt is not only a practice, but a philosophical activity from below, which activates and expresses the organic intellect of insurrection. We have much to learn from revolt, and we need it.

We have no need for a theory that has no need for revolt.

IV Insurrection everywhere

At this juncture, I would like to recommend both an antagonistic and agonistic politics of revolt. Antagonistic means a politics of opposition and contestation, which involves the identification of some objectionable power, and active modalities of going against it. Agonistic means that we do not act alone, for there are ways of acting together, which in agonistic terms means *voluntarily*, *cooperatively*, and with some *common cause*. Through antagonistic and agonistic activity, we seek to combine negation and affirmation, to combine being-against with being-for. And we do so recognizing that we cannot confront the wretchedness of the world alone. There is, inevitably, a communist comportment to the antithetical (antagonistic) and associative (agonistic) commitments of this formulation. Indeed, there is always some communist content in an insurrection.

There is a long history of pointing out that state power was capitalist even when various ideologues called it "communist." Cornelius Castoriadis observed in 1949 that the mode of production in Russia was fundamentally capitalist, that the Soviet Union was state capitalist, whereas the US was free-market capitalist.[223] Guy Debord attacked the Russian and Chinese bureaucracies as pretending to represent the impoverished and marginalized while abusing those populations in actual fact.[224] And *Solidarity*, a working-class organization in Poland, came together to oppose

---

223 See Chapters 5 and 6 in Castoriadis, Cornelius, *Political and Social Writings, Volume 1, 1946-1955: From the Critique of Bureaucracy to the Positive Content of Socialism*, trans. David Ames Curtis (Minneapolis: University of Minnesota Press, 1988).

224 Debord, Guy, Theses 100 and 107 in *The Society of the Spectacle*, trans. Donald Nicholson-Smith (New York: Zone Books, 1995) and "The Explosion Point of Ideology in China" in *A Sick Planet*, trans. Donald Nicholson-Smith (London: Seagull Books, 2008).

the working-class government of Poland.[225] Numerous other cases, notably in Hungary (1956) and Romania (1989), but also elsewhere in the 20th century, provide evidence of "communist states" opposed by communist activity in civil society. This was a communism by way of an antagonistic and agonistic politics from below. Hence, even when world politics was ideologized as a grand stand-off between communists and capitalists, it was widely held that the so-called communist states were no less a betrayal of everyday people than were the capitalist ones. We know this from a rich documentary record of a communist politics from below that opposed itself to both capitalist and so-called communist government.

And now, well over twenty years after the Cold War came to an end, it should finally be noncontroversial to observe that most (indeed, all, to varying degrees) of the world's official institutions of governance are capitalist. In the 1990s, there was some debate about the socialism of the former Yugoslavia, and in early millennium, there have been more or less "socialistic" leaders in Latin America and Europe, but these states are only more or less cooperative with a logic of capital they ultimately accept. Today's "socialist" regime only exercises some amount of democratic socialism, which distinguishes itself by not allowing the market logic of capital to decide every last question.

In any case, we can no longer pretend that capitalism has nothing to do with present global miseries. As cited above, not even the IMF can pretend to do this in light of their own research today. Yet, ideological analysis of the economic crisis in the United States persists, despite the fact that Occupy Wall Street interrupted dominant discourse with a temporary return to the question of capital. When the capitalist economy breaks down, ideological

225 Alain Touraine, *Solidarity: The Analysis of a Social Movement: Poland 1980-81*, trans. David Denby (Cambridge, UK and New York: Cambridge University Press, 1983).

analyses maintain that the breakdown has nothing to do with capital. They do this primarily by ignoring the question of capital altogether. Some even blame the global economic crisis on one, two, or three men, Barney Frank, Ben Bernanke, Barack Obama, etc. The central and most difficult task is making and sustaining a critique of capital, instead of personal villains. Such a critique must not be academic. Such a critique may take the form of revolt, and would do well to heed the aesthetic and imaginative insights discussed in Chapter 3. That is, to make and sustain a critique of capital today, the critique will have to be artistic, visual, sonic, funny, sexy, disruptive, pervasive, and expressed in a million different ways. This is the task of insurrection. The critique of capital is far better when it comes from a collectivity of everyday people in public, joyful, riveting, provocative, and often dangerous and illegal interruptions of everyday life — from the Greek uprising of 2008, for example, or from the occupation movements of present and past generations, or from the mountains of Chiapas.[226]

And, while the Egyptian uprising of 2011 was too heterogeneous to articulate any ideal end state, the resounding content of the message coming from the streets of Cairo was that the existing state of affairs must end, igniting imaginations of the possible over and against the actual. Immediately, we heard too much worry from the West about the "results" of the popular insurrection in Egypt. Discourses that pathologically fixate on the end result as the ultimate measure of success or failure must be rejected. Let us propose instead that the uprisings — as a rejection of the old and effective lie that existing society is the *only* one the people could ever have — are already a successful realization of the power of revolt.

---

226 The argument here is developed in different directions and complemented by discussions in my books *Unbounded Publics* (2008), *Spectacular Capitalism* (2011), and *Precarious Communism* (2014).

Political questions, especially those that are interested in collective action and revolution, will find little guidance in the works of Nietzsche, although the rebel will surely find solace and inspiration. Hence, the quote from Nietzsche that opens this chapter may appear strangely out of place, or misfit altogether. The quote comes from the famous passage # 341 in *The Gay Science,* one of the places where Nietzsche considers eternal recurrence, a meditation on the possibility of an eternal return and what that means for living human action. To plunder the eternal recurrence for political theory, we might pose it as follows: For how long must we bear the ongoing and growing anxiety and material insecurity of the world, while waiting patiently for some tremendous historic breakthrough? Such breakthroughs always leave much to be desired. If we cannot find any real solution in politics, and we have to bear it all over again, would the insurrection be the dreadful part of life, the part to make us gnash our teeth? Or perhaps, is the everyday life in between each uprising the part that is the nightmare for far too many people? And isn't insurrection precisely the tremendous moment or breakthrough when human societies define themselves against the eternal return of the existing state of affairs? Human history reveals insurrection as a global event that societies seem to desire once more and innumerable times more.

Of course we don't want to see a military regime in Egypt. The good news is that the problematic results of an uprising can be addressed through another uprising. Of course, we like to see the people of Egypt, Tunisia, Bahrain, Syria, Yemen, the United States, the UK (and elsewhere and hopefully everywhere) enter into emancipated spaces of transition. Of course, we want to see insurrections capable of sustaining a serious structural critique of capital that can open up concrete possibilities for transformation. The insurrectionists are not decisively or overwhelmingly communist or anarchist, and they are obviously not primitivist. But inflexible identifications don't matter or help much here. As discussed in Chapter 2, we do not look forward to the ends of insurrection because we understand that the ends of insurrection are never the end of insurrection as a transformative social force.

This last point is the main one. It is necessary in the 21st century to oppose any revolutionary eschatology. Thus, we look forward to the beginnings of insurrection everywhere.

v Epilogue (after the end)

Revolution betrays its own logic when it claims to have reached the end.

CHAPTER 5

A Graveyard for Orthodoxies

Now it is seen that socialism in the sense of State-directed planned economy means state-capitalism, and that socialism in the sense of workers' emancipation is only possible as a new orientation.
  — ANTON PANNEKOEK, *Workers' Councils* [227]

Like name tags display the wearer's name, political discourse is an ideological marker. *Communism*... now *communisation*. We do not know how communist insurgents will call themselves, most likely not "communist." The 20th century has given communism a bad name... Maybe insurgents will be weary of what Victor Klemperer called the "depreciation of the superlatives." Maybe they will prefer to experience the darkness of a missing word, and they will make do with off-target terms, until they complete the phrase.
  — GILLES DAUVÉ, *Everything Must Go!* [228]

In this book we have self-consciously taken up theoretical and political source material that indicates certain ideological preferences. As the reader knows well by now, we have taken up works in French and German critical theory, Marx and Marxism, autonomist and anarchist trajectories, Italian political philosophy, and psychoanalytic theory, among other usual suspects in contemporary Continental social and political thought. Thus, we inevitably

227   Pannekoek, Anton, *Workers' Councils* in *Left Communism Reader* (New York: Prism Key Press, 2013), p. 433.
228   Astarian, Bruno and Dauvé, Gilles, *Everything Must Go! The Abolition of Value* (Berkeley: LBC Books, 2015), pp. 192 and 194.

arrive at a question of whether or not we can make use of these sources beyond and/or against their own ideological boundaries. In this chapter, I argue that we can and must extricate this source material from its ideological trappings and limitations.

In the social theory, political philosophy, and revolutionary movements of the 19th and 20th centuries, certain orthodoxies made good sense. The stakes of world affairs seemed to hinge upon choosing one ideology or another. In the political debates of the late 19th century and early 20th, there was a palpable sense that the prevailing worldview would shape the future. This was especially true in the debates of thinkers who sought to throw the world of capital into question.

Within European radicalism was the idea that following the influence of Pierre-Joseph Proudhon or Karl Marx could lead to hell or heaven on Earth, depending on one's point of view. Everything was submitted as evidence for one side or the other, from the Paris Commune and its catastrophic fate to debates between Paul Lafargue and the anarchists, and between Lafargue and the Marxists, too. The notion that there should be a decisive ideology for world affairs did not die easily, although one might have seen a possibly-final embodiment in the reactionary discourses of the Cold War. But alas, as the current phase of neoliberal ideology meets with the materiality of capitalist crisis, and governments struggle for enduring relevance in transnational politics, all the old ideologies have come back again, like zombies hungry for life.

But in the 21st century, good work is a graveyard for orthodoxies. This means that good works today don't contribute to the revitalization of the dead language of ideological purity. This does not mean that we cannot call ourselves "anarchists" or "communists," or that there are no longer "capitalists" in the world. Such conclusions would be absurd. We do not live in a "post-capitalist" world, since most of the whole of human affairs is governed by exchange relations according to the logic of capital. What it means to insist on a graveyard for orthodoxies is that we must rethink old traditions and trajectories against their calcified and vilified forms, burying zombified ideologies for good. A less ideological and more philosophical conversation has become necessary.

Indeed, one of the many places where Marx got it wrong was in his conceit in the poverty of philosophy. To be fair, Marx had good reasons at the time of *The German Ideology* and *Theses on Feuerbach* (1845-1846) to worry about the prominence of philosophers and to oppose Berlin's youth culture of a Hegelian contemplation floating above the real world of human suffering. However, times have changed, the world is not overly philosophical today, and philosophy is not ideology (and arguably, never was). Philosophy is the process of open questioning that comes to an end in the rigid "comprehensive" worldviews of ideology. Philosophy is more practical than ideology. If we have learned anything from the failures and frustrations of 170 years of revolutionary theory and practice, it should be that ideological narrowness prevents an open approach to all available resources, and is a dangerous dead end.

It is important today to recover the work of Anton Pannekoek, a left communist and fierce critic of Lenin and other socialist derailments in the Soviet Union. It is critical to engage the communism of thinkers like Pannekoek, Sylvia Pankhurst, Herman Gorter, Amadeo Bordiga, and Jacques Camatte, among others. Today, there are influential theoretical movements operating under the name of "communization," which inadvertently makes communist anti-statism appear as if it were a new thing. The very existence of a long history of anti-"communist" communists, along with a real reckoning with Marx's own complex theory of the state, helps to expose the false pretenses of ideological orthodoxy.

When I teach my course on Marxist Philosophy, students are always surprised to learn that Marx was not an enthusiastic statist, that he wrote so much about the problems of state power, and so little about alternative forms of government. These facts are hard to see when we only consult ideological narratives about

Marx, instead of Marx directly. A few weeks into the semester, and students can no longer make use of the ideological apparatus they brought with them on the first day. They can of course return to their ideological comforts later on if they like, and sadly, many of them do. But the ideological position they start with is always reliably challenged and broken apart in the course of sustained and honest engagement with the material.

Ideology has also held hostage many streams of anarchist thought. There are still anarchist journals, magazines, and publishers that get squeamish around any serious consideration of Marxism, as if an affirmation of a single Marxist idea is tantamount to ideological betrayal. Now, it has to be finally and fully comprehended that Kropotkin, Bakunin, Proudhon, Malatesta, Goldman, and so many other anarchists have shared much in common with Marx, and even used his critique of capitalism as a basis for their own work. While Emma Goldman wrote about her disillusionment with Russia, so too did many communists, like Antonio Gramsci and Cornelius Castoriadis, and critical theorists in the decades following World War II. Despite real common ground, there has been insufficient crosspollination (and insufficient contamination) across the cleavages of different radical currents. What revolutionary theory needs to find out — *what needs to be explored in both scholarship and in the world* — is what can grow in the graveyard for orthodoxies.

Repressed desires can and do unpredictably explode, and insubordination is never totally foreclosed. Riot and revolt are never in permanent abeyance, and the "elite" are never as safe as they would like to be from the many ways we can unsettle the "social order" of this world. What we have seen in recent years is that the "elite" in many countries, in Egypt, Turkey, Brazil, Greece, the US, the UK, Tunisia, Spain, and elsewhere, are not beyond being taken by surprise by everyday people at various breaking points around the world. No matter how repressed, disintegrated, manipulated, or exploited, human beings do possess real desires for a life defined by something other than the precarity of capitalist work, unemployment, passive entertainment, and other diversions. Real human desire is, fundamentally, a non-ideological force, by which I mean that it exists before, beneath, and beyond particular worldviews. On the most superficial level, we often see the difference and distance between what a politician claims to desire and actually desires — in the media, this is called exposé and scandal. The manifold of human desires is diverse and unruly, but its content can be specified in the absence of ideology. One does not need Marxism or anarchism to answer the question of what one wants. There are many good examples over the last twenty years (1994-2015), which demonstrate that revolutionary desires can and do come alive even after they're considered extinguished, and that they do not always fit easily into the molds of ideological orthodoxy.

The key point here, however, is that public expressions of disaffection (including riot and revolt) frequently take radical thinkers by surprise, thus surprising others than the so-called ruling class.

Insurrections do not ask for academic guidance. We do not teach social movements. At our best, we learn from them, for they test and reveal the limits of possibility within the contexts in which they occur. To take one of my favorite examples, the 1994 uprising of the Mexican Zapatistas revealed and recommended to theorists — *and especially to anarchists and communists* — certain possibilities that were not grasped until that point. And it is clear that recent insurrectionary activity in the Middle Eastern and North African (MENA) countries south of the Mediterranean Sea, as well as in Greece, Spain, Turkey, and Brazil, is once again forcing analysis to consider (a) its own limitations and (b) new emancipatory possibilities.[229]

---

229 These limitations and possibilities are directly taken up, for example, in Berardi, Franco, *The Uprising: On Poetry and Finance* (Los Angeles: Semiotext(e), 2012).

Here, Marx's famous line comes to mind: "The weapon of criticism cannot, of course, replace criticism of the weapon, material force must be overthrown by material force; but theory also becomes a material force as soon as it has gripped the masses."[230]

It is the last clause of this quote that forms a recurring question for me, which is taken up more fully in the present chapter and remainder of this book: Are those participating in the many modes of uprising looking for or demanding an alternative program? Or: Is there an alternative program capable of answering the heterogeneous and often contradictory demands of global revolt? Many critics and onlookers from outside insisted that movements like Occupy Wall Street needed to adopt a platform for an alternative program, and today, many of the same people point to the absence of such a program as the reason for the dissolution of Occupy X activities. Of course, there are many possible programs that could be defined, but none of them were practical from the multifarious perspective of the many minds of Occupy X.

The range of radical criticism found in Tahrir Square, Gezi Park, and Taksim Square, or in any occupation from 1968 to the present, cannot be resolved in a good plan. Such social upheavals, when they are indeed upheavals, are ungovernable. The more they specify, the more they shrink. From the point of view of "governmentality," this may sound hopeless. But riot, revolt, and insurrection do not proceed from or with a "govern" mentality, that is, they neither pretend to become government, nor do they want to be governed. The uprising is itself the most important achievement, perhaps, precisely for this reason: *the governed become ungovernable*. That is the significance of the *hyperpotentia* of revolt. In a world where uprisings are too few and far between, and where each insurrection is separated from the next by indefi-

---

230 Marx, Karl, *Critique of Hegel's 'Philosophy of Right'*, trans. Annette Jolin and Joseph O'Malley (Cambridge, UK: Cambridge University Press, 1970), p. 133.

nite periods of relative quiescence, such upheaval always makes a critique and breaks with the banality of everyday life. Revolt shows the world that there are those who want a different world, and that real revolutionary desires are available to be discussed, debated, and developed. Revolt shows us that the world can still be thrown into question, and that we need not let existing conditions decide what is practical.

In many ways, writing is a more desperate (and less dangerous) act than insurrection. After all, text calls out for readers, and depends on their serious and sustained attention. Securing committed readers is no easy thing, as any honest author (or publisher) will tell you. Authors who have truly impacted world events are fewer in number than the old bourgeoisie and its heirs. But revolt is another kind of writing, a human drama that demands and commands attention, and concrete political proposals do frequently come from it.

Perhaps revolt is the writing that matters most. We do not know what any given insurrection will say, what it will demand, what theory will "grip the masses" and become material reality. We do know that in between every insurrection, there is another one on the horizon.

But so what? What is all that social energy good for? It comes and goes, and when it's gone, too much is always left the same. What does it do? What can it do for real people in the real world? Can we (and who is that?) organize the energies of insurrection into a concrete platform, into a unitary politics? Don't we need a political party, an organization, an infrastructure, or else won't all this revolutionary energy just be wasted in brief saturnalias of opposition that city officials can clean up on Monday morning? These questions, one way or another, are questions about organization, about the implementation of structural changes that matter to real people in the real world. If we care about the real lives of real people, if we want to avoid the relative smallness of anarchist uprisings and experiments, and if we want to move beyond the pornography of riots, then don't we need to finally confront the questions of the state and the party? Yes, but only if these questions are taken up with a different comportment than has been done in most of the Marxist and anarchist discourses.

Since the life and times of Bakunin, Marx's theory of the state has been caricatured as "authoritarian" by a great many anarchists who have not understood it. At the same time, too many Marxists have accepted the premise by engaging in apologetics for the socialist state as an idea and historical practice.

Throughout his many decades of writing, Michael Parenti has argued in defense of the socialist state as both an idea and historical practice, as can be seen in his *To Kill a Nation*, *Contrary Notions*, *Profit Pathology and Other Indecencies*, and indeed, in most of his other books.[231] Parenti has consistently worked to establish the qualitatively better conditions of life in both historical and possible societies governed by a socialist state. The socialist state is the major praxis of his Marxism, which does not diminish the usefulness of all his astute criticism and analysis of capitalist society, economy, media, history, and culture. More recently, in the celebrity Left theory of Jodi Dean, Slavoj Žižek, and Alain Badiou, the socialist state and the communist party have been making a peculiar kind of comeback, even including qualified apologetics for Stalin (especially in the works of Žižek and Badiou, though Parenti has offered some such apologetics as well). In *The Communist Hypothesis*, Badiou argues against the consensus that the communist experiments of the 20th century were failures. He argues that the pervasive ideological narrative of the Cold War poisoned our ability to see anything but catastrophe and terror in the so-called communist regimes of the previous century.

---

231   Parenti, Michael, *To Kill a Nation: The Attack on Yugoslavia* (London and New York: Verso Books, 2000); *Contrary Notions: The Michael Parenti Reader* (San Francisco: City Lights Books, 2007); *Profit Pathology and Other Indecencies* (Boulder and London: Paradigm Publishers, 2015).

"Lumping together Stalin and Hitler was already a sign of extreme intellectual poverty."[232] And:

What exactly do we mean by 'failure' when we refer to a historical sequence that experimented with one or another form of the communist hypothesis? What do we mean when we say that all the socialist experiments that took place under the sign of that hypothesis ended in total 'failure'? Was it a complete failure?[233]

Badiou spends a large part of *The Communist Hypothesis* challenging the discourse of communist failure from the 20th century that we have inherited in the 21st.

Yet, by the end of the book, Badiou takes a position surprisingly close to this chapter's epigraph from Anton Pannekoek. On the word and idea of communism, Badiou concludes that "the word's function can no longer be that of an adjective, as in 'Communist Party', or 'communist regimes'. The Party-form, like that of the Socialist State, is no longer suitable for providing real support for the Idea."[234] In this, Badiou breaks from recent efforts to revitalize the party-form and the socialist state, problematizing the positions of Dean and Žižek. Dean has been arguing for a militant international communist party, for example, while Žižek staked great hope in the Syriza party in recent election cycles in Greece, and has argued disdainfully against all autonomist tendencies.[235]

Parenti argues that

232 Badiou, Alain, *The Communist Hypothesis* (London and New York: Verso Books, 2010), p. 3.

233 Ibid., p. 6.

234 Ibid., p. 257.

235 Dean, Jodi, "The Party and Communist Solidarity" at the Eighth International Rethinking Marxism Conference, Amherst, MA, September 21, 2013 and Žižek, Slavoj, "On the Role of the European Left" at the 6th Subversive Festival, Zagreb, Croatia, May 15, 2013.

the former communist states transformed impoverished semi-feudal countries into relatively advanced societies. Whatever their mistakes and crimes, they achieved what capitalism has no intention of accomplishing: adequate food, housing, and clothing for all; economic security in old age; free medical care; free education at all levels; and a guaranteed adequate income.[236]

Parenti often observes that the collapse of these so-called communist states has been bad news for their citizens:

As the peoples in these former communist countries are now discovering, the free market means freedom mostly for those who have money and a drastic decline in living standards for most everyone else. With the advent of free market reforms in the former USSR and Eastern Europe, workers saw their real wages, pensions, and savings dissolve.[237]

Indeed, macroeconomic and social data confirm that Parenti is correct on the basic points.[238] In these examples of state capitalism, from the USSR and Eastern Europe, capital was regulated for the greater benefit of people far more effectively than increasingly unbounded capital has done since the 1990s, with its ever-withering social concerns. However, Parenti's long-standing confusion of state capitalism with communism is deeply problematic on theoretical and conceptual grounds for many reasons, not the least of which being that his critique of capital is essentially a call for

---

236 Parenti, Michael, *Profit Pathology and Other Indecencies* (Boulder and London: Paradigm Publishers, 2015), pp. 144-145.

237 Ibid., p. 145.

238 Parenti's books provide documentation of these basic macroeconomic claims. I provide confirmatory citations about growing inequality and the failures of capitalist economy in my own work, throughout the present book as well as in *Spectacular Capitalism* (2011) and *Precarious Communism* (2014).

its re-regulation.[239] He often makes no distinction between communism and socialism, on the one hand, and state capitalism, on the other. And in his voluminous work, Parenti scarcely examines the importance (or necessity) of revolution. Thus, Parenti defines communism as no antithetical force against capital, as no process from below, but mainly as the social and political administration of economy and public law. From a practical and historical point of view, none of the failures and disappearances of the so-called socialist state have dissuaded Parenti from calling for its reemergence, even as revolt itself appears to have only diminishing faith in the administrative proposal. Today, faith in state capitalism is viewed with the deep distrust of radicals, yet remains the optimistic hope of liberals.

Most importantly, this wave of apologetics for the socialist state and the communist party has not pooled together with recent waves of insurrection that appear to occur in different waters. In recent years, we have seen multifarious and ideologically variegated uprisings around the world, some of which have overthrown governments, while others have changed conversations and given the experience of revolt to new generations. Waves of global uprising since 2008 have created real moments of recognition and realization of the social energies of everyday people capable of throwing the existing world into question. A central problem for the theories of Dean, Žižek, Badiou, and Parenti is that the communist desire that has been expressed in recent insurrectionary activity is *not* calling for a communist party, has little faith in the state to solve the problems of everyday

239 It is important to point out that "democratic socialism" is today used as the more communistic-sounding name for state capitalism. During the Democratic Party presidential primary in the US in 2015 and 2016, Bernie Sanders repeatedly clarified that his "democratic socialism" is fully capitalist (just not "casino capitalist") and that it should not be mistaken for any form of communism or any anti-capitalist position. He is correct in that clarification.

life, and makes no enduring connections to the communist projects of the previous century. Leftist intellectuals may insist on
the *practical* political necessity of party and state organizations,
but if real revolt does not want them, such practical recommendations are more impractical than their theorists can see.

It is one thing for theory to imagine itself in an advisory role
for social movements, and another for theory to learn from them.
I argue that theory always has more to learn from social movements than it has to teach them. And, if we are paying attention
to actually-existing revolt in the world, and not forcing it into
the frame of an ideological worldview (*weltanschauung*), then we
simply cannot conclude that new uprisings want communist parties, socialist states, or any continuation of Soviet "experiments."
This does not mean that there is no communist desire here. This
does not mean that nothing can come from revolt. To say otherwise is to assume that nothing is happening until it starts to
look like something else that has already happened before. I think
that what we are seeing is what Pannekoek called for over seventy
years ago, the emergence of "a new orientation."

This new orientation is more important now than ever before
in the history of communist theory and action. Indeed, a new orientation seems almost inevitable. Ongoing vilifications of communism depend upon a conversation haunted by the specter of
statist catastrophes. I argue that we must bury the ideologized
anarchist-Marxist debate, *along with statism itself*, as casualties
of the 20th century. While autonomist Marxist trajectories offer
the most promising pathways, they often retain too much of the
old dichotomies that foreclose the use of important theoretical,
historical, and political resources. I have argued for a "precarious
communism," which should not be confused with an acceptance
of the whole fashionable discourse on precarity.[240] Simply, precarious communism is a communism that self-consciously lacks con-

240 Throughout *Precarious Communism* (2014).

fidence about some particular, alternative future. And, precarious communism is not reassured by the old revolutionary imaginary of communist state power. Rather, it sees the "communist state" as a contradiction in terms (as did Marx, I would claim), and thus has other positive identifications, as follows:

(a) Precarious communism is *communist* on the grounds of its single most confident claim: A world organized by the logic of capital is a world set against the diverse interests of most people on Earth. Thus, precarious communism is communist on the grounds of its total critique of capital.

(b) Precarious communism is *precarious* inasmuch as it accepts that concrete proposals for new ways of being-in-the-world will be differentially developed as nodal points within the contexts of actually-existing revolt. Thus, precarious communism is precarious on the grounds of its practical uncertainty about how to abolish the rule of capital.

What does it mean to be a precarious communist? It is something like being a non-ideological communist who is honest about the past, present, and the future. While ideology makes communism more confident, precarious communism is more philosophical, less ideological, and therefore more self-consciously uncertain.

Communism today requires an open Marxism that synthesizes theoretical trajectories across the cleavages of left-communist currents and anarchism. From Cornelius Castoriadis and Guy Debord, to Raya Dunayevskaya and C.L.R. James, to Gilles Deleuze and Félix Guattari, to Antonio Negri, Franco Berardi, Silvia Federici, George Caffentzis, and John Holloway, efforts to unmoor communism from the ideological encrustations of the 20th century are increasingly resonant. We can take it as good news that there is a growing appeal to what is called "communization theory." Within earlier left-communist milieus, in the works of Sylvia Pankhurst,

Herman Gorter, Anton Pannekoek, and Jacques Camatte, there was a practice of communization theory during and against the dominance of the Soviet Union and an expanding Cold War narrative. It is not that so-called "communization theory" is new, but rather that the meaning of communism has been decided against the favor of such communist currents, until now.

Consider again Marx's abovementioned declaration that "theory also becomes a material force as soon as it has gripped the masses."[241] The theory of the left communists comes especially to mind here. It would seem that all of the statist transpositions of Marxism into the world had to reveal their limitations and dangers before the conditions were created for anti-statist Marxism to finally be taken seriously. Lenin's fierce critique of what he called the "infantile disorder" of "left communism" survived in one way or another, as part of the longer Marxist tradition (going back to Marx himself) of condemning a caricatured anarchist foolishness.[242] But now, the "infantile disorder" appears as a possible maturation point of 21st-century communism. In the 1970s, Camatte wrote: "Forced to take account of the strength of the proletariat, Stalinist Russia had to disguise itself and realize the triumph of capital under the mask of socialism."[243] Today, there appears to be little interest in a more convincing, or a more faithful, mask, and what we find in the 21st century is a widespread "post-socialist" sensibility that political parties *are* masks, and that states always wear them.

To accompany and support these sensibilities-from-below, this *Gemeingeist* of revolt, the whole heterogeneous bevy of the more neglected communist theorization must move from margin to center. There is what could be called a subaltern communist

241 Marx, Karl, *Critique of Hegel's 'Philosophy of Right'*, op. cit., p. 133.
242 Lenin, V.I., *"Left-Wing" Communism, An Infantile Disorder: A Popular Essay in Marxist Strategy and Tactics* (New York: International Publishers, 1940).
243 Camatte, Jacques, *Capital and Community*, trans. David Brown (New York: Prism Key Press, 2011), p. 203.

history of theory and practice to recover, a legacy of Marxism without statism. Can we not finally say that every good Marxist is more than a bit of an anarchist these days?[244]

Of course, we can't reduce a long history of oppositions to nothing. The disagreements between Marx and Proudhon, for example, raised critical questions in the debates of the 19th century that would take all of the next century to settle, and they have not yet been finally settled. But there is another history, less sordid and less scandalous, which has been eclipsed by strong personalities and rhetorical bluster.

Marx gave us the most systematic, rigorous, and exhaustive analysis of the history, tendencies, and crises of capital that he was capable of producing in a single lifetime — all of his energies were ultimately given over to that task. When one reads the anarchist literature contemporaneous with Marx and the Marxism of the early 20th century, certain things are undeniable. Proudhon, Bakunin, Kropotkin, Malatesta, and so many others, made dependable use of Marx's analyses of capitalism, so much so that one could find them fully agreeable on *at least* three broad premises: (i) the impossibility of an acceptable/sustainable capitalist world; (ii) the desirability and possibility of a different world organized on *other* principles or logics; (iii) the necessity of revolution, although many different and incompatible conceptions of revolution are at play within this history.

When one reads Errico Malatesta's little book, *At the Café: Conversations on Anarchism*, the analysis of capitalism and class follows Marx right up to the question of revolution, at which point Malatesta distinguishes his position in a discussion of "free communism."[245] And while Bakunin had a famously tumultuous

---

244 Perhaps this was already true in Marx's time, as could be argued in the case of Paul Lafargue.

245 Malatesta, Errico, *At the Café: Conversations on Anarchism* (London: Freedom Press, 2005), p. 65.

relationship with Marx, we cannot reduce that relationship to its oppositions alone. Bakunin joined the Geneva section of the First International, helped create new branches in Italy and Spain, and translated and circulated many of Marx's works, including the first Russian edition of *The Communist Manifesto*. One year after his expulsion from the International, Bakunin would admit: "Rarely can a man be found who knows so much and reads so much, and reads so intelligently, as Marx... Undoubtedly there is a good deal of truth in the merciless critique he directed against Proudhon."[246] Proudhon advocated a different conception of revolution, which he thought would be more enduring, albeit slower. In his letter to Marx of May 17, 1846, he wrote: "I would prefer to burn property slowly with a small fire than to give it new strength by carrying out a Saint Bartholomew's Night of the Proprietors..."[247] Anarchists have long been capable of critiquing Marx, while crediting him for the foundation on which so much of anarchism rested.[248] Additionally, serious Marxist thinkers have long rejected major features of Marx's arguments, a tradition that goes back at least to Paul Lafargue, to Antonio Gramsci's essay "The Revolution against *Capital*," and to Georg Lukács' denouement of vulgar Marxists.

Despite this, ideological allergies persist. Consider one prominent example, which I have taken up elsewhere:[249] Michael Hardt and Antonio Negri have retained a strange insistence on distinguishing an ideological divide that dissolves in their own work. It is important to highlight the problem here, in the case of Hardt

246 Bakunin, Michael, *Statism and Anarchy*, trans. Marshall S. Shatz (Cambridge, UK: Cambridge University Press, 1994), p. 142.

247 Proudhon, Pierre-Joseph, "Letter to Karl Marx" in *Property Is Theft!*, ed. Iain McKay (Edinburgh, Oakland, Baltimore: AK Press, 2011), p. 164.

248 See also "Bakunin's Reminiscence" of Marx in *The Portable Karl Marx* (New York: Viking Penguin, 1983), p. 26 and Emma Goldman's *My Disillusionment in Russia* (New York: Dover, 2003).

249 *Precarious Communism* (2014), pp. 120-122.

and Negri, because they are now among the most iconic representatives of Marxism without statism — especially Negri, who has written two autonomist Marxist manifestos.[250] Hardt and Negri declare that it is their time, as communists, to give voice to the cry: *"Big government is over!"* They acknowledge the old socialistic aspiration to use government to redistribute wealth, and they confess: *"Today, however, those times are over."* Hardt and Negri define the revolutionary aspiration of the multitude in terms of a quest for *"autonomous self-government."*[251] No anarchist would disagree with that aspiration. Hardt and Negri know this well, and immediately anticipate the accusation that they are anarchists. They make the following pre-emptive rebuttal:

> *That is not true. We would be anarchists if we were not to speak (as did Thrasymachus and Callicles, Plato's immortal interlocutors) from the standpoint of a materiality constituted in the networks of productive cooperation, in other words, from the perspective of a humanity that is constructed productively, that is constituted through the "common name" of freedom. No, we are not anarchists but communists who have seen how much repression and destruction of humanity have been wrought by liberal and socialist big governments.*[252]

What is *"the standpoint of a materiality constituted in the networks of productive cooperation"*? What is *"the perspective of a humanity that is constructed productively"*? Hardt and Negri mean that they

---

250 The two "manifestos" I am referring to are *The Politics of Subversion: A Manifesto for the Twenty-First Century*, trans. James Newell (Cambridge, UK and Malden, MA: Polity Press, 2005) and, with Félix Guattari, *New Lines of Alliance, New Spaces of Liberty* (Brooklyn: Autonomedia/Minor Compositions, 2010).

251 Hardt, Michael and Negri, Antonio, *Empire* (Cambridge, MA and London: Harvard University Press, 2001), p. 349.

252 Ibid., p. 350 (italics in original).

are not anarchists because they accept the materialist premises of Marx's political-economy. It is thus reasonable to assume that they have not read the rich history of anarchism in which those very premises are also accepted, a history in which such premises are often accepted with a self-conscious debt to Marx. The perspective of a humanity constructed productively can be found throughout the history of anarchism, in the diverse writings of Lucy Parsons, Peter Kropotkin, Charlotte Wilson, and Rudolph Rocker, to name just some examples.

There is ultimately nothing to take seriously in Hardt and Negri's peculiar insistence that they "*are not anarchists but communists who have seen the repression and destruction wrought by liberal and socialist big governments.*" Anarchists have long been communists who have seen how much repression and destruction of humanity have been wrought by governments. Indeed, the anarchist prescience about such repression and destruction defined them in the 19th century, when their theory of power only looked like a fearful wager, and vindicated them in the 20th century, when it appeared as prophecy. Why does this matter? Because ongoing ideological dichotomies continue to haunt and over-determine the development of new autonomist Marxisms, which do not then make use of the theoretical, historical, and political resources of other anti-capitalist tendencies. Thus, the purported heterodoxy of open Marxism is belied by the fact that it remains a too-narrow enclosure.

To be fair, many anarchists have made worse mistakes when it comes to ideologizing the divide between communist forms. Many anarchists have become so sectarian that they've produced a little cottage industry of anarchist broadsides against other anarchists.[253] As well, in much of the anarchist press, there

---

253 See, for example, the published record of disputes between Murray Bookchin, John Zerzan, Bob Black, David Watson, Hakim Bey, etc.

remains a misguided ideological rule against taking anything Marx said seriously.[254]

In *Anti-Oedipus: Capitalism and Schizophrenia*, Deleuze and Guattari famously discuss the body without organs (BwO), an idea borrowed from Antonin Artaud, and made to mean a plane of indeterminacy, of open possibilities, a terrain of our becoming, of our fighting, of our losing and winning, a terrain on which we see ourselves as a body without organs.

> Every coupling of machines, every production of a machine, every sound of a machine running, becomes unbearable to the body without organs. Beneath its organs it senses that there are larvae and loathsome worms, and a God at work messing it all up or strangling it by organizing it.[255]

Biologically, organs define the purposes of a body as a specific kind of machine, its constitutive parts make up a reference for what that machine can do, what it is designed for. For the human machine, for the question of what we can do or what we are made for, this comes down to a question of purposes. The BwO points to a politics of subversive repurposing. The point is: We can rethink our purposes, and not leave the question up to God, up to the mode of production, or up to any ideological tradition.

Guattari was especially interested in the politics of subversion. He wrote about "becoming-woman" with an understanding of the subversive repurposing of gender.[256] A body without organs is a subject that is subject to change. When I propose a precarious

---

254 There are many examples of this, but to take one recent indication: The long-standing anarchist magazine, *Fifth Estate* (established in 1965), published a Spring 2015 issue (# 393) entitled "Anti-Marx."

255 Deleuze, Gilles and Guattari, Félix, *Anti-Oedipus: Capitalism and Schizophrenia* (New York: Penguin Books, 2009), p. 9.

256 See Guattari, "Becoming-Woman" in *Hatred of Capitalism: A Semiotext(e) Reader* (Los Angeles: Semiotext(e), 2001).

communism, I mean that we need a communism as the body without organs of the "communists," that is, we need a new communist becoming, a becoming-ungovernable, as we could imagine Guattari might say.

What is the empirical side of this? If we look at the major post-Cold War uprisings over the twenty years from 1994 to 2014, from the uprising of the Mexican Zapatistas to the more recent insurrectionary activity in the Middle Eastern and North African countries south of the Mediterranean Sea, as well as in Greece, Spain, Turkey, the US, and Brazil, we see that actually-existing revolt has turned away from the question of administrative modes of problem-solving. For a brief moment in Egypt it might have appeared that Morsi was the answer to Mubarak, but it is now clear that — in Egypt and elsewhere — *revolutionary politics is less about governance than about various processes of becoming-ungovernable*.

In a post-orthodox, non-ideological communism, there is nonetheless a generalized purposiveness, an "open hope" for an everyday life of dignity, autonomy, and association.[257] Therefore, we can understand revolutionary processes of becoming-ungovernable as activities in search of the structural transformation of everyday life. Today's uprisings are not only not calling for a resuscitated "socialist" state, but also, they reject the capitalist substitutes for transformative solutions — like the cultural commons in a shopping mall, as was proposed for Gezi Park and Taksim Square. Actually-existing revolt in recent years has expressed just such an "open hope," and has helped prepare a graveyard for orthodoxies.

That revolt does not speak with one brain does not mean that uprisings in Greece, Egypt, Turkey, Brazil, and elsewhere do not speak at all. Uprisings are full of legible communicative content that demands unpacking. They speak volumes about sovereignty, democracy, racism, exclusions, economic crisis, and structural

257 See Part III of *Precarious Communism* (2014).

transformation, among other things, and concrete proposals *do* come out of them.[258]

For example, the Greek leftist party Syriza, in power with Prime Minister Alexis Tsipras in 2015, was founded as a political party in 2012, four years after sustained social upheaval, revolt, and sporadic insurrection coming from impoverished, unemployed, and otherwise disaffected people throughout the country. From 2004 to 2012, Syriza was an alliance and coalition of leftist and radical parties and civil-society organizations, many of them anti-capitalist. As such, Syriza inevitably generated participation and support throughout Greek civil society in the revolts from 2008. But, mainly and fundamentally, Syriza benefitted from the social energies of revolt, which catapulted and consolidated its viability as a popular political party. The Greek revolts from 2008 neither clearly nor overwhelmingly identified Syriza from the start as part of a practicable political proposal for the national stage for many reasons, not the least of which being that Syriza was not yet founded as a national party.

Basic facts about the relationship between actually existing revolt and Syriza have scarcely been noted in the Western media, as well as in alternative and left-wing sources. But it is in fact not possible to understand the viability of Syriza without the critical content of the foregoing revolt. It is precisely such critical content that theorists should attend to, for it is there that new proposals are seeded and grow. The revolt prepares the ground for the articulation of new proposals in a graveyard for orthodoxies, where there are no foregone conclusions, and where the communist hypothesis comes to life. This does not mean that Syriza is the realization of the communist hypothesis, for communist contestation (communist aspiration) is acted out long before its vari-

---

258 The communicative content and proposals of revolt will be the sustained focus of Chapter 7, and thus more fully (and finally) worked out there.

ous (and always disfigured) institutional forms. And of course, Syriza is not the end of communist revolt, not even in Greece. A different hypothesis: It is likely that Syriza would have failed if it had been a national party with electoral aspirations in 2008; if it would have then tried to seize upon the energies of revolt, we could imagine how quickly the revolt would have rejected its self-serving solicitations. But now, after the regime has enough time to generate new disaffections against itself, the possibility of new revolt can grow again, similar to how Morsi was targeted shortly after Mubarak.

Syriza also shows how the statist solution is immediately problematic from the very perspective of the insurgent forces that empower it, although Syriza shows this in a different way than did Morsi. The demand for Syriza and Tsipras to stand up and vote "NO" to European austerity deals was both reasonable and predictable given Syriza's political history from its pre-party origins in 2004 to its formal commitments as a political party after 2012. And, of course, the social upheaval that enabled Tsipras to win state power was fiercely anti-austerity, anti-neoliberal, anti-IMF debt, anti-neocolonial, etc. Unsurprisingly, Tsipras totally agreed with the popular opposition to the EU's austerity deals, but nonetheless eventually and very painfully went on to cooperate and accept more than he or Syriza's social support wanted.

I maintain that Tsipras' sincerity and commitments were not the problem, and that to claim that a "more radical" prime minister would have done differently is only to personalize a much larger historical and institutional problem with state power exercised in a global capitalist context. To point out the weaknesses in Tsipras' personality is, fundamentally, to misunderstand how state power works in a global capitalist context. The fact that so many Marxist commentators and radical critics were quick to criticize Tsipras, but much slower (or altogether silent) to criticize the limitations of his instruments and office, reveals a stubborn reluctance to recognize the real limitations of those instruments and office. I consider the Syriza victory as good news — perhaps it was the best available through the hobbled procedural apparatus of Greek electoral politics at the time. But it is not the only victory or power in the Greek story. The revolt that empowered Syriza is, now, the ghost that haunts every new compromise and failure of Syriza, the ghost that haunts every move Tsipras makes. Moreover, Greek revolt is left to confront the next great betrayal or capitalist concession of the Greek state, and indeed, the revolt is the more reliable power.[259]

To prepare and cultivate a graveyard for orthodoxies is not, therefore, to take no positions at all, or to have no point of view. A graveyard for orthodoxies does not require the corpses of all forms of Marxism, anarchism, liberalism, feminism, etc. Rather, it requires the willingness to learn from the *communiques* of the disaffections of everyday people. It does, however, require the corpses of every ideological orthodoxy that fought a war of position in the 20th century.

Insurrectionary expressions of disaffection will not always be decisively anarchist or communist, and their success in affecting and effecting the world does not depend upon their making such commitments. Revolt does not need to choose a party. Indeed, if it had one to choose, it would not occur in the first place.

Ideological orthodoxy and its political commitments (from the identity of group members to tactics and strategies) may well seize upon the disorder of generalized disaffection, but they break apart within it. The problem is not with the becoming-ungovernable, but rather with the ideological impatience to rule it.

---

259 We should keep these lessons in mind also in light of the more recent left-wing celebration of Jeremy Corbyn's electoral victory as the Leader of the Labour Party in the UK in 2015.

CHAPTER 6

The Ferguson Revolt
Did Not Take Place

Black people desire to determine their own destiny. As a result, they are constantly inflicted with brutality from the occupying army, embodied by the police department. There is a great similarity between the occupying army in Southeast Asia and the occupation of our communities by the racist police. The armies were sent not to protect the people of South Vietnam but to brutalize and oppress them in the self-interests of the imperial powers.

  – HUEY P. NEWTON, "A Functional Definition of Politics" (1969)[260]

We don't need anybody to agree with our tactics, right? We're disrupting business as usual. That is the whole idea. We're not going to stand in a corner and protest, because nobody pays attention to that. We are going to disrupt your life. You are going to know that business as usual in America and the world is not going to continue while black people — unarmed black people — are literally being shot and killed by law enforcement in the street every day.

  – MISKI NOOR, Black Lives Matter Minneapolis (2015)[261]

---

260 Newton, Huey P., "A Functional Definition of Politics, January 17, 1969" in *The Huey P. Newton Reader*, ed. David Hilliard and Donald Weise (New York: Seven Stories Press, 2002), p. 149.
261 Noor, Miski, "Interview on CNN with Carol Costello about the Black Lives Matter Protest Planned for the Mall of America" (12/22/2015), accessed January 11, 2016, http://archives.cnn.com/TRANSCRIPTS/1512/22/cnr.02. html.

The Ferguson revolt did not take place; the Baltimore revolt is proof.[262] The Ferguson revolt did not take place because it has occurred and is still happening in different ways in other places. In so many uprisings, from Shays' Rebellion in 1786 to the many North American slave revolts of the 18th and 19th centuries, to the race riots of the 20th century, from Springfield, Illinois in 1908 to Watts, Los Angeles in 1965, to current insurrections in Ferguson 2014 and Baltimore 2015, to the Black Lives Matter disruptions at the Mall of America and Minneapolis airport in Minnesota in December 2015, there is always some part of the event that expresses disaffections carried over from the previous ones. Revolts are nodal points in the elaboration of a transformative "politics" that exceeds them. To historicize revolt by marking its beginning and its end is to cut it off from itself, to misunderstand it. In particular, the fixation on the end of revolt disguises that old quotidian hope for a *retour à la normale*.

Riot and revolt are difficult to predict. And yet, as soon as they break out, the reasons for their occurrence are easy to see. The hardest part of processing riot and revolt in an intellectual register is always: not why they happen, but why they do not happen (until now). They are difficult to predict because of the remarkable capacity of societies to bear the unbearable, to suffer the insufferable.

Historians have a difficult time with the continuity of discontinuous events. But we can find a close connection between any two coordinates in the history of black revolt in North America. In the recent examples of Ferguson and Baltimore, the linkages are clear (i.e. killer cops, poverty, racism). Yet, historical accounts always want to identify the start and end dates of each uprising,

262   This short chapter is a *détournement* of Gilles Deleuze and Félix Guattari's shorter essay, "May '68 Did Not Take Place" in *Hatred of Capitalism: A Semiotext(e) Reader*, ed. Chris Kraus and Sylvère Lotringer (Los Angeles: Semiotext(e), 2001).

especially because discrete and isolated events can be treated as local aberrations, not expansive fabrics of discontent.

What if Baltimore does not *begin* with the case of Freddie Gray? What if Baltimore does not *end* in Baltimore (which we discover when it is taken up again in six months, in one year, in two years, in another city)? Each revolt is itself, as Deleuze and Guattari claimed, "an unstable condition that opens up a new field of the possible."[263]

But what exactly is possible here beyond the possibility of posing old questions in new ways? First of all, the whole question of revolt is thoroughly imbricated with selective concerns about violence. Violence pervades and disfigures everything from the start. Every revolt, every riot, is haunted by the figure of violence. On April 28, 2015, *The Wall Street Journal* declared that "violence breaks out" in Baltimore.[264] That is the basic treatment: "Violence breaks out" whenever black people revolt against racist violence. For *The Wall Street Journal,* there is no violence when the cops kill black people, there is no violence on Wall Street, let alone any consideration of the violence of capital more broadly. The article could have been written by the Baltimore Police Department, and the fact that it wasn't is indicative of the depth of the problem. Bakunin's basic understanding of revolt from 1872 far exceeds the understanding from *The Wall Street Journal* in 2015. Bakunin said: "To revolt is a natural tendency of life. Even a worm turns against the foot that crushes it. In general, the vitality and relative dignity of an animal can be measured by the intensity of its instinct to revolt."[265] Contrary to racist caricatures of insurgents as wild

---

263 Deleuze and Guattari, "May '68 Did Not Take Place," op. cit., p. 209.

264 Calvert, Scott and Maher, Kris, "Violence Breaks Out in Baltimore After Freddie Gray's Funeral," accessed May 6, 2015, http://www.wsj.com/articles/violence-breaks-out-in-baltimore-as-freddie-gray-is-laid-to-rest-1430169131.

265 Bakunin, Mikhail, "On the International Workingmen's Association and Karl Marx," accessed January 7, 2016, https://www.marxists.org/reference/archive/bakunin/works/1872/karl-marx.htm.

animals, revolt is — for the human animal — a modality of indignation, a measure of dignity.

Nonetheless, ideological and idiotic depictions of "violence" remain effective and reliable mechanisms for the disqualification of the critical content of revolt. Georg Lukács explained that "the radical and mechanical separation of the concepts of violence and economics" are the result of the fetishization of economics as a nonviolent and legal field, and the fetishization of violence as always outside economy and law.[266] Revolt exposes the "invisible" violence of economy and law, challenging that separation. Economy and law establish themselves as the normalization of the non-violent order, so anything that opposes them is identified and condemned as violence and disorder. Voltairine de Cleyre had it right when she observed the violence of the social order: "watch a policeman arrest a shoeless tramp for stealing a pair of boots. Say to your self, this is civil order and must be preserved... Aye, I would destroy, to the last vestige, this mockery of order, this travesty upon justice!"[267] What the revolt invites, encourages, and makes possible, is to worry less about "violence" *to* capital (its inanimate objects and commodities), and more about the violence *of* capital. A broken window, looted food, a burning bank, a burning car, are violence from the perspective of property law. From what perspective, however, is the police killing of Amadou Diallo, Oscar Grant, Abner Louima, Michael Brown, Eric Garner, Walter Scott, Freddie Gray, Tamir Rice, Laquan McDonald, Jamar Clark, and so many others, called violence? So many others indeed: On August 9, Michael Brown became the 668th person killed in the US by the police in 2014, and he was far from the last. Police killed over 1,000 people in the US in 2014, and in between every killing

---

266 Lukács, Georg, *History and Class Consciousness: Studies in Marxist Dialectics* (Cambridge, MA: The MIT Press, 1988), p. 240.

267 de Cleyre, Voltairine, *The Votairine de Cleyre Reader* (Oakland and Edinburgh: AK Press, 2004), pp. 71-72.

you do hear of, there are hundreds of others you don't. Someone is killed every day by police in the US. In fact, it's usually several each day.[268]

It is therefore necessary to reject all efforts to reduce each revolt to the stories of the murdered individuals who trigger them. We all know that the "Arab Spring" was not about Mohamed Bouazizi, the Tunisian street vendor who lit himself on fire in December of 2010. We must try instead to see the violence in the conditions that made self-immolation appear sensible to Bouazizi. Can we ask, as Bouazizi's sister asked: "What kind of repression do you imagine it takes for a young man to do this?"[269] Treatments of particular cases matter, but even "justice" in a verdict, as suggested by the indictments of the six officers responsible for the death of Freddie Gray, resolves none of the everyday violence of capital and law.

Everyday violence indeed, and one which it is necessary to confront as an overwhelmingly racist violence. Angela Davis points out: "The sheer persistence of police killings of Black youth contradicts the assumption that these are isolated aberrations."[270] She refers to "an unbroken stream of racist violence, both official and extralegal, from slave patrols and the Ku Klux Klan to contemporary profiling practices and present-day vigilantes."[271] In light of this everyday violence, which is of course not the only form of violence, revolt is patient, revolt is kind. Revolt may even appear too moderate, too restrained, and too peaceable.

Professional academics are typically part of the problem. We

268   Killed By Police, accessed February 8, 2016, http://www.killedbypolice.net/.

269   Reuters, "Peddler's martyrdom launched Tunisia's revolution (1/19/11)," accessed January 8, 2016, http://af.reuters.com/article/libyaNews/idAFLDE70G18J20110119?pageNumber=2&virtualBrandChannel=0&sp=true.

270   Davis, Angela Y., *Freedom Is a Constant Struggle: Ferguson, Palestine, and the Foundations of a Movement* (Chicago: Haymarket Books, 2016), p. 77.

271   Ibid.

need less intellectual analysis of revolt, and more consideration of the active intellect of revolt, revolt as analysis itself. Can we only hear the *demos* when it speaks in ballots? One participant in the Baltimore revolt answered in the midst of the uprising: "They tell us when we 'vote' we are being heard. No THIS is an example of us young people being heard!"[272] That revolt does not need to speak through experts, elections, figureheads, and analysts is a lesson that even the most sympathetic political scientists are slow to learn.

Academics can be helpful only if they possess a deep and abiding understanding — as did Socrates and Jacques Rancière — that intelligence is not the private property of professionals. Discourse in the form of text can be useful indeed. Rancière's beautiful book, *Hatred of Democracy*, diagnoses the hatred of democracy that hides behind the professed love of democracy.[273] I propose the following variation on Rancière's theme:

Those who condemn the riots secretly love them — the purported hatred of the "violence" of the riots conceals a special love for that "violence." They love the riots they condemn, for their own reasons, most of them racist. The riots are made to serve as evidence for what liberals and conservatives already think about politics, race, class, and capital.[274] This is particularly clear with the media, but can also be seen throughout society (universities included) in the surrounding conversation.

Deleuze and Guattari claimed that what "we institutionalize for the unemployed, the retired, or in school, are controlled 'situa-

272 *The 2015 Baltimore Uprising: A Teen Epistolary* (New York: Research and Destroy, 2015), no page numbers.

273 Rancière, Jacques, *Hatred of Democracy*, trans. Steve Corcoran (London and New York: Verso, 2006).

274 In short, liberals and conservatives hold in common that procedural and electoral politics and reform are sufficient, that racism is a shrinking or minor difficulty, that socio-economic class positions are more-or-less negotiable through hard work and upward mobility, and that capital is either neutral or good, respectively.

tions of abandonment'."[275] This is also true of impoverished black communities throughout the US. Institutionalized abandonment and everyday violence are always more the causal factors of revolt than the personal immorality and intellect of participants.

In the Baltimore revolt of 2015, there was an early celebration of a black mother, Toya Graham, who discovered her son participating in the uprising. She chased him down in the street, grabbing him and hitting him in the head, scolding him loudly. Forget the National Guard, said her fan club, send in the moms to tame the revolt. Graham knows well what the police do to young black men like her son, but she was not applauded for concern over his well-being. Rather, she was applauded for berating and beating him in the streets. The message in her celebration was clear: Black people in revolt are like out-of-control children, and what they really need is the paternalistic power of containment.

Meanwhile, capital hides behind the scenes of revolt, staying aloof and quiet. But what of the peculiar silence of capital? Even those who acknowledge the class dimensions of the problem often do not acknowledge that capital has nothing to offer impoverished communities that face a dilapidated opportunity structure with no future.

Over 63% of Baltimore's population is black, but the median income of the black population ($33,000) is roughly half that of whites in the city. Maryland is the richest state in the country, which exacerbates the already abysmal conditions of life for the poor. Young black men in Baltimore were unemployed at the startling rate of 37% in 2013. Compare that with 10% unemployment for white men of the same age. One-third of Maryland residents live in the state's prisons, and they come from the mostly black communities of Baltimore.[276]

---

275   Deleuze and Guattari, "May '68 Did Not Take Place," op. cit., p. 211.
276   Malter, Jordan, "Baltimore's Economy in Black and White," accessed January 8, 2016, http://money.cnn.com/2015/04/29/news/economy/baltimore-economy/index.html.

Impoverished black people in the US don't need to be taught how to stand up for themselves. Everyday life shapes and informs the knowledge and experience of the disaffected, and indicates that "the field of the possible lives elsewhere."[277] You cannot simultaneously reproduce everyday life and transform it. Revolt understands that basic logic.

Thinking about May '68, Deleuze and Guattari argued: "There can only be creative solutions. These are the creative redeployments that can contribute to a resolution of the current crisis and that can take over where a generalized May '68, amplified bifurcation or fluctuation, left off."[278]

Baltimore 2015 takes over where Ferguson 2014 left off, keeping Ferguson (and Springfield 1908 and Watts 1965) on the list of unfinished business. But the creative solutions and redeployments that Deleuze and Guattari call for may still be premature. Creativity is a productive activity, but there is still much to abolish. Perhaps the abolition of racism calls for creative solutions, and perhaps abolitionists need to get more creative. Yet, we cannot create new worlds without transformation, and transformation implicates abolition. Hegel and Marx understood well that there is an abolitionist force in the negations of transformation. The abolition of old forms of life, political institutions, and social structures implies the creation of new ones, implies creativity. There is always an abolition of old understandings in the creation of new ones, even if, in Hegel's sense, the new understandings carry forth much from the old. And there is always an abolition of the present state of things in the construction of a new state of things, even if some things stay the same.

Those who condemn the revolts actually love them because they get to condemn a "violence" that justifies the violence they defend, the violence they love. Critics of revolt do not, therefore,

277   Deleuze and Guattari, "May '68 Did Not Take Place," op. cit., p. 211.
278   Ibid.

fear the violence, but rather the transformative potentialities of revolt, its abolitionist (and creative) content. Their wager and hope is that nothing they love will be abolished, that the present state of things will be defended against every revolt. And if the existing order is maintained against revolt, as it often is, that existing order will be haunted by the specters of future revolt. Defenders of this present capitalist society know well that surviving a revolt is not busting the ghosts, is not laying them finally to rest. The conditions that give rise to revolt, left unchanged, also leave the abolitionist impetus in place. If the imprecators of upheaval tremble, perhaps they know: Efforts to realize abolitionist dreams continue on where previous ones leave off. Nothing is over and done.

CHAPTER 7

Reason and Revolt: Philosophy from Below

Well then, philosophy, too, must create worlds of thought, a whole new conception of thought, of "what it means to think," and it must be adequate to what is happening around us. It must adopt as its own those revolutions going on elsewhere, in other domains, or those that are being prepared. Philosophy is inseparable from "critique."

— GILLES DELEUZE, *Desert Islands and Other Texts*[279]

But it is not enough for me to stand before you tonight and condemn riots. It would be morally irresponsible for me to do that without, at the same time, condemning the contingent, intolerable conditions that exist in our society... And I must say tonight that a riot is the language of the unheard.

— MARTIN LUTHER KING, JR., "The Other America" (1968)[280]

This final chapter is not a summarizing conclusion, but rather the culminating stage in the development of the theory of revolt as philosophy from below. As such, the present aim is to bring the distinctive movements of each preceding chapter into a cohesive synthesis, proving a clear picture of how the intellect of insurrec-

---

279 Deleuze, Gilles, *Desert Islands and Other Texts: 1953-1974*, trans. Michael Taormina (Los Angeles and New York: Semiotext(e), 2004), p. 138.
280 King, Jr., Martin Luther, "The Other America," Speech at Grosse Pointe High School, March 14, 1968, accessed January 18, 2016, http://www.gphistorical.org/mlk/mlkspeech/mlk-gp-speech.pdf.

tion works, and a full answer to the question of why we must learn from the reason of revolt.

In the existing world, largely governed by the logic of capital and the pathologies of accumulation, revolt is an expression of reason. In light of so many measures, such as the basic macro-economic facts of global poverty and inequality, the absence of revolt may even appear as the height of unreason. A society that does not revolt against a social order that damages it with such escalating facility — psychologically, collectively, ecologically — is a society that, if it were a person, would be living at the terminal stage. Revolt functions like an antidote, or like part of the immune system of the body politic, generating forces against what kills us. In this opening flourish, much needs defining. We must finally and fully define revolt and reason, in light of what has been argued up to this point, and only then can we take up the normative claims of these statements.

Here, the work of George Katsiaficas provides an invaluable resource. Katsiaficas has been arguing for the reasonable content of social movements and rebellions for nearly thirty years, and has applied that general perspective to an analysis of historic and recent revolt around the world, including to uprisings in Asia, Latin America, Europe, the US, and in other geographic and historic locations. Katsiaficas is not alone in seeing the reason of revolt, since many thinkers before him have accepted the logic of this general perspective. Some of those thinkers will also be consulted in the present consideration of the praxis of philosophy from below.

In addition to making the case for understanding revolt *as* reason and reason *as* revolt, I shall argue for a certain twist, not against, but beyond the work of Katsiaficas. I argue for an extension of Katsiaficas' general theory into a rethinking of theory itself. Specifically, we need to shift from understanding the affective and reasonable dimensions of upheaval, to an understanding of the philosophical content of revolt, to an understanding of revolt as philosophical work. This shift, at bottom, can be understood as a shift from an explanatory and descriptive mode of analysis, conducted by social scientists on the *object* of revolt, to recognizing that much of the work of social science is itself carried out more effectively by the *subjects* of revolt. In short, we need another inversion, from the intellectual analysis of revolt, to revolt as intellectual analysis itself.

But, before engaging this bigger question, let us establish our basic terms and concepts.

I Revolt and reason

For brevity's sake, I shall retrieve some basic understandings of revolt and reason from sources that stipulate the meanings I would like to defend and deploy.

Julia Kristeva has thought about the conceptual and etymological meaning of revolt perhaps more than any other scholar of our time. Kristeva, a critical theorist, psychoanalyst, and philosopher, has written many books and novels dedicated to the topic of revolt. She is particularly useful here because, as we shall see, Katsiaficas' theory of the eros effect draws out the psychoanalytic dimension of revolt by way of Freud and Fromm through Marcuse, and that dimension is also the central preoccupation of Kristeva's work on revolt. In her book *Intimate Revolt*, Kristeva writes: "The word 'revolt,' with its rich and complex etymology, acquired its current, distinctly political meaning with the French Revolution. Thus when we speak of revolt today we first understand a protest against already established norms, values, and powers."[281]

Kristeva affirms that revolt is protest against already established norms, values, and powers, but she also wants to retrieve certain meanings of revolt that date back before the French Revolution,

281 Kristeva, Julia, *Intimate Revolt*, trans. Jeanine Herman (New York: Columbia University Press, 2002), p. 3.

and to expand revolt into psychological and affective spheres of life. Kristeva does not depoliticize revolt, and she understands its ongoing and necessary connection to politics and revolution, but rather she wants "to wrest it, etymologically, from the overly narrow political sense it has taken in our time."[282] She sees

> revolt as a dialectical process... Today the word "revolt" has become assimilated to Revolution, to political action. The events of the Twentieth Century, however, have shown us that political "revolts" — Revolutions — ultimately betrayed revolt, especially the psychic sense of the term. Why? Because revolt, as I understand it... refers to a state of permanent questioning, of transformation, of change, an endless probing of appearances.[283]

Kristeva argues that, after the French and Russian Revolutions, those revolutions stopped calling into question their own values, and started to defend themselves rather than to continually question themselves, and in this way, the revolutions came to betray revolt itself.

In his 1989 essay, "The Eros Effect," Katsiaficas focuses on how social upheavals "imagine a new way of life and a different social reality" and "may be considered collective liberatory sublimation — a rational way of clearing collective psychological blockages."[284] Thus, Katsiaficas explicitly connects revolt to processes of working through psychological, as well as social and political, problems. His sense of revolt is both consistent and resonant with

282 Kristeva, Julia, *The Sense and Non-Sense of Revolt*, trans. Jeanine Herman (New York: Columbia University Press, 2000), p. 3.

283 Kristeva, Julia, *Revolt, She Said*, trans. Brian O'Keeffe (Los Angeles: Semiotext(e), 2002), p. 120.

284 Katsiaficas, George, "The Eros Effect" (paper presented at the annual meeting of the American Sociological Association, San Francisco, California, 1989), accessed August 12, 2014, http://www.eroseffect.com/articles/eroseffectpaper.PDF.

that of Kristeva. And it is important to notice that Katsiaficas finds in revolt a critical text full of "imaginative" proposals and "rational" activity.[285] Following this, revolt may be defined as a permanent state of questioning, transformation, and change, as a form of reason or critique; it is an active feature of the psychological health of society, and embodies and expresses the social imagination and desire for new ways of life.

Next, what are reason and rationality? The liberal political philosophy of John Rawls is of little use for a discussion of revolt, making him a rather strange place to start. A general position of liberals, held faithfully by Rawls, is that revolt is superfluous in liberal societies, which can address most problems within the limits of the law. Moreover, Rawls fundamentally disagrees with the basic premises of my own work, in that he holds out hope for a fair capitalist society, which I take as a contradiction in terms. Rawls devoted his life's work to theorizing a "practical" way toward that great contradiction. Rawls' premises continue to ground the most fundamental of liberal conceits, including that perplexingly unshakeable faith in "capitalist democracy." Like most liberals, Rawls never placed his faith in riot, revolt, or revolution.

Having said this, Rawls' famous distinction between the "reasonable" and the "rational" is convincing and useful for purposes other than his own. Here, I shall use it to make the case for both the rationality and reason of revolt. Rawls writes:

> Reasonable persons are ready to propose, or to acknowledge when proposed by others, the principles needed to specify what can be seen by all as fair terms of cooperation... Some have a superior political power or are placed in more fortunate circumstances;

285 One excellent discussion of these themes can be found in Katsiaficas, Georgy, *The Subversion of Politics: European Autonomous Movements and the Decolonization of Everyday Life* (Oakland and Edinburgh: AK Press, 2006). See, specifically, the section "Toward a Rationality of the Heart," pp. 228-233. See also tables 7.2 and 7.3 and the corresponding discussion, pp. 246-248.

...it may be rational for those so placed to take advantage of their situation... Common sense views the reasonable but not, in general, the rational as a moral idea involving moral sensibility.[286]

In other words, if something (in thought or action) can be made to make sense, then it has an accessible rationale, and is thereby "rational." Everything that is understandable, explicable, or that can be comprehended from someone's experience and point of view, is rational. If you murder someone in a jealous rage, in a "crime of passion," the action is rational to the extent that we understand *why* you did it, even though we can say it was unreasonable at the same time. Some things are both rational and unreasonable. What makes something reasonable, according to Rawls, is its "moral sensibility," the idea that it is the right thing to do, and especially for Rawls, that it is fair. There is always your rational self-interest, and then there is what is good for the community, and sometimes (not always) the two are mutually exclusive. In many cases, there is a rationale for doing X, but it is more reasonable to do Y instead.

Part of what is good in Rawls' definition is that he makes it difficult to be "irrational." To be irrational, one has to do or think something that cannot be understood, that is totally inexplicable — that cannot be made to make any sense. Throughout history, this has been the plight of the "mad," of "madness" — a history of horrific and often deliberate misunderstanding, wherein failing to understand a person's rationale for doing something leads to the conclusion of irrationality.[287]

286 Rawls, John, *Justice as Fairness: A Restatement* (Cambridge, MA and London: Harvard University Press, 2001), pp. 6–7.
287 In many interviews and books, Michel Foucault has discussed how "madness" has been used to establish and maintain relations of power in society and politics. His most extensive study, which supports the claim here, is *Madness and Civilization: A History of Insanity in the Age of Reason*, trans. Richard Howard (New York: Vintage Books/Random House, 1988).

But if something can be given a rationale, then it is at least rational, even if it is not the right thing to do (i.e. reasonable). On this view, we can say that rioting and terrorism are rational, even when we do not want to call them reasonable. What is nice about Rawls' distinction is that it creates the space for us to acknowledge the rationality of an action, but to denounce the action on the grounds of reason. With Rawls, we can say for example that we understand the rationality of a war, but condemn it as unreasonable at the same time. We cannot disqualify thoughts and actions as irrational as long as they embody and reflect grievances we are capable of understanding. Whereas, revolt is often characterized as being both irrational and unreasonable, I argue the opposite, that revolt is both rational and reasonable.

ii Intellect of revolt, not analysis of revolt

We can agree with Hamid Dabashi's assessment of the "Arab Spring" where he claims: "When they were shouting 'People Demand the Overthrow of the Regime,' they did not mean just the political regime; they meant also the régime du savoir and the language with which we understand and criticize things."[288] I resist, however, Dabashi's insistence throughout his book *The Arab Spring* that the content of the uprisings is "gloriously simple."[289] I think the content of the uprisings is, to the contrary, quite complex, and complex enough to have warned us against replacing the reductionist readings we don't like with the reductionist readings we prefer. Similarly, Dabashi also warns that "we need to decipher the new revolutionary language" and to not assimilate events "retrogressively" to "false assumptions."[290]

288 Dabashi, Hamid, *The Arab Spring: The End of Postcolonialism* (London and New York: Zed Books, 2012), p. 75.
289 Ibid., p. 77.
290 Ibid., p. 63.

Nonetheless, he ultimately claims that we should read revolt "as a novel," whereas I would regard it more as a difficult philosophical work.[291]

In 2000, in a conversation about the 1999 Seattle protests against the World Trade Organization, Katsiaficas said:

> It seems the revolutionary subject, as Marcuse said, emerges in the course of revolution. Regions are another way of organizing ourselves, and they would emerge in the course of making themselves real. We can't just have our alternative to capitalist globalization emerge full blown from our brains. Some people have attempted to create models for how this country could be organized. I'm not sure that's the way. I think the way is for people to do it, to actually reorganize, live it.[292]

Here, both Katsiaficas and Marcuse are right to highlight the productive and formative work that revolt does. Marcuse wrote about a "new sensibility" that emerges directly out of "*praxis;* it emerges in the struggle against violence and exploitation where this struggle is waged for essentially new ways and forms of life."[293] Marcuse also wrote about "the changing composition of the working class," about the possibility for a "new working class" that, "by virtue of its position, could disrupt, reorganize, and redirect the mode and relationships of production" (although he was doubtful they would do so).[294] Katsiaficas understood that the 1999 Seattle protests expressed a new sensibility, and potentially a new com-

291 Ibid.

292 Katsiaficas, George, "Is there an Alternative to Capitalist Globalization?" in *The Battle of Seattle: The New Challenge to Capitalist Globalization*, ed. Eddie Yuen et al. (New York: Soft Skull Press, 2001), pp. 321-322.

293 Marcuse, Herbert, *An Essay on Liberation* (Boston: Beacon Press, 1969), p. 25.

294 Ibid., p. 55.

position of the revolutionary subject position, which seemed to confirm Marcuse's contention that revolt is a process of shaping, of actually producing new subject positions, and of working out alternatives to capitalism.

Yet, there is another line in Katsiaficas' thinking that expresses his affinity for the politics of prefiguration, which can be seen in the above passage, for example, in the closing call to construct and to live alternatives to the existing society in the here and now. The politics of prefiguration, which has seen a resurgence of interest during recent uprisings, especially since 2011, and has the good favor of too many anarchists, is the wrong orientation. I want to suggest that prefiguration leads to misdiagnoses in the analysis of revolt, and that the rich critical content of revolt is always more important than what it prefigures.

Prefiguration suggests that actors construct and experience new ways and forms of life by directly organizing and living them in the present. Advocates of prefiguration generally adopt the praxis of "learning by doing," suggesting that a liberatory politics reveals both its desirability and possibility when we directly experiment with and experience alternatives to the capitalist present. The politics of prefiguration can be found in many diverse places, for example, in John Holloway's discussion of "other-doing," Hakim Bey's idea of the "temporary autonomous zone," and goes back at least to Michael Bakunin's arguments in *Statism and Anarchy*.[295] More recent articulations and defenses have been taken up by many anarchists, including Uri Gordon, Cindy Milstein, and

295   See Holloway, John, *Crack Capitalism* (London and New York: Pluto, 2010), p. 3; Bey, Hakim, *T.A.Z. The Temporary Autonomous Zone, Ontological Anarchy, Poetic Terrorism,* (Brooklyn: Autonomedia, 1991), pp. 97-103; Bakunin, Michael, *Statism and Anarchy*, trans. Marshall S. Shatz (Cambridge, UK and New York: Cambridge University Press, 1994), p. 133.

Benjamin Franks.[296] As Franks briefly summarizes: "Prefiguration involves using means that are in accordance with the goals, creating in the present desired for features of the future."[297]

To be clear, I do not deny the importance of experiments in prefiguration, of learning and building alternatives directly by trying to make and to live them; a radical politics of "experiential learning" as it's often called in academia. In fact, I agree with Bakunin, Bey, Holloway, Katsiaficas, and others that prefigurative politics can reveal alternative logics of life than those governing the capitalist lifeworld. At the same time, however, prefiguration neglects the more significant, impactful dimensions of revolt, which regard its theoretical content. As shall become clear in the remaining pages of this book, by "theoretical" I do not mean "academic," "textual," or "impractical." I intend this as good news, for if prefiguration was the way to construct real alternatives, then any hope for real alternatives would be lost.

Of course, on a micropolitical scale, anarchist co-ops, community gardens, and groups like Food Not Bombs *do* challenge the logic of capital. They have a different operational logic than the logic of capital, and they are good for communities and good for people. But the capitalist world is mostly untroubled by them. Unless there is a direct conflict of interest, capital can even (and often does) encourage the existence of such projects. The peaceful coexistence of grocery stores and community gardens, for example, can be invoked to bolster the defenses of the tolerant, flexible, and "democratic" present. When we create lived experiences that model alternative lifeworlds, we personally participate in

296 See Gordon, Uri, *Anarchy Alive! Anti-Authoritarian Politics from Practice to Theory* (London: Pluto Press, 2008); Milstein, Cindy, *Anarchism and Its Aspirations* (Oakland: AK Press, 2010); Franks, Benjamin, "Anti-Fascism and Prefigurative Ethics" in *Affinities: A Journal of Radical Theory, Culture, and Action*, Volume 8, Number 1, Summer 2014.

297 Franks, Benjamin, "Anti-Fascism and Prefigurative Ethics," op. cit., p. 53.

meaningful human experience, but not in revolutionary activity that disrupts or publicly challenges the conditions of life. Experiences of life are not conditions of life. And diverse experience and experimentation is possible within existing conditions. For this reason, I am critical of any praxis that overdetermines the transformative power of prefigurative politics. In all politics, it is critical to pay attention to the significance of the real mismatch of scale between our position and our opponent's, even if we do not know how to solve that problem. However, so much of prefiguration does not do this with sufficient seriousness. Therefore, most prefiguration only contests the existing world in ways that are compatible with the reproduction of the existing world indefinitely into the future.

It is therefore good news that prefiguration — or building alternatives by living them in the present — makes up a miniscule part of what happens in revolt. Revolt throws the world into question far more effectively than it makes new worlds. Revolt aspires to be a world-making power, and that is its most precarious endeavor. Revolt is a much more effective world-questioning power. We must seriously consider the severe limitations imposed on us by this world to create new worlds within it. Indeed, if there were no severe limitations to creating alternatives to the existing world in the here and now, radicals would have little to criticize. What can be done to create alternatives to capitalism in a world organized largely (even if not totally) by the logic of capital? What could be prefigured in Seattle in 1999, or later, in the Occupy encampments of 2011? In capitalist society, most of what we do in school and work is governed by the logic of capital, and even leisure time is determined as the time left over after work (and that time is rapidly disappearing for reasons I have discussed elsewhere).[298]

298 See Gilman-Opalsky, Richard, *Precarious Communism: Manifest Mutations, Manifesto Detourned* (Wivenhoe, New York, and Port Watson: Autonomedia/Minor Compositions, 2014) and also Crary, Jonathan, *24/7: Late Capitalism and the Ends of Sleep* (London and Brooklyn: Verso, 2013).

Without a doubt, certain forms of alter-relationality (relations beyond exchange-relations) and human solidarity are available for direct experience in social movements, and these are all good things, and good reasons to participate. But, in the existing capitalist world, people invariably *"retour à la normale,"* as appeared on the popular poster in Paris during the uprisings of May-June 1968.[299] Seattle and Occupy protestors rupture the normality of everyday life, but the call to return to normal can only be resisted for so long before having to go back to work, school, etc. The return to normal demonstrates the power and pull of capital.

And we cannot stay in park encampments for at least two good reasons: First, we never intended to choose homelessness (we do not want to sleep outside in subzero temperatures), and work is necessary even (and especially) for those who hate it. Second, and more importantly, we do not choose to live in park encampments *in order to live in park encampments*, but for other reasons worked out in the activity of occupying the park. That is to say, the critical content of the occupation, *and not the occupation itself*, expresses the radical thinking of the practice.

Historically, revolt does not have the perpetuity of its opponent, for revolt occurs in saturnalias, festivals of resistance and spontaneity that flourish and dissipate over short durations of time (typically days, sometimes weeks). Saturnalias of revolt cannot reverse the logic of the capitalist world, and they cannot produce alternative forms of life that can be selected over the capitalist reality. Our opponent, on the other hand, is not temporary like a saturnalia, but deeply entrenched, reproduced by everyday life, and enjoys enough confidence in its own permanence such that, in most countries, it can allow room for revolt without too much worry.

299 *Atelier Populaire: Posters from the Revolution, Paris, May 1968* (London: Dobson Books Ltd., 1969).

The foregoing analysis would seem dissuasive of revolt, were it not for the fact that revolt can be understood as accomplishing a very different thing. Revolt is an organic intellect at work, a collective philosopher, the old kind of philosopher, not a professional thinker in a university. Revolt does what all good philosophy has always done; it throws the reality and justice of the world into question. The most striking difference is that revolt accomplishes this far better than anything or anyone else, far better than a professional philosopher or book.

As discussed in the preceding chapter, Deleuze and Guattari argue that events like the revolution of 1789, the Paris Commune, the revolution of 1917, and the uprising of 1968 enact

> a lawless deviation, an unstable condition that opens up a new field of the possible... There can only be creative solutions. These are the creative redeployments that can contribute to a resolution of the current crisis and that can take over where a generalized May '68, amplified bifurcation or fluctuation, left off.[300]

Deleuze and Guattari argue against the historian's demand to establish insurrectionary events as phenomena with certain start and end dates, like birthday parties or protest demonstrations. We have agreed with Deleuze and Guattari in rejecting this historicization on the grounds that it fundamentally misunderstands the eventuality of the events. What is most interesting about revolt is the way in which it opens up an unfinished questioning, which other insurrections had previously begun, and which new ones can pick up where they have left off. Thus, Deleuze and Guattari also shift the emphasis from what is concretely prefigured or

---

300   Deleuze and Guattari, "May '68 Did Not Take Place" in *Hatred of Capitalism*, ed. Chris Kraus and Sylvère Lontringer (Los Angeles: Semiotext(e), 2001), pp. 209 and 211.

achieved by revolt, to how the revolt participates in a philosophical inquiry (unfinished questioning) about radical possibilities, about creative solutions to crises.

As stated at the outset of this chapter, there is no hard disagreement here with Katsiaficas, but rather a twist, a turn, an extension, a critical emphasis with consequences, which changes the way we understand the relationship between revolt and philosophy.

In *The Subversion of Politics*, Katsiaficas writes: "As expressions of antisystemic participatory politics, autonomous social movements seek to live without a control center, no matter how rationalized its operation may be."[301] What Katsiaficas emphasizes here is an aspiration to live without a control center. This great aspiration, however, cannot be realized in existing capitalist societies, save for short-lived experiments in marginal and radical milieus. On the question of control, capital is decisive (though not totalitarian). Most of what we do, and when and where we do it, is decided by capital. Indeed, while our leisure time may be used as we wish (within certain and sometimes severe limitations), what time is leisure time, when it is available, what we can do in it, and how much we have, are all largely decided by capital, by the existential demands of work and money.

But Katsiaficas also touches upon another point that I must elaborate more fully here, and that is the objectionable rationality of the control center itself. Revolt opposes that rationality with a different rationality, a different reason. If we do not want to temporarily prefigure other forms of life, but to actually create the conditions where we can live alternatives in perpetuity, this is what is called "revolution" or "transformation." Revolution or transformation, first of all, engages in the negation of the constituted reality, or as Marx put it, "abolishes the present state of

---

301   Katsiaficas, *The Subversion of Politics*, op. cit., p. 257.

things."[302] New forms of life that come about but that leave the present state of things essentially unchanged are not new forms of life at all, but only developments or experiments within the limits of capital.

To be clear, I am by no means stating that nothing can be done until after capitalism is already in a museum or a graveyard. To the contrary, there are many forces of negation working against capitalism, from within capitalism itself. This dialectical sensibility reveals a certain Marxist orientation on my part, which many autonomists and autonomous social movements have also grasped, and which should be argued against the coterie of anarchists who cling to a politics of lifestyle and prefiguration. Revolt is only one form of negation.[303] Negation can also come in the form of crisis, such as the global economic crisis that has been fueling insurrectionary activity around the world since 2008, or in growing climate and ecological crisis.

One thinker who expressed a profound understanding of the intellect of revolt was Raya Dunayevskaya. She focused on the philosophical content of what she called "spontaneous mass

302 Marx, Karl, "The German Ideology" in *The Portable Karl Marx*, trans. Eugene Kamenka (New York and London: Penguin, 1983), p. 179.

303 Throughout this chapter, I variously consider both the negative and positive dimensions of revolt. Here, negative, in the sense of revolt's negation, refers to the critical refusal of and opposition to the constituted reality. Positive, in the sense of the creative and purposeful dimension of revolt, refers to the imaginative anticipation of desirable possibilities and the social energy that expresses such desire. I cannot suggest that one of these dimensions comes first, or that they do or must always occur simultaneously. I do not think we can or even should foreclose the possibility of any order (or of the simultaneity) of these dimensions in an active revolt. What I would assert with more confidence is that *the transformative power of revolt is bolstered by the depth and clarity of both its positive and its negative content.*

action," which she argued emerges as a dialectical force within and against the capitalist lifeworld.[304] In 1981, Dunayevskaya wrote

> that there are certain creative moments in history when the objective movement and the subjective movement so coincide that the self-determination of ideas and the self-determination of masses readying for revolt explode. Something is in the air, and you catch it. That is, you catch it if you have a clear head and if you have good ears to hear *what is upsurging from below*.[305]

On the one hand, there is a certain spontaneity to revolt, and yet revolt articulates and communicates a critical content that those with "clear heads" and "good ears" can hear. Often, the spontaneity of revolt masks its rationality and reason, because the iconic image of the reasonable is calm, objective, and carefully presented. Revolt does not look reasonable in that conventional way, because it is unsettling, subjective, and unruly. But Dunayevskaya contends that those who are willing to think and to listen can and do receive the messages of revolt.

In *Philosophy and Revolution*, Dunayevskaya explicitly addresses the intellect of revolt, arguing that revolt is itself a form of theory, that revolt embodies and reflects "a new stage of cognition."[306] She focuses on Marx's concept of praxis, contending that the word "praxis" cannot and must not be reduced to a synonym for the word "practice." Reducing praxis to practice strips the concept of praxis of its theoretical and critical dimensions. Dunayevskaya

---

304 See, for example: Dunayevskaya, Raya, *Rosa Luxemburg, Women's Liberation, and Marx's Philosophy of Revolution* (Urbana and Chicago: University of Illinois Press, 1991), Chapter XI, and Dunayevskaya, Raya, *Marxism and Freedom: From 1776 until Today* (New York: Humanity Books, 2000), Chapter Eleven.

305 Dunayevskaya, *Rosa Luxemburg*, op. cit., p. xxvii.

306 Dunayevskaya, Raya, *Philosophy and Revolution: From Hegel to Sartre, and from Marx to Mao* (New Jersey: Humanities Press, 1982), p. 255.

maintains that, for Marx, praxis never simply means action, but also a form of theory, and not theory in any narrow academic sense, but rather, a "critical-practical activity" that sees revolt as a form of philosophy from below.[307] Perhaps most sharply, Dunayevskaya ripostes:

It is fantastic that some of those who hail new forms of revolt still do not see the masses as Reason. Instead, they interpret these upsurges as if praxis meant the workers practicing what the theoreticians hand down... No new stage of cognition is born out of thin air. It can be born only out of praxis. When workers are ready for a new plunge to freedom, that is when we reach also a new stage of cognition.[308]

It would be fair to say that the intellect of insurrection was Dunayevskaya's central and enduring interest. Marcuse was closely following her work and always learning from her analyses, as is well documented in their extensive correspondence, and also reflected in his preface to her book, *Marxism and Freedom*.[309] For Dunayevskaya, to be a Marxist was to oppose every statist transposition of Marx's work in the 20th century, to critically condemn so-called socialist states as "state capitalism" in disguise. In her view, to be a Marxist was to always return to "spontaneous action," to "upsurging from below," as the source of revolutionary negation. "The core of all of Marxism begins with and centers around the activity of labor in the process of production itself. It is here that the living laborer revolts against the domination of

307 Dunayevskaya, *Philosophy and Revolution*, op. cit., p. 265.

308 Ibid., p. 265.

309 See *The Dunayevskaya-Marcuse-Fromm Correspondence, 1954-1978: Dialogues on Hegel, Marx, and Critical Theory*, ed. Kevin B. Anderson and Russell Rockwell (Lanham: Lexington, 2012) and Dunayevskaya, *Marxism and Freedom*, op. cit.

dead labor, against being made an appendage to the machine."[310] Dunayevskaya reads the revolts of everyday people around the world, which she constantly watched with a close eye throughout her life, as both an oppositional force to, and a philosophical questioning of, the capitalist reality.

Key to bringing these considerations of revolt together is the understanding that they integrate (1) the psychological and affective dimensions of revolt, with (2) sociological and political-economic analysis of life conditions, and (3) the importance of spontaneity. An everyday life tied to the productive and consumptive apparatus of capital gives rise not only to certain social conditions, forms of life, but also to certain pathologies, and to certain feelings against it. Here, despite other differences, Dunayevskaya, Kristeva, Katsiaficas, and Marcuse are in full agreement. And it is worth pointing out that this was a fairly consistent feature of the critical theory of Marcuse's generation. Erich Fromm, for example, a close colleague of both Dunayevskaya and Marcuse, was a practicing psychoanalyst. In Fromm's *Escape from Freedom*, he offers a psychoanalytic critique of contemporary social life:

> Today the vast majority of the people not only have no control over the whole of the economic machine, but they have little chance to develop genuine initiative and spontaneity at the particular job they are doing. They are "employed," and nothing more is expected from them than that they do what they are told.[311]

In this short passage from Fromm (which comes from the concluding section of his book, on the subject of spontaneity), you can see the integration of (1) psychoanalytic and (2) political-economic concerns with (3) the importance of spontaneity.

310 Dunayevskaya, *Marxism and Freedom*, op. cit., p. 177.
311 Fromm, Erich, *Escape from Freedom* (New York and Toronto: Rinehart & Company, Inc., 1941), pp. 272-273.

Yet within this milieu, only Dunayevskaya regularly insisted upon seeing revolt as a philosophical event. In a 1960 letter to Marcuse, she put it this way:

> Subjectivity as objectivity absorbed is not for the philosophers, but for the masses and it is they who are writing the new page of history which is at the same time a new stage in cognition. Even as every previous great step in philosophic cognition was made only when a new leap to freedom became possible, so presently the new struggles for freedom the *world* over will certainly shake the intellectuals out of the stupors so that they too can create freely a new "category."[312]

Like Katsiaficas, Dunayevskaya took very seriously what Marcuse wrote about eros in *Eros and Civilization: A Philosophical Inquiry into Freud*. According to Marcuse: "The world of nature is a world of oppression, cruelty, and pain, as is the human world; like the latter, it awaits its liberation. This liberation is the work of Eros."[313] And although Marcuse understands the opposition of Eros to Logos, the antagonism of Eros against what is conventionally accepted as "reasonable," he stresses that "Eros redefines reason in his own terms."[314]

Beyond this, and as expressed in the passage above, Dunayevskaya articulates a distinct position that connects mass rebellion to "philosophic cognition." Eros is indeed a liberatory and libidinal force that gives rise to (and lives in) revolt, but for Dunayevskaya, it dies in state power. For Dunayevskaya, if we follow the reason of revolt, the reason that eros defines, we dis-

---

312   Dunayevskaya, *The Dunayevskaya-Marcuse-Fromm Correspondence*, op. cit., p. 74.

313   Marcuse, Herbert, *Eros and Civilization: A Philosophical Inquiry into Freud* (Boston: Beacon Press, 1974), p. 166.

314   Marcuse, *Eros and Civilization*, op. cit., p. 224.

cover that the real continuity of the currents of radical theory, of Marx's thought, cannot be found in Stalinism or in any state power.[315] Eros redefines reason in revolt, showing us the opposition between (1) *Gemeinwesen* (commons, public good/commonwealth) and *Gemeingeist* (common spirit/sensibility), on the one hand, and (2) purportedly representative states, on the other. In other words, states always claim to embody and reflect the eros of the polity, the *Gemeinwesen* and *Gemeingeist*. But the embodiment of eros in revolt directly and clearly refutes such claims, making it difficult for states to defend their reason (and sometimes, their *raison d'être*).[316]

III Sketching the logic of revolt

Much of Katsiaficas' thinking about the transnational contagiousness of the eros effect predicts perfectly what has happened in the "Arab Spring". In his essay, "Seattle Was Not the Beginning," Katsiaficas wrote:

> Because of the power of the media and the global village character of the world today, the eros effect has become increasingly important. Social movements are less and less confined to one city, region or nation; they do not exist in isolation in distant corners of the globe; actions are often synchronically related.

315 See Dunayevskaya's discussion of Marcuse in Dunayevskaya, *The Dunayevskaya-Marcuse-Fromm Correspondence*, op. cit., p. 222.
316 While I'm not taking it up more fully here, I acknowledge that the question of the relationship between revolt and the state is a large and complex one. For example, can't revolt democratize the state rather than undermine its legitimacy? Or, can't the state be the reasonable side of the antagonism in some cases? While it is tempting to take a detour into such questions here, I will only note that the thinkers cited above (Dunayevskaya, Fromm, and Marcuse) do take up the question of the state extensively in their work. I have also done so in my book, *Unbounded Publics: Transgressive Publics Spheres, Zapatismo, and Political Theory* (Lanham: Lexington, 2008).

Social movements in one country are affected sometimes more by events and actions outside their own national context than they are by domestic dynamics.[317]

Katsiaficas viewed Seattle in 1999 very similarly to how Deleuze and Guattari viewed Paris in May-June 1968. Seattle, Katsiaficas argued, was yet another nodal point in a recent history of revolt in various geographic locations. The expressions of disaffection in Seattle would inevitably continue on elsewhere in other ways, as we saw shortly thereafter in mass protests at the International Monetary Fund and World Bank meeting in April 2000 in Washington D.C., during the 2001 G8 summit in Genoa, Italy, at the first World Social Forum in 2001 in Porto Alegre, Brazil, and at many other locations on up to the present.

In this way, the eros effect helps to explain how, for example, upheaval in Tunisia in 2010 resonates with (and helps to detonate) Egyptian disaffection under Hosni Mubarak in 2011, and how the spirit of revolt there seems to "catch on" in other countries, such as in Yemen, Bahrain, and Syria, among others. One thing we have to keep in mind in the present macro-level view of revolt is the fact that within each specific location there is an incredible and even overwhelming amount of complexity. We must be careful to avoid a reductionist view of upheaval that sees it as being the same across countries and time, to avoid stripping each occurrence of its particular communicative content. One of the places where you can see this complexity very well is in Jehane Noujaim's remarkable film, *The Square* (2013). Despite some of the faults of this film (a discussion of which is not relevant here), it succeeds in conveying the difficulty and complexity of the communicative content expressed by and through revolt. The intel-

---

317 Katsiaficas, George, "Seattle Was Not the Beginning" in *The Battle of Seattle: The New Challenge to Capitalist Globalization*, ed. Eddie Yuen et al. (New York: Soft Skull Press, 2001), p. 32

lect of insurrection does not share a single brain. Throughout the waves of revolt in Egypt, positions on the military, Muslim Brotherhood, and Morsi were developing and shifting in relation to very particular political moves, and religious and cultural commitments.

National and sub-national levels of analysis of the specificity of the distinct philosophical movements of revolt is an important endeavor, but that is not my current concern.[318] There is a different comportment involved in explaining what has happened, on the one hand, and in coming to terms with the critical content of revolt as an unceasing human phenomenon, on the other. I am thus concerned with the question: What is the general schematic of such critical content?

Katsiaficas explains distinctions that help to define a certain schematic in *The Subversion of Politics*. On the characteristics of autonomous social movements in Europe, in the three decades after 1968, Katsiaficas writes:

> Parliamentary groups operate according to the logic of the established political system. The first rule of any party must be to obey the law. To ensure members' compliance with existing rules for participation in the government, a structure must be maintained that is compatible with the state. Insurgent social movements aimed at limiting the power of government and creating autonomy seek forms of decision-making of a qualitatively different kind.[319]

318 I have and would of course read such analysis, which is mainly historical and documentary, like Jehane Noujaim's *The Square* (2013), or descriptive works of political science or sociology. Such documentary and explanatory work is important, but it is not my work. I am interested in the theoretical dimensions and the practical and political implications of revolt as a persistent, interminable human activity with emancipatory motivations.
319 Katsiaficas, *The Subversion of Politics*, op. cit., p. 100.

So what is the critical content, at least paradigmatically, that the qualitatively different logic of revolt poses to the logic of the established order? Here, I shall provide a rudimentary sketch of the content and logic of revolt in both positive and negative (and normative) terms:[320]

(a) Revolt is communicative action by means other than words, by means other than text. That is to say, revolt articulates questions, criticisms, visions, and expresses disaffections. Following Immanuel Kant, we might say that revolt is a "public use of reason," and yet contrary to Kant, revolt writes and speaks by other means than those he recommended.[321] Revolt is an experimental form of writing and speaking in that it makes use of non-textual and non-verbal communicative action, for example, musical, visual, symbolic, eventual, performative, and theatrical forms.

(b) Revolt thinks, acts, writes, and speaks *against* the existing state of affairs. Revolt rejects the world as it is, not wholly *per se*, but in some defining regard.

(c) Revolt calls *for* some other state of affairs (or states of affairs) that can be imagined. Revolt imagines a state of affairs that does not exist, yet seems both possible and desirable to insurgents. That is, revolt imagines possible and desirable transformation.

320 I should briefly define what is meant in this new and distinct context, in the following rudimentary sketch, by "positive and negative (and normative) terms." By "positive," I mean to indicate what revolt *is* and *is for*. By "negative," I mean to indicate what revolt *is not* and *is against* (as in negation). The *is/is not* distinction belongs to the descriptive account of the critical content and logic of revolt. The *for/against* distinction belongs to the normative account of the critical content and logic of revolt.

321 See Kant, Immanuel, "An Answer to the Question: 'What is Enlightenment?'" in *Political Writings*, trans. H.B. Nisbet (Cambridge, UK and New York: Cambridge University Press, 1991). Kant favors the public speech and, especially, the published writing of "men of learning."

(d) Revolt thinks, acts, writes, and speaks *against* conventional politics and established channels of reform. Revolt emerges in the face of frustrated and failed reform. Or, revolt addresses reformist failure.

(e) Revolt speaks *for* positions that are marginal or invisible without it. Revolt seeks to eliminate the invisibility and oblivion of its own reasonable content.

(f) Revolt thinks, acts, writes, and speaks *against* the boredom and acceptance of everyday life by way of their opposites, excitement and rejection. Revolt is an ecstatic refutation of acceptance. Raoul Vaneigem declares that "wherever passionate acts of refusal and a passionate consciousness of the necessity of resistance trigger stoppages in the factories of collective illusion, there the revolution of everyday life is underway."[322] Revolt is a rupture with everyday life and its ideological defenses.

(g) Revolt calls *for* and enacts the direct experience of autonomy and spontaneity (this acknowledges the prefigurative aspects of the rupture with everyday life).

(h) Revolt thinks, acts, writes, and speaks *against* the separation of theory from praxis. This is, perhaps strangely, another Kantian dimension of revolt; like Kant, revolt rejects the notion that what makes sense in theory (i.e. justice, freedom, dignity, liberation) is impractical.[323]

(i) Revolt calls *for* resolutions of anguish and hope. Revolt is not, in-and-of-itself, a solution to a problem, and yet it conceives of and presents itself as part of (and participant in) resolutions.

322 Vaneigem, Raoul, *The Revolution of Everyday Life*, trans. Donald Nicholson-Smith (London: Rebel Press, 2006), p. 271.
323 See Kant, Immanuel, "On the Common Saying: 'This May be True in Theory, but it does not Apply in Practice'" in *Political Writings* (Cambridge, UK and New York: Cambridge University Press, 1991).

(j) Revolt thinks, acts, writes, and speaks more desperately and dangerously than in conventional communicative formats, such as textual writing and political speech. Even where revolt wants (and attempts) to be non-violent, it self-consciously risks various forms of violence, and in confronting a quotidian violence, is incapable of promising the absence of violence.[324]

Of course, given a particular case of revolt, in Germany, Italy, France, Egypt, Turkey, Mexico, Spain, the United States, or Brazil, we can and must make further qualifications. Locations and eruptions of revolt are not generic. Revolt arises from circumstances, within historical contexts, and in response to changing material and immaterial conditions, even specific policies or verdicts in some cases. The above sketch is not, therefore, offered in the place of contextual accounts of specific instances of revolt, but rather as a conceptual and analytical rubric that could be applied to reading the reason of revolt in any instance.

I offer the general picture of revolt above, which I maintain does something important and productive. It stipulates a logic and content of revolt that distinguishes revolt from other forms of praxis. This is precisely a qualitative distinction that expands upon and helps us to understand the logic of insurgent social movements that Katsiaficas speaks about, an oppositional logic to that of the established social, political, and economic system.

---

324 Revolt cannot guarantee the total absence of violence because (1) it directly challenges some form of already-existing violence in the world and (2) counterinsurgent forces may variously introduce or multiply violence. It is also worth noting that categorical positions against violence, however much we may wish to take them, reassure the opponents of revolt of their safety. Fundamentally, a revolt that makes categorical promises to peace and safety can't be considered a revolt. It would purport to be, in that sense, a non-disruptive disruption. I claim that while revolt *need not* result in violence, the risk or possibility of violence is necessarily part of it.

IV The praxis of philosophy from below

Why should there be any enduring interest in exploring old and making new connections between philosophy and revolt here in the concluding pages of this book? We do not do this to come to the aid of philosophy as discipline or tradition. Rather, we do this to help discover and appreciate the deep thinking of a society in the places, spaces, and events where thought is commonly proclaimed to be absent. I claim that unpacking philosophy from below is fundamental to the tasks of revealing the reason of revolt, on the one hand, and to revealing the praxis of philosophy, on the other. Moreover, the carrying out of either one of these tasks is critical to the carrying out of the other. But how, precisely, is that the case?

First, revolt — and especially seemingly spontaneous uprising — is typically characterized as the opposite of thinking, as an emotional outburst that is entirely destructive and always condemnably violent. This old and ongoing characterization rests upon the familiar idea that reason must be dispassionate, purely objective at its best, and that it is impossible to be reasonable while also being affected by anger or indignation, among other tumultuous feeling. That old, erroneous characterization, I would add, owes much to an anti-feminist and misogynistic scientism that degrades and disqualifies subjectivity and feeling writ large. Thus, exploring and establishing the reason of revolt, and even more, the notion of revolt *as* reason, challenges widespread assumptions about how reasonable persons act, challenges the common claim that good thinking is always dispassionate, just as it also challenges the image of revolt as a "masculine" physical confrontation of macho powers. As has been more fully argued above, unpacking the critical content of revolt produces new understandings of what thinking is and may be, and about how and where thinking happens.

Second, philosophy as an academic field can be seen as the discipline that stood before and gave rise to all the others.[325] From the point of view that identifies philosophy as the first form of all the sciences — natural, mathematical, and social — philosophy works with the unknown to search out and discover truths, which it collects, and eventually to establish formal bodies of knowledge. Philosophy typically claims to systematize the separation of good thinking from bad, truth from falsehood, much of which can be measured by logic. These fundamentally epistemological and moral dimensions of philosophy define so much of the analytical school.

Friedrich Nietzsche has been taken far more seriously outside of the analytical tradition. In many ways, Nietzsche's critique of philosophy was more ferocious and unsparing than Marx's. Claiming that the purportedly dispassionate objectivity of philosophy conceals its ulterior and moralizing motivations, Nietzsche famously wrote: "I distrust all systematizers, and avoid them."[326] In the same book, *Twilight of the Idols*, alternatively titled *How to Philosophize with a Hammer*, Nietzsche devotes whole sections of criticism to Socrates and the assumptions of "reason" in philosophy.[327]

> All the ideas that philosophers have treated for thousands of years have been mummied concepts; nothing real has ever come out of their hands alive. These idolaters of concepts merely kill and stuff things when they worship — they threaten the life of everything they adore.[328]

In Nietzsche's work, a key problem in the history of philosophy is that it purports virtue in its distance from the living world. Whereas for Nietzsche, feeling and thinking are not antithetical, and any pretension to their separation is a lie, indeed, one of philosophy's favorite deceptions.

325 See Russell, Bertrand, *The Problems of Philosophy* (Oxford and New York: Oxford University press, 2001), pp. 89-94.

326 Nietzsche, Friedrich, *Twilight of the Idols*, trans. Anthony M. Ludovici (New York: Barnes & Noble, 2008), p. 4.

327 Nietzsche, *Twilight of the Idols*, op. cit., pp. 7-17.

328 Ibid., p. 13.

Philosophy has long suffered its own caricature, the very one Nietzsche attacked, and has mostly positioned itself (and has been positioned by others) as being so far removed from the world of real life that what it offers to human practice is always unclear. In teaching political philosophy and social theory in a department of political science, the same demand to answer the question of practice haunts every session. Much like Kant, I have chosen to substantiate the connections between philosophy and praxis, between theory and practice, rather than to accept some metaphysical conceit that the real world is somewhere beneath philosophy. What philosophy offers, at its best, are transformative understandings of the world that can reveal the limits of ideology, and radical reevaluations of the principles that organize our lives. Following this, when other practices than philosophy offer such transformative understandings and radical reevaluations, we must consider the other ways that philosophy happens, challenging the notion that the most serious thinking is the purview of professionals.

Finally, how do these two tasks intersect, and why does the intersection matter for a theory of revolt?

There is a long history of people in positions of power calling everyone who opposes their position "irrational." There is also a long history of turning that inverted perspective on its head. Despite Nietzsche's derisions, Plato understood this point well, as he and Socrates argued against the Sophists (who Nietzsche, interestingly, defends), against those "professional intellectuals" who sold ideas to the sons of wealthy families. Since the time of Plato and Socrates, one defining vision for philosophy was as a discursive and dialectical force against the existing state of affairs. Central to this philosophic vision was an opposition to professional philosophy. Beyond Socrates' notoriously pejorative regard for the Sophists, we might also consider the argument of Socrates in Plato's *Meno* that the formally uneducated slave was already fully capable of doing philosophy. In Plato's *Meno*,

Socrates engages in discussion with one of Meno's slaves to prove that the slave possesses intellectual capabilities that must not be denied. Eventually, Meno's slave comes to feel that he has "spontaneously recovered" knowledge, an epiphany that was dialectically aroused.[329]

Now remember our figure of Spartacus from the book's introduction. Certainly, there is a philosophy from below in the slave revolt, that is, a deep, challenging thinking about power, freedom, human suffering, and human desire, all coming from the dungeon bowels of the ludus. From underneath the highfalutin education of the lanista and the culture of the ruling Roman elite, the thought that breaks the unjust reality is forced upon that world not by the critics of barbarism, but by the "barbarians" themselves. And we must also consider the fact that Socrates — iconic philosopher of philosophers — was an enemy of the state, ultimately put to death for doing philosophy in the streets. Different villains, Socrates and Spartacus, but their "crimes" risked a similar danger. In many ways, the guiding question of the present chapter has been: *Who else does philosophy in the streets*?

The problem with the case in the *Meno* is that the midwife for the slave's epiphany is the guidance of the great philosopher; so the slave cannot take full credit for his achievement in the end, since Socrates appears as the one to thank for the revelation. But often, as in the case of Spartacus and the slave revolts, there aren't any formal philosophers, iconic, professional, self-proclaimed, or otherwise, helping make philosophy happen. Sometimes social upheavals articulate and arouse the deep questioning and epiphanies that philosophers seek to articulate and arouse. Often, nothing does philosophy better than revolt. Socrates did not go far enough.[330]

329   Plato, *Meno* in *Protagoras and Meno*, trans. W.K.C. Guthrie (London and New York: Penguin Books, 1956), at 85d.
330   This is also because, while Socrates insists on philosophical currents that test the limits of the laws, he ultimately accepts and defends the laws, as can be seen in Plato's *Crito*, as well as in other dialogues.

Inasmuch as Thoreau was an abolitionist philosopher, we should appreciate his profound appreciation and active defense of John Brown's insurrection. Thoreau, who called for civil disobedience and peaceable revolution, came to the defense of an insurgent who believed in armed insurrection.[331] Brown's revolt was not as much a contradiction of Thoreau's pacifism as was the slave system they both abhorred. And Thoreau observed that Brown was declared insane because his insurrectionist raid had to be condemned "unreasonable" by the perspective of the slave system, and "that it was necessary that the bravest and humanest man in all the country should be hung."[332] In *The Impending Crisis*, David Potter recognizes how effectively the emotional power of Brown's uprising focused peoples' attention on the horrors of slavery.[333] Brown's insurrection was more effective in this regard than any philosophical treatise on abolition. Indeed, philosophy longs for the power of insurrection.

Yet, I would also affirm Alain Badiou's statement that "as a philosopher, I never accept the world as it is because it is as it is... from the very beginning, from Socrates... it is not the job of the philosopher to accept the opinion because the opinion is dominant."[334] Indeed, good philosophy has always thrown the world as we know it into question. But no conventional text can expect to be as provocative or compelling as creative, unpredictable uprisings that seize attention and ignite imaginations. Revolt is a philosophical modality, a way of doing and surpassing the work of professional intellectuals. If we fail to recognize reason as revolt

331 Thoreau, Henry David, "A Plea for Captain John Brown" in *Civil Disobedience and Other Essays* (New York: Dover, 1993).

332 Thoreau, "A Plea for Captain John Brown," op. cit., p. 48.

333 Potter, David M., *The Impending Crisis: America Before the Civil War 1848-1861* (New York: Harper Perennial, 2011), p. 380.

334 Badiou, Alain, "BBC HARDtalk Interview," March 24, 2009, with Stephen Sackur, accessed February 15, 2016, https://www.youtube.com/watch?v=NPCCNmE7b9g.

and revolt as reason, then we fail to see that the Greek uprisings in 2008, the "Arab Spring," Occupy, and uprisings in Turkey, Brazil, and Spain, for example, are doing the most important philosophy of our time. It is necessary to theorize a "philosophy from below," which understands that professional thinkers have more to learn from insurrectionary movements than to teach them, and also, that understands the deficiencies of reason within the limits of law. Is it even possible to take seriously the claim that authors of books on politics, morality, and philosophy can throw the reality and justice of the world into question as well as Spartacus, John Brown, occupied buildings, and public squares? A philosophical text may conceal or confess its aspiration to be as provocative as a riot, but such an epiphanous power of rethinking the established and accepted reality remains an enduring and lofty goal.

In the wake of the riots around London in early August 2011, Darcus Howe, a West Indian writer and broadcaster in London, was interviewed on the BBC. From his perspective, it was quite clear that the riots were an insurrectionary expression of youth defiance against police brutality and racism throughout many London boroughs. Howe understood the riots to be telling us that there was something seriously wrong in the country. As he put it:

> What is obvious is that these young people will go on relentlessly... They've seen Syrians, Libyans, Egyptians and insurrection. I don't think four months jailed in a miserable little hole will change them. It's a different set of youths today... That's been going on since I landed here 50 years ago, now it's almost complete. I think this insurrection is the last stop in its completeness.[335]

335 Howe, Darcus, "My father curfewed me and I jumped through the window," *Socialist Worker*, Issue # 2265, August 16, 2011, accessed January 11, 2016, https://socialistworker.co.uk/art/25261/Dar-cus+Howe%3A+%E2%80%98My+father+curfewed+me+and+I+-jumped+through+the+window%E2%80%99.

Whether or not one agrees with Howe's analysis (and he was at least wrong about the insurrection of 2011 being the "last stop"), he is rightly interested in the rational *and* reasonable content of the events. Meanwhile, Howe's interviewer at the BBC would not recognize the presence of anything sensible in the riots, because her position expressed the general view of the opposition in power, denying the upheavals any rationality or reason, reducing the whole expression to an aberrant, senseless episode of violence.[336] The same methods used in 1859 to deny the rationality and reason of John Brown have been used time and again on up to the present to condemn philosophy from below.

But when we speak of insurrection, we have not simply meant armed militant factions fighting the police forces of state power, and we do not mean violent conflict and murder. We have recovered the word's 15th-century meaning in this book, defined by the idea of "a rising up." The risings-up of insurrection seek systemic-structural transformations from within the lifeworld they want to transform. Insurrection is a trouble-making from the inside, but not simply the subversive insubordination of administrators, or lone-wolf insurgents. No, insurrection implies some form of collective action, no matter how micropolitical. Spartacus and John Brown did not act alone, and could not have. Insurrection says something legible about the system in which it rises up, even when its opponents deem it "irrational." This was not only the case of Spartacus and John Brown, but of the 2011 London riots, and the 2014 and 2015 uprisings in Ferguson and Baltimore. Insurrection does not, as we have seen, necessarily seek political solutions like "new government." For we have also seen new government make new betrayals in very short order, and bring forth the reasonable criticisms of new insurrection, as in the Egyptian uprisings against Morsi in the summer of 2013.

---

336 Howe, Darcus, "BBC News Interview on UK Riots," accessed January 11, 2016, http://www.youtube.com/watch?v=mzDQCToAJcw.

To be sure, many uprisings do not have what we could reasonably call "revolutionary" effects. Many successful insurrections, from Spartacus and Brown, to those in Egypt, Greece, Ferguson, and Baltimore, are not successful revolutions. They accomplish some things, not everything. If, by revolution, we mean some kind of structural transformation, some kind of transformation of power relations, or of everyday life, then we cannot necessarily call uprisings that occur in response to contested election results, court decisions, or even electrical blackouts "revolutionary." Some uprisings neither seek nor result in transformations of power or conditions of life. For example, masses of unruly people breaking down doors are sometimes mobilized by the shopping prospects of Black Friday in the US, or by a new Nike sneaker debut (i.e. a so-called riot at a mall in Orlando, Florida, in February 2012).[337] But even a frenzied mass of consumers stealing sneakers in a mall or TVs during a blackout expresses something quite serious about a society and a culture, if we want to listen.

Often, rioting and looting are easier to read, as in the case of the tumultuous response to the police shooting and killing of an unarmed black teenager, Michael Brown, in Ferguson, Missouri in August 2014. This typically calm St. Louis suburb was rocked for days by rioting, smashed shop windows, protests, fires, confrontations with police, and looting by people outraged by the murder. While news reports openly and reliably condemned these uprisings, never hesitating to call them "violent," some participants in the upheavals have been interviewed explaining their rationality and reason. Participants have expressed the need for exceptional outrage against exceptional injustice, to show the police that even if the law allows the police to use *their* violence, the community will not. One participant in the rioting, DeAndre Smith, told the

337 *The Daily Caller*, "New Nike sneaker causes riot at Orlando mall," February 24, 2012, accessed January 11, 2016, http://dailycaller.com/2012/02/24/new-nike-sneaker-causes-riot-at-orlando-mall/#ixzz3wxxbRjnc.

St. Louis Post-Dispatch that the Ferguson revolt was exactly the right response to the injustice, saying "I think they got a taste of what fighting back means."[338]

The primary source material is the revolt itself. To that end, I was inspired to see the publication of *The 2015 Baltimore Uprising: A Teen Epistolary*, first published as a zine compiling tweets from Baltimore teens outraged by the murder of Freddie Gray and active in upheaval throughout the city.[339] Taking up such content as this with seriousness, it would seem, is a more promising pathway to comprehending the direct thinking of the Baltimore uprising than, for example, to have it explained by professional social scientists. The same could be said of the edited volume, *We are an Image from the Future*, which compiled first-hand insurgent reportage from the Greek revolt.[340] We need more primary source materials such as these. While I have developed a theory of revolt as philosophy from below, I have never intended *Specters of Revolt* to be a book-length study of the intellect of some one particular uprising. However, though that is not the aim of my book, according to its theory, any such dedicated study should centralize the importance of primary source material compiled in publications like *The 2015 Baltimore Uprising* and *We are an Image from the Future*.

Once we abandon the disqualifying and vilifying discourses of irrationality and violence, it is obvious that any honest consideration of the Ferguson and Baltimore uprisings, for example, will require a confrontation with questions of racism, power, poverty,

338 "DeAndre Smith speaks with the St. Louis Post-Dispatch," accessed January 11, 2016, http://www.stltoday.com/news/multimedia/video-man-justifies-the-looting-in-ferguson/html_7699be22-bb74-5d4f-aa49-fc-c46f5cb025.html.

339 *The 2015 Baltimore Uprising: A Teen Epistolary* (New York: Research and Destroy, 2015).

340 *We are an Image from the Future: The Greek Revolt of December 2008* (Oakland, Edinburgh, and Baltimore: AK Press, 2010).

justice, and police brutality. These are just some, among many other contents that a dedicated reading could explore.

Nonetheless, on the issue of reading the rational and reasonable content of revolt, I must address the fact that outsiders consuming unsympathetic reports of the uprising from a distance are unlikely to carry out the close and dedicated reading I've been discussing. For many observers at a distance, the communicative content of revolt may not be sufficient to overturn the vilification of the uprising as irrational violence, or to shift their ideological commitments against it.

While revolt gets more attention than a book, and more effectively and directly communicates than intellectual analysis, a network of supportive activities — outside of and after the uprising — can help revolt defend itself against reductionist and ideological reading. The usual activities come to mind: articles, books, blogs and social media, independent media, radio shows like *Democracy Now!*, public forums, documentary films, sit-ins, die-ins, solidarity demonstrations, university classes, conversation with family and friends, etc. One example, in response to Ferguson, was the organization of the Black Lives Matter reading list and the Ferguson Reads Discussion Group at Left Bank Books in St. Louis. As described by Left Bank Books: "The events in Ferguson have been upsetting for nearly everyone in our community. This reading group is an attempt to add some civility and context to the mix by exploring race, not only in St. Louis, but America as a whole."[341] The group started meeting to discuss Ferguson in September 2014, and continued on into 2015.

Regarding this example, and others in Missouri and around the world, in the network of supportive activities for a close reading of the content and contemplation of revolt, we mustn't lose

---

341   Left Bank Books has multiple pages on their website dedicated to their efforts to further an understanding of the events in Ferguson, accessed February 15, 2016, http://www.left-bank.com/fergusonreads.

sight of the fact that the revolt itself is the catalyst, often both the mode of analysis *and* the unit of study, the agenda-setting event. All of the follow-up analysis about race and class, economic crisis, capital, the opportunity structure in impoverished black communities, tactics and rebellion, police brutality, and the sociological and historical context of violence in society, emerges from the *communiqué* of revolt. Dozens of teenagers were killed by police from the time of the Michael Brown shooting to the time of this writing — and over 1,100 people in 2014 and over 1,200 in 2015 — and sadly, we know that the number is far greater by the time you are reading this. The difference that makes the difference between the ones we know about and the ones we don't is revolt. It is therefore clear that revolt is a discourse that participates in the proliferation and production of knowledge.

Beyond the old idea of "permanent revolution," which goes back to Marx and Trotsky, among others, I recommend something like "permanent revolt," which is close to what Kristeva calls a "culture of revolt." Kristeva says:

> The permanence of contradiction, the temporariness of reconciliation, the bringing to the fore of everything that puts the very possibility of unitary meaning to the test (such as the drive, the unnamable feminine, destructivity, psychosis, etc.): these are what the culture of revolt explores.[342]

She further claims that the culture of revolt "poses the question of another politics, that of permanent conflictuality."[343] Seen this way, revolt participates in revolutionary transformation inasmuch as it is an active, physical and philosophical force of negation that throws the existing state of affairs into question. It is not only philosophical in a narrow intellectual sense, for it is

---

342 Kristeva, Julia, *Intimate Revolt*, trans. Jeanine Herman (New York: Columbia University Press, 2002), p. 10.
343 Ibid., p. 11.

also visible, public, and eventual (as only some philosophy is). Following Kristeva, I see revolt as the conflictual activity of ongoing challenges to every celebratory discourse that defends each new reconciliation in society and politics. Thus, for example, revolt opposes the intrinsically conciliatory dispositions of liberalism and conservatism. This means that liberal and conservative revolt are yet two more contradictions in terms, much like the concept of fair capitalist democracy. Despite meaningful differences in their classical forms, liberalism and conservatism present themselves as political alternatives to revolt. Revolt is an enemy of liberal and conservative politics.

Still, revolt is not a clear step toward revolution in any certain or linear sense. It is, rather, an activity that reveals problems and generates real, concrete thinking about the problems. The position I have outlined is self-consciously precarious: Those who make revolt do not share a single blueprint for the different world(s) they desire, and revolt does not *know* how to make new worlds. Indeed, even after the establishment of some new lifeworld, revolt would return again to challenge its limits and failures. In this way, revolt is a precarious politics of world-making.

In the beginning of every revolt, the only great confidence is that the present state of affairs is unacceptable. Yet, we should never minimize the significance of that epiphany. It is an epiphany far away from the defensive quotidian routine of liberal-to-conservative political discourse. In between every revolt, we are accustomed to accepting the unacceptable, to tolerating the intolerable. Revolt breaks that pathological obedience. The practical hope of revolt is a reasonable aspiration that what emerges from it may constitute a nodal point in the development of transformative politics.

Because the messages of insurrection are written by those who want to live in a different world, but who cannot say exactly what that world is, uprisings always appear irrational from the point of view of power. They speak a different language altogether. And it turns out that demanding revolt to "be rational" and "be practical" is never a good-faith interest in either the sense or success of the revolt. Such demands to be rational and practical are invariably the defensive reactions of the existing society against anything that throws it profoundly, existentially, into question. Such demands always posit the rational and practical people as those who write letters to the editors, vote, take seriously the established liberal-conservative debate, and of course, as those who insist that justice always follows the law. But it is the rational-practicality of the present situation that insurrection rejects, on the grounds of an insistence that there are *other reasons* and *other rationalities* excluded by the ideological narrowness of the defensive position. Revolt is largely about wrenching open that narrowness so that we can see other rationalities, another reason.

Insurrectionary movements exceed the diagnostic and prescriptive efforts of scholars, and everyday people are capable of discovering (as they have been discovering in uprisings across Middle Eastern and North African countries, in the wave of occupation movements, and in Spain, Turkey, Brazil, Ferguson, Baltimore, and elsewhere) that *they are the midwives*, which puts them beyond the subordinate relationship of Meno's slave to Socrates.

From philosophical, psychological, social, political, and ethical perspectives, the absence of revolt is more frightening than its presence. As deep questioning of what is, revolt is good philosophically. As vigorous expression of disaffection and desire, revolt is good psychologically. As human solidarity (reanimated *Gemeingeist*) and democracy realized (reanimated *demos*), revolt is good socially and politically. As moral indignation, revolt is good ethically.

The absence of revolt signals the acceptance — *or at least the toleration* — of what is. But an acceptance of the reality and justice of the existing world is an acceptance that good philosophy never grants easily. We therefore have good reason to be reassured by occurrences of riot, insurrection, and revolt, understanding these as modalities of the collective questioning of the world. The various risings-up of insurrection, the activities of everyday people who throw the world into question, are writing philosophy from below. And it is philosophy from below — not the professional thinking of academics — that raises the most pressing questions.

This calls for a reversal of general perspectives commonly held in both society and science. In society, this calls for reversals of perspective on notions of practicality, violence, and irrationality. We have seen revolt as a practical response to various forms of already-existing normalized violence — and as a response that usually makes good sense (and typically, good arguments) in the light of its historical and social context. In science, this calls for reversals of perspective on notions of objectivity, intelligence, and analysis. We have seen revolt as a legible subjective analysis, as the activity of an organic general intellect helping us to understand real problems in the world.

In between every revolt we are haunted by the specter of its possibility. It is in the possibility of revolt that the possibility for radically rethinking and remaking the world resides. Revolt tells us that real desire for a transformed world can, and inexorably will, express itself in powerful disruptions of our upside-down reality. Revolt has been communicating this to us with intensified frequency in recent years, and even if it is not now happening, we know that it will.

It's always *anterivolta*. But we don't have to wait for the next revolt to think. While the next one will help us, there is much in the last ones still to be taken up.

Repeater Books

is dedicated to the creation of a new reality. The landscape of twenty-first-century arts and letters is faded and inert, riven by fashionable cynicism, egotistical self-reference and a nostalgia for the recent past. Repeater intends to add its voice to those movements that wish to enter history and assert control over its currents, gathering together scattered and isolated voices with those who have already called for an escape from Capitalist Realism. Our desire is to publish in every sphere and genre, combining vigorous dissent and a pragmatic willingness to succeed where messianic abstraction and quiescent co-option have stalled: abstention is not an option: we are alive and we don't agree.